Good Books Lately

ST. MARTIN'S GRIFFIN

New York

Good Books Lately

The One-Stop Resource for Book Groups
and Other Greedy Readers

Ellen Moore *and* Kira Stevens

www.stmartins.com

BOOK DESIGN BY AMANDA DEWEY

Library of Congress Cataloging-in-Publication Data

Moore, Ellen.
    Good books lately : the one-stop resource for book groups and other greedy readers / Ellen Moore and Kira Stevens.—1st ed.
            p. cm.
    ISBN 0-312-30961-9
    1. Book clubs (Discussion groups)—Handbooks, manuals, etc. 2. Group reading—Handbooks, manuals, etc. 3. Books and reading.   I. Stevens, Kira.   II. Title.
    LC6619.M66 2004
    374'.22—dc22

                                    2003058692

First Edition: March 2004

2 4 6 8 10 9 7 5 3 1

For our parents, who so kindly passed down their passion for the written word, and for our husbands, who were so patient and supportive as we struggled to produce a hundred thousand of our own.

Contents

Acknowledgments

We'd like to begin by thanking all the book group members who contributed to this book by sharing their stories. Our entrance into the world of book groups began when Kira worked with Virginia Valentine, book club coordinator at Denver's Tattered Cover Book Store. Virginia's charisma, enthusiasm, and wealth of knowledge inspire us. We are most grateful to Eleanor Hardy, the "Angel Investigator" who helped get Good Books Lately off the ground. We're indebted to Elizabeth Geiser, director of the Publishing Institute, who was kind enough to guide us to our agent, Deirdre Mullane, of the Spieler Agency. Our deepest appreciation goes to Deirdre: we depend on her years of experience in publishing, tireless attention to detail, and articulate advice. We'd like to pay tribute to Jane Rosenman, formerly an editor at St. Martin's Press, whose suggestions helped us create some of the most "delicious" pieces of our book. Jane's editorial work was continued with great care by Ethan Friedman, whose swift editorial pen managed to cut a much-too-long manuscript in half and to make it twice as good. We'd like to acknowledge other folks at St. Martin's for their invaluable work: John Karle and Emily Gewitz, for assiduous publicity; Karen Resnick, for innovative marketing; Amanda Dewey, for her fabulous design; and Olga Gardner Galvin, for flawless copyediting. When developing our book group survey, we relied on the astute advice of Diane Waldman, mass communication professor at the University of Denver. And once again, thanks to our readers. We've spoken with you on the phone, chatted with you over E-mail, and met with you in your living rooms; and without your candid anecdotes, smart suggestions, and creative ideas, this book wouldn't have been possible.

Introduction

This book is for readers—most specifically, for readers who also belong, or want to belong, to book groups. We have worked with thousands of book club members from all over the country in the past five years and are continually surprised by their diversity, drive, and determination to create a comfortable space for shared intellectual pursuits and emotional revelations. In writing this book we have tried to look at the book group experience from every angle that seems to be important to book group readers—ourselves included. If you remember the old Hair Club for Men commercials, you probably remember Cy Sperling's famous tag line, "I'm not only the president of the Hair Club for Men, I'm also a client!" Well, our line isn't as snappy (nor can we doff our hair weaves to reveal our shiny bald heads), but it shares something of the same spirit: "We're not only cofounders of a book group consulting company, we're also a book group!" Since we spend so much of our time hanging around other people's groups, the Good Books Lately book group, composed of every member of our company team, can only meet every three months. But our group faces the same challenges—if only four times a year—that every other book group in the world confronts: how to choose the best books, how to read for meaning, how to find materials and questions to spur the most energetic discussion, how to get the talkative people to shut up so the more reserved get a chance to speak, how to balance between social time and book time, and how to sneak off with the forgotten unopened bottle of wine that got left on the counter.

If you're the cover-to-cover kind of reader, by all means feel free to sit down and dive right into chapter 1, where you will discover a side of book group history that we think may intrigue you—you'll never feel quite the same about your participation in this long-standing and surprisingly controversial tradition. Or perhaps you need to come up with some good discussion techniques and questions for the meeting that's taking place in two hours, in which case you'd best skip ahead immediately to chapter 4. Because we are writing this handbook for a such a wide spectrum of readers—voluntary students of literature, also known as book group members, come in an astounding variety of ages, experiences, levels of education, ambitions, preferences, and reading tastes—we expect and anticipate that the majority of those who pick it up will use it as exactly that, a handbook, something to look through for the ideas and information that may be of personal interest. We have tried to organize this book in such a way that you can dip in and out of any chapter or section to find the material you want quickly—or proceed through it slowly, building your book group expertise and talents from the ground up. We've included numerous recommendations in each chapter from those truly at the battlefront of the book group enterprise—that would be you folks, the book group members, readers, and leaders. Wherever possible, we have cited examples from the works that occupy the most exclusive echelon in the published word—the books that are favorites with book group readers in living rooms across the globe.

In case you're curious, a note about the phrase "book group" for your consideration. In Britain they're usually known as reading groups. American and British publishers call them reading groups or reading clubs—probably in the desire to differentiate these numerous small pockets of readers from the old staple, the Book-of-the-Month Club. Most Americans involved in these reading groups or clubs generally refer to their organizations as book clubs or book groups. In this book we'll usually refer to them as book groups because that's the term that we like best, for some reason. However, between you, us, and the kitchen sink, all these terms are pretty much interchangeable, so use whichever one you like.

We talk to many book group members every day over the phone and through E-mail, and after we're done sharing book suggestions or discussion tips, we often get asked, "How did you start doing this?" In case you are also wondering, we fell into our line of work by virtue of two crucial factors: many painstaking years of concentrated study and a single random evening of idle speculation. In the summer of 1999 we were finally nearing the end of our postgraduate program (to the relief of our long-suffering husbands and families), the Ph.D. in English at the University of Denver. Our "real lives" as college professors were (hopefully) about to begin. Then one of us asked the fatal question that knocked our career paths in a whole new direction: "I wonder if there's anything else that you can do with a doctorate in English besides teach at a school?" Because of her ten years of work at Denver's Tattered Cover Book Store, Kira Stevens knew that many local book groups were eager to find professional facilitators to lead special book discussions. We figured maybe we should give this a try. We had been teaching literature classes at the university for four years, so why couldn't we start a business working with book groups? After all that schooling, how hard could it be to start a company?

Ah, the poignant naïveté and vainglorious dreams of two sequestered academics! As you might have guessed, entrepreneurial success turned out to be a little more complicated than we had initially anticipated. But we floundered on, buoyed by the infectious intellectual enthusiasm of the devoted readers we encountered, readers who kept coming up with new and interesting requests for book group help and services. We still facilitate several meetings each week for book group members in the Denver/Boulder area. We also offer customized help in book selections, write a series of reading guides (called Read*Smart*Guides®) on specific books, and try to keep up with the racing pulse of the expanding book group community in our monthly on-line newsletter, *LATELIES*. In 2004 we will start a membership program for book groups, the National Book Group Association of America, encouraging readers to create their own individual book group Web sites and allowing them access to a wide variety of resources provided by writers, publishers, book group leaders, and friendly bibliophiles eager to lend a hand. You can learn more about all our book group offerings at www.goodbookslately.com. We're trying to make our site a valuable gathering place for book group readers across the English-speaking world, much as we attempted to make this book a one-stop resource for all you greedy readers who just won't quit devouring and talking about books. Anyway, that's us, so far. Give us a call sometime and talk with Ellen Moore if you want to know any of the juicier details.

We hope you enjoy this book as much as we have enjoyed all the original ideas and fantastic stories that you have shared with us while we were writing it. Our most profound thanks go to the hundreds upon hundreds of you who so generously completed the exhaustive surveys we conducted in the process of putting this book together. For all those about to read, we salute you.

Good Books Lately

Sewing Circles and Salons: Tracing the Ramified Roots of Book Groups in the United States

"I think we're a salon group," Jill said, nodding emphatically. *"Most definitely."*

"Really?" Nancy raised an eyebrow. *"I was thinking we're more of a sewing circle, but we like to* think *we're a salon."*

"What's the big deal, anyway?" asked Marjorie. *"I mean, can't we be both?"*

When we meet with a book group for the first time, we ask some basic "getting-to-know-you" questions about the group's history, literary tastes, and reading habits. Sometimes we share our thoughts on the possible origins of reading groups in two seemingly different traditions—sewing circles and intellectual salons. We can usually guess how members might perceive themselves in light of our theory, and often we witness the kind of friendly debate we see between Jill, Nancy, and Marjorie. It's no surprise that book group members might disagree about how to define themselves and what they do together— the literary and cultural foundations of book groups are widespread and complex.

Because book groups are a grassroots phenomenon, it's difficult to trace their beginnings back to one moment in time and say with confidence, "This is where it all began." After working with book groups for years, we noticed that most members have two goals: one, to grow intellectually and explore the world through great books; and two, to join a community of readers who share, through literary discussion, their life experience. We wondered what institutions or customs might connect these two aims, and after researching the history of reading and the development of women's groups in the United States, we came up with the aforementioned sewing circles and intellectual salons. But in order to be sure our intuition was right, we had to do some digging.

How far back should we go? We surveyed the most dramatic literary developments in history. Two thousand years ago the Chinese began experimenting with paper-making techniques. Five hundred and fifty years ago Gutenberg invented the printing press in Germany. Three hundred years later the eighteenth century saw the rise of the novel. From the very beginning, novelists were often denigrated along with London's "Grub Street" writers, who wrote sensationalist pieces for pamphlets that we might today call tabloids. Just read a little Samuel Johnson, and you'll understand that the relevant reverence in which we hold writers of popular literature today did not come easily.

So when did book groups start? They may have started among the leisure class in the earliest days of the eighteenth century; books were very expensive, and people often gathered together to read aloud or shared books to save money. But way before that, people have been gathering together to exchange stories. For instance, in *The Decameron,* a collection of tales by Giovanni Boccaccio, which takes place during the Black Death epidemic in 1348, a group of young men and women go to the Italian countryside to escape the plague and spend their time there telling stories. In 1559 French aristocrat Margaret de Navarre reworked Boccaccio's famous tales into a similar collection called *The Heptameron.* When considered this way, even Chaucer's ride to Canterbury in *The Canterbury Tales* can be considered a sort of "book group on the go."

The revolutionary print culture of the eighteenth century got women involved in reading outside the home: the Shakespeare Ladies'

Club was popular, and reading groups were created for women prisoners. In the mid-nineteenth century, English mill workers met at dawn each morning to read and discuss Shakespeare. In 1816, in his villa on Lake Geneva, Mary Wollstonecraft Godwin and her lover, Percy Bysshe Shelley, visited Lord Byron and some of their friends in what could be called a *really* long book group meeting where, among other things, they read ghost stories. Byron challenged his guests to write one of their own, and the result was the now-married Mary Shelley's *Frankenstein*.

About 140 years ago, cheap paperbacks and the newly literate middle and lower classes created a huge transformation in readership demographics: more and more people could afford books. In the mid-nineteenth century, in Europe, the notion of "the author as star" began, with groups meeting to discuss the work of Robert Browning and others. In the United States, this tradition was continued by the National American Lyceum, formed in 1831 to organize a grassroots movement of readers, who gathered in each other's parlors to read books and discuss important ideas of the day. In just twenty years, there were an estimated three thousand groups from communities of all sizes in the association. As these groups formalized their agenda, they moved their meetings to more public spaces, invited celebrated speakers, and began charging fees. In 1878 Bishop John Heyl Vincent spearheaded the creation of Chautauqua Literary and Scientific Circles. These popular lecture circuits gave women access to education not available to them at universities, and "Chautauqua Circles" played an important role in the genesis of the modern American book group.

While we can never be certain, there are a few things we know for sure. Women have been reading fiction since novels first came on the scene in Europe. Women and men have gathered together in intellectual salons since at least the seventeenth century. These groups have taken many forms—from communal to political to aesthetic. They have had many missions—community building, intellectual growth, self-improvement. In order to understand how book groups developed, we need to look at all these possibilities and put them together in a way that allows room for the diverse experience of book groups today.

WOMEN AND READING

As we said, women have been reading novels since they were first published. Early on reading fiction was seen as a leisurely activity available only to educated men and to upper-class women. As books became more available, reading for pleasure was understood to be a solitary act. In many ways women reading was seen as unwholesome—society couldn't trust a woman who sat by herself reading all kinds of trashy stories (many early novels were torrid tales of fallen women). Think of all those iconic paintings you've seen of a woman reading alone in a private domestic space—this is just one image, an image dependent on the notion that a woman's place was in the home, that her aspirations should never leave the private domestic sphere.

This image was challenged by women in seventeenth- and eighteenth-century France; women who ran salons that attracted the most powerful politicians and revolutionaries of the day. One such *salonnière*—Germaine de Stael—was eventually exiled from Paris by Napoleon, who feared her political influence. Likewise, Anne Hutchinson was banished and eventually died in the American wilderness after causing the Antinomian Crisis, the most serious challenge to Puritan power the New World had ever seen. What did Hutchinson do to cause such a fuss? She gathered readers together in her home to discuss Scripture. She formed a book group.

This kind of literary activism continued in the United States through the Progressive Era and up through the political turbulence of the 1960s and the women's consciousness-raising groups in the 1970s. Even Harold Bloom, that cranky leviathan of literary criticism, admits: "For many, many years now, the majority of my best students—that is to say, the most sensitive and brilliant and dedicated readers—have been women."

So this rich history of reading—reading together with other women, more specifically—may help to explain why the majority of book group members are women. But we'd like to offer the perceptive analysis of a male book group member, Bob Lamm, who argues that women dominate book groups because men don't want to violate what he calls "the Guy Code." Part of this code defines book groups as either "women's work to be avoided at all costs" or "too feminist." Lamm also believes that "since most men want their sexism to remain unchallenged, staying out of reading groups makes a certain kind of sense." He goes on to suggest that

> The prevalence of women's reading groups in an equal-opportunity world underscores several controversial clichés that carpet either side of the gender divide. Namely, that men read "how-to" manuals and speak in grunts of less than two syllables, while women love literature and discourse.

Is it true that women and men are so different? Can we really say that women like to talk for hours and men just grumble? It does seem possible that women are socialized to view conversation as a pastime and to share their feelings in a way that men aren't. There's always an exception to the rule, of course, but we agree with one of our editors, Jane Rosenman, who suggests that women like to "dissect" things verbally more than men do. One of our own book group members prefers the verb "masticate" to describe how women tend to gnaw on a topic for hours. At any rate, women and book groups have come a long way, baby. In the words of one writer, "The [book club] tradition has survived like a whalebone corset at the bottom of a drawerful of sports bras."

Book Groups and Women's Communities in the United States

"Are book discussion groups really bitch-and-stitch sessions without the needle and thread?" asks Marilyn Poole in her 1999 study of Australian book groups. The sense of communal support that many women value in their book group is related to the sewing-circle tradition, among others. When we researched women's communities in the United States, we discovered how many of them are literary, and how many of them have a long and distinguished history. For instance, here's a statistic you may not know: 75 percent of public libraries in the United States were founded by women. But here's the amazing part: they were founded as civic institutions by women who didn't have the right to vote. Reading groups were, in many ways, the backbone of the suffrage movement and provided an opportunity for self-education at a time when women weren't allowed access to higher education. Women made a commitment to their own intellectual growth and to each other, a commitment that motivates many book groups today.

During the late nineteenth century, there were two types of reading groups: one type for professional women and the other for women devoted to charity work. The first groups included Sorosis and the New England Woman's Club. These early clubs were primarily made up of middle- to upper-class women and were derided by New York upper-crust society embodied by novelist Edith Wharton. In her short story "Xingu" Wharton describes these "club women":

> Mrs. Ballinger is one of the ladies who pursue Culture in bands, as though it were dangerous to meet it alone. To this end she had founded the Lunch Club, an association of herself and several other indomitable huntresses of erudition.

The snobbery we hear in the voice of Wharton's narrator was shared by many who felt that these "club women" were overstepping their bounds by seeking "Culture." However, by 1906, five thousand clubs had joined the General Federation of Women's Clubs. It wasn't just white ladies who dared to "pursue Culture in bands." African-American women started their own clubs in the North before the Civil War. In New York in the 1830s, the Colored Ladies Society was created, followed by the Afric-American Female Intelligence Society of Boston and the Library Company of Colored Persons in Philadelphia.

Shortly after the turn of the century, the Progressive Era began, and middle-class ladies formed reading groups for women in poor communities, convinced that the urban despair brought on by the Industrial Revolution could be eradicated through education. In the 1950s the

Great Books Foundation started a reading revolution with the radical suggestion that *anyone* could read and understand the classics. In the 1960s women's book groups became informed by the social activism of the era, and in the 1990s the book group phenomenon reached a peak. Even before Oprah's Book Club, which aired for the first time in 1996, book groups were on the rise. Why? In *The Reading Group Book* Virginia Valentine, book club coordinator at Tattered Cover Book Store in Denver, Colorado, offers this explanation:

> My feeling is that the current movement gained momentum from the generation of people now in their thirties and forties. This was the first generation to grow up with television as their primary stimulus and the first generation in which women took working for granted. These young women were working very hard and didn't really have the chance to read. They wanted companionship, intellectual stimulation. They wanted to go back and repattern themselves, and they found they could do this by sitting down and reading a book.

Book Groups on TV

Book groups have come of age. If being featured on a prime-time drama or a sitcom is any kind of litmus test, it's fair to say that book groups have thoroughly permeated our popular culture. But as we point out in this chapter, book groups have a long and complex history that should ensure that—unlike beehive hairdos and wood paneling on station wagons—they're here to stay.

Did you catch the scene in the first season of HBO's hit series *The Sopranos* where mob boss's wife, Carmela Soprano, and her book group are discussing *Memoirs of a Geisha*? "She's just so trapped, so confined by her culture," states one member of the group when talking about Sayuri, the novel's main character. All the other expertly manicured and superbly coifed mob wives nod in ardent agreement, "Yes, yes, she is." Do you think *The Sopranos*'s creator David Chase intended a little irony here?

Didn't see that episode of *The Sopranos*? Ever watch *Malcolm in the Middle*? In an uncharacteristic move, Lois—the frazzled mother of four unruly sons—decides to join a book group. She diligently reads the book and shows up excited to talk about it, but it turns out the women just use the book group as an excuse to get together, get drunk, and complain bitterly about their families. Things go from bad to worse, and Lois ends up hiding from the police in a Dumpster with a member of the book group, crying about how all she wanted to do was discuss the wonderful book she read.

Didn't watch that one, either? My my, what do you do all day—read? In late 2002 a new CBS sitcom called *Still Standing* took a chance and devoted an entire episode to the laugh-track possibilities of book groups. The main characters—Bill and Judy Miller—are a middle-class Chicago couple. When it's Judy's turn to host her group, Bill joins them and compares the nineteenth-century mystery they're reading to an Arnold Schwarzenegger movie. Bill's simple, homespun wisdom makes him the star of the group, and he easily dominates the group's male leader, Terry, who comes across as a snooty wimp. Later that night, Judy explodes at Bill, and their argument disintegrates into a childish competition of "who's better at book club."

On to a more flattering portrayal of book groups on television. In summer 2003, we watched an episode of HBO's drama *The Wire* that featured a men's-prison book group. The group discusses *The Great Gatsby,* and surprisingly, the young black men from Baltimore relate to this "white cat" of long ago, to his "frontin' like he's a playa." One group member argues that Gatsby's downfall isn't his love for Daisy. In fact, he suggests, all the guys in the group—sporting their orange department-of-correction scrubs—share Gatsby's fatal flaw: he wanted something fast, and he wanted to be someone different from who he was, so he made up a story of his not-so-glamorous past. The camera pans over the men's faces, and viewers can see the recognition in their eyes, the way they've connected Gatsby's story with their own. It's a poignant moment that conveys the way the best book group discussions invite us to understand our own experience in new ways.

From what we've heard, TV viewers in the United Kingdom don't want to miss an episode of *The Book Group,* the sleeper hit sitcom that began in 2001. Clare is an American girl in Glasgow, who starts a book group with the idea that she'll meet some interesting people. She was right, but they're not the kind of interesting people she was hoping for. There's wheelchair-bound and shy Kenny, punk Ph.D. English student Barney, and the two slutty footballers' wives, Dirka and Fist. Imagine all the crazy adventures this zany group of readers will have! Now that's must-see TV. In some ways *The Book Group* sounds like the same old tired idea, a sort of bookish British *Seinfeld* for the twenty-first century. Gather some wacky and not-altogether-likable characters, trap them in a small space, give them nothing much to talk about, and see what happens. One critic of the show thinks that while the premise is intriguing, the book group in the show is not believable. Why would a Ph.D. English student be in a book group? (Read our bios on the back cover of this book, and you'll get our little joke.)

Sewing Circles, Quilting Bees

Speaking of patterns, let's take a look at sewing circles and quilting bees—those great gatherings of women—to see how they relate to book groups today. Sewing circles peaked around the time of the Civil War, when women sewed supplies for soldiers and made clothes for the sick and needy in their communities. Of course, it wasn't all about volunteer work and charity events and fund-raising projects. Sewing circles were about self-expression, too. Some of the oldest sewing circles in the country are still in existence and still making some of the most beautiful textile crafts in the United States. Book groups often tell us this sense of historical continuity and shared experience is what drew them to the experience. The fascinating thing about sewing circles is that because they were deemed "women's work," no one took them too seriously. Women could gather with other women and stay below the cultural radar, so to speak. That's why sewing circles were the perfect place to begin the suffrage movement. Scholars have speculated that groups devoted to women's rights may have grown out of small informal get-togethers like sewing circles. Some literary salons were named bluestocking societies because women gathered in their most relaxed clothes, their blue stockings. Turns out maybe those sewing circles were doing more than just darning their socks. They might have been hatching plans to get women the right to vote.

Saturday Evening Girls Club

During the Progressive Era, after the massive industrialization following the Civil War, middle-class reformers entered the slums and began establishing self-help programs. Energies shifted after the United States entered WWI, but the New Deal (1933–37) continued the work of these Progressive women and established the foundation of U.S. social policy. One of the earliest and most influential women-run literacy programs of the Progressive Era was the Saturday Evening Girls Club (SEGC), which was founded in 1899 in the North End of Boston. Most of the women involved in SEGC were second-generation immigrants, and their intellectual hunger threatened some of their parents, who were afraid their vulnerable daughters would lose a sense of connection with their cultural roots. Nonetheless, education was so important, some girls defied their parents' wishes in attending SEGC. These young women were Americanized not just through what they studied but through the democratic way in which the groups were run. The founders of SEGC wanted to do more than just train these young women for a life of work in a factory or in the home.

Other Associations of American Women

A member of SEGC called it a "happy refuge," one that provided a place for women to develop their minds. This work continues in the American Association of University Women (AAUW), whose mission is "to promote education and equity for all women and girls." With fifteen hundred branches and more than 150,000 members, the AAUW is a forceful testament to the power of women's education. Some of the first book discussions Kira facilitated were for AAUW groups, and she found them to be some of the most intellectually insatiable women she's ever had the pleasure to meet. The League of Women Voters and the Junior League grow out of this same tradition of women's communities with a mission. Like many Junior league organizations, the Junior League of Boston began as a sewing circle. The Boston league's purpose when it was founded in 1901 was to get young women of a certain social position involved in urban problems as part of the Progressive movement. To this day, Junior Leagues across the country combine debutante balls with social philanthropy, inspiring their members to be as schooled in social justice as they are in the social graces—now that's what we call a well-rounded woman.

BOOK GROUP MEMBER
AS INTELLECTUAL

The Famous Salons of Paris

"To talk of literature, morals, and fine arts, and everything under the sun, is to indulge in politics," Napoleon argued. "Women should knit. If I let [Germaine de Stael] come to Paris she would make trouble; she would lose me the men around me." Can you hear Napoleon just quaking in his little boots? He sure had reason to—even after he had banished de Stael from Paris. De Stael commanded the attention of the most influential men and women in revolutionary France and was the grande dame in the salon's finest hour. (Picture your own book group, only really, really fancy and full of political intrigue.) The salons themselves were made up primarily of men—but women stood at the core, the glue that held the whole thing together.

In late seventeenth-century and early eighteenth-century Paris, women were generally understood to be morally superior to men and therefore responsible for the moral regeneration of society. No pressure, really! The salons were more than just a way to cultivate talented aristocracy. Because women were not allowed to be educated, their taste was seen as "pure" and "natural," their intuition in matters of art and literature and music believed to be superior to that of men. Women were also honored for their expertise in matters of propriety and harmony as carriers of moral values (inside the home, of course, and only women of a certain class). These "women of quality" had a certain power as arbiters of taste, and in some cases their influence expanded into the public, male-dominated realm of politics. In 1791 there were eleven hundred *sociétés politiques* in France; by 1793 there were close to six thousand. But just because these societies were popular doesn't mean they changed the basic definition of proper French womanhood: to reign supreme in the domestic sphere and to care for the men. Germaine de Stael obviously didn't pay attention. While other salon women focused on apolitical topics, Stael demanded that her salon mean something and do something beyond the walls of her luxurious home. Napoleon banished her because he wanted to contain the power of salon culture; he thought women shouldn't try to be "something other than their sex."

Salon women in the eighteenth century were caught in a nasty catch-22: they were not allowed to be educated, and they were not allowed in the public sphere because they weren't educated. That left the salons as the one place they could develop themselves intellectually. However, the value that had previously been placed on women's "pure" intuition had given way to a belief that because their authority rested only in intuition and not in education, women couldn't comment and be taken seriously on public matters. As the century wore on, salons were increasingly seen as frivolous social events; the role of the *salonnière* was limited to that of a hostess. Her job was to move the conversation of enlightened men along without adding her own opinions. She was supposed to send out the invitations, hand out the hors d'oeuvres, and look pretty.

During the nineteenth century, salon life had become male dominated, with powerful intellectuals attending less and less. The rise of modern institutions designed to increase the power of the middle class also had an effect on the salons, moving the centers of power firmly out of the grip of aristocratic women, who couldn't participate in public dialogue because of their lack of education. By 1837 salons were sterile, the conversation no longer seen as the path to civic change. The salon became a haven from the world instead of a center of cultural change, reinforcing the idea that the feminine domestic sphere was a refuge from the world. Women were relegated to the role of passive muse, marginalized from the channels of political power.

The salon didn't disappear from Paris, however. Gertrude Stein's 1920s expatriate salon attracted the most promising young artists of what would become the modernist movement. Sherwood Anderson, F. Scott Fitzgerald, Ernest Hemingway, Pablo Picasso—they all spent time in the home of Stein and her lifelong partner, Alice B. Toklas, where artists were given the space they needed to develop their work away from the chaos of the modern world. Dorothy Parker and other literary tastemakers continued this tradition with the Algonquin Round Table in New York in the 1920s and 1930s. Parker's biting wit was something to be feared like de Stael's influence over a hundred years before. When Napoleon was in exile, he admitted that de Stael was "very dangerous." Indeed, at one point he went as far as to say "her salon was fatal."

Reading as Subversive

Who would have guessed that book groups could be dangerous and threatening? Not us certainly, until we learned more about de Stael and the radical power of the salon to change the political and social climate. This got us thinking about whether or not this subversive quality of women's groups made its way over the Atlantic. The answer, we discovered, was yes, as we can see in the story of a woman named Anne Hutchinson, who arrived in 1634 at the Massachusetts Bay Colony.

Perhaps it's no coincidence that many book groups trace their origins to church groups. Some would even argue that America's first book group was a church group formed by Anne Hutchinson, when she gathered women in her Boston parlor twice a week for sermon discussions. In her parlor talks, Hutchinson encouraged women to discuss everything, from literature to theology, for self-education. When the authorities finally cracked down on her group, she was accused of "troubling the peace of the Commonwealth" and "maintaining a meeting and an assembly in [her] house that hath been condemned by the general assembly as a thing not tolerable nor comely in the sight of God nor fitting for [her] sex."

If you remember reading the sermons of John Cotton or John Winthrop in high school (two Puritan leaders of the Massachusetts Bay Colony), you'll know what kind of fundamentalism Hutchinson was up against. Here are the inspiring words of Jonathan Edwards, who preached many years after Cotton and Winthrop had met their

Maker, but his view of the relationship between humanity and God was directly descended from his Puritan forefathers:

> The God that holds you over the pit of hell, much as one holds a spider, or some loathesome insect, over the fire, abhors you, and is dreadfully provoked; his wrath towards you burns like fire.

Hutchinson's seditious crime was that she didn't believe in this view of humanity as a "loathesome insect." In fact, she didn't believe in the covenant of works. If you don't know anything else about the Puritans, you probably know a little something about the Puritan work ethic. This great American value wasn't always about working hard just so you could buy that new Honda Accord. No, back in those days, that Puritan work ethic was presented as the only way to get into Heaven. Hutchinson didn't believe it. Instead, she suggested that faith alone was necessary for salvation, and in 1637 the general court decided she was an antinomian heretic.

Puritans weren't too fond of those who didn't toe the line. Remember poor Hester Prynne in *The Scarlet Letter*? She paid a very public price for her adultery, and no one in the village had to ask what that letter "A" on Hester's chest meant. The condemnation of her sin was unanimous—no interpretation necessary, although the same can't be said for the "A" in the story as generations have argued about its meaning. Hawthorne sure did have his finger on the pulse of the Puritan mentality. Too bad for Hester, there was no community at all for her once she broke the rules.

Things didn't end well for Hutchinson either. After she was found guilty and exiled, she moved to Long Island, where she and her family were killed by Native Americans. Her work wasn't forgotten, however, and this spirit of candid and vigorous debate was continued by Margaret Fuller, who in the 1840s hosted bookstore "conversations" on literature and culture and encouraged women to claim the right and responsibility of self-realization.

❧ READING FOR SELF-IMPROVEMENT ❧

Every man in his lifetime needs to thank his faults. As no man thoroughly understands a truth until he has contended against it, so no man has a thorough acquaintance with the hindrances or talents of men, until he has suffered from the one, and seen the triumph of the other over his own want of the same. Has he a defect of temper that unfits him to live in society? Thereby he is driven to entertain himself alone, and acquire habits of self-help; and thus, like the wounded oyster, he mends his shell with pearl.

—RALPH WALDO EMERSON, "Compensation"

BOOK GROUPS TODAY

Where's Waldo? How Emerson Helped Launch Oprah's Book Club

Now let's move to the biggest book group event of the twentieth century: Oprah's Book Club. We've seen that book groups can trace their roots to women's communities, sewing circles, literacy organizations, and intellectual salons. In a similar way, Oprah's literary mission can be linked to ideas that are deeply embedded in our shared American consciousness.

Many critics have argued that Oprah Winfrey is responsible not only for encouraging people to read but for getting them to read in a new way. You'd think this would earn her accolades, and it has from many. But some book-industry insiders have criticized her. As one critic sees it, "The true legacy of Oprah's Book Club has been turning reading novels into self-help."

Just take a look at a few of the short passages from Ralph Waldo Emerson's famous essay "Self-Reliance," and you'll see how wrong this critic is. Oprah didn't do it—at least not by herself. This phenomenon preceded Oprah; it preceded Emerson and his transcendentalist friends. Self-help is as American as apple pie. We could say that America is a Self-Help Nation. As our learned Founding Father Benjamin Franklin advised us in *Poor Richard's Almanac*, "God helps them that help themselves." Self-reliance is what Emerson calls it, and it's the reason the pop psychology section of your local bookstore is bursting at the seams. Most of us believe—or at least want to believe—that we can help ourselves and make our lives better through conscious living. It's just a short step between that fundamental belief and the idea that reading books can help you discover yourself and improve your life. You might think the following words have a certain Oprah ring to them, but no, this is Ralph Waldo Emerson speaking:

- Nothing is at last sacred but the integrity of your own mind.
- Nothing can bring you peace but yourself.

Oprah's Book Club

On September 17, 1996, Oprah Winfrey proclaimed, "I want to get the whole country reading again!" and launched Oprah's Book Club, the most powerful one-woman literacy program in the history of our nation. Six successful years later, on April 4, 2002, Oprah shocked everyone by announcing the end of her book club, admitting to her disappointed audience, "It has been harder and harder to find books on a monthly basis that I feel absolutely compelled to share."

Oprah's Book Club (in its first manifestation) was an integral part of her talk-show's mission expressed in the tagline "Change Your Life TV," which, Oprah says, works to "help people create the highest vision for themselves." It's true that Oprah treated novels as springboards for self-reflection, and this therapeutic approach has a long history. Whatever you think of Oprah and her book club, there's no denying that she was the reading cheerleader, the book club evangelist the industry needed. She spoke eloquently and passionately about how books had changed her life, and she chose books based on her own tastes and the recommendations of friends. As long as her book club lasted, she refused to consider publisher recommendations in order to keep her choices "pure," relying only on her own taste and intuition (sounds a bit like Emerson, doesn't it?).

We were lucky enough to meet Oprah and to talk to her about books. Needless to say, chatting with her was incredible. In fact, we have never quite recovered from the excitement of meeting Oprah and her staff (check out our special feature "The Day We Met Oprah" for details). We don't think we're speaking in hyperbole when we say that Oprah's Book Club is a phenomenon that changed the face of book clubs forever, saved a struggling publishing industry, established its own "canon" of literary works, created millions of new active readers, and transformed the reading, writing, and emotional lives of countless people around the globe. Oprah has spoken publicly about her belief in the power of books many times. Here's one poignant example:

> I feel strongly that, no matter who you are, reading opens doors and provides, in your personal sanctuary, an opportunity to explore and feel things, the way other forms of media cannot. I want books to become part of my audience's lifestyle, for reading to become a natural phenomenon for them.

At its peak in 1999, Oprah's Book Club segment had more than thirteen million viewers, with foreign distribution in over 130 countries from Afghanistan to Zimbabwe. In most cases, by the time the book club segment aired, more than five hundred thousand people had already purchased the book. Oprah's recommendation meant a minimum of an additional five hundred thousand to upward of a million copies sold, or an additional five to ten million dollars for the publisher. According to *Publishers Weekly*, all forty-eight books selected for Oprah's Book Club became best-sellers. Even Starbucks got involved, selling Oprah books (and only Oprah books) in its stores, with profits going to the Starbucks Foundation, a literacy program. Oprah convinced publishers to donate ten thousand copies of each book club pick to libraries nationwide, and her "Pass It On" service project donates used books to selected organizations, like schools and prisons.

In 1999 Oprah was awarded the 50th Anniversary gold medal at the National Book Awards as "the most influential force in publishing." By 2000 the book club had slowed down with only nine titles featured, and in 2001 that number had fallen to six. The ratings were dropping, and we imagine Oprah might have been a bit worn out. Jonathan Franzen (author of *The Corrections*) couldn't have helped matters any when—after Oprah gave him the phone call most authors only dream about—he told reporters he had mixed feelings about being chosen as an "Oprah book." Some of her previous choices were "schmaltzy and one-dimensional," he said, and he didn't like the idea of Oprah's Book Club label appearing on his cover as a symbol of "corporate ownership." Oprah retracted her invitation to have Franzen on her show, and after just a few more choices she ended her original book group with Toni Morrison's novel *Sula*.

When Oprah's producers came to her in 1996 with the idea of a book club segment, she thought they had lost their minds. Books don't make good TV. How could she and her staff make the show engaging? One solution was to have the author appear (which meant the club could select only books by living authors), and the other was to have viewers on the show, chosen from among many who submitted deeply personal stories about how the book had changed their lives. Oprah and her staff decided to do both. The segment featuring *White Oleander* was a perfect example of what one critic calls "confessional TV." Janet Fitch's novel is the story of a young woman who comes of age in foster homes after her mother is sent to prison for murder. On the book club show, two guests grew up in troubled homes, one was a foster parent, and the other was a social worker. Unlike the critic mentioned above, we don't believe this was cynical "confessional TV" plotting; rather, featuring guests whose lives resemble the book goes along with what Oprah has said all along about why she adores reading:

> You read about somebody else's life, but it makes you think about your own. That's the beauty of it. That's why I love books. . . . Reading is like everything else. You're drawn to people who are like yourself.

The Day We Met Oprah

I'm calling from Oprah's Book Club," the woman said, "we've been checking out your book group Web site and wondered if you'd be interested in meeting with us to talk about some books and authors?"

Talk about surreal. For the record, we are huge fans of Oprah and Oprah's Book Club. Oprah's decision to share her love of reading with her public inspired hundreds of thousands of people (many of whom, by their own admission, hadn't read for pleasure since the Carter administration) to become passionate, regular readers. Let's say we know exactly whom we have to thank for the chance to start a book group business.

In the cab on the way to Harpo Studios, Kira pulled her copy of the May *O* magazine out of her bag. "Look!" she gulped spastically, waving Oprah's smiling face bravely back and forth. "We're going to meet her in a few minutes!" Ellen recoiled from the proffered cover in panic. "Are you crazy? Get that thing away from me!" The cab driver, impressively oblivious to the shrieks and scuffle emanating from his backseat, proceeded to maneuver at a maddeningly slow crawl through the streets of the Chicago meat-packing district. We emerged from the taxi, limp and babbling like toddlers steeped to the gills in Novocain.

Later we agreed that the marble path that twists and turns from the outer reaches of Harpo Studios to the inner sanctum of Oprah's office resembled nothing so much, in our fevered brains, as the spiraling yellow-brick road that Judy Garland's Dorothy traversed to the Emerald City. As the coordinator of Oprah's Book Club inquired pleasantly about our trip, we tried to respond in kind, in English. Our laden attempts at wit fell on our own ears as the garbled keenings of a pair of particularly troubled Munchkins. At last we reached the closed door of Oprah's office, dropping in momentary relief on the luxurious sofa outside. The door opened as somebody else came out, offering a shattering glimpse of Oprah's regal head. Fortunately, Oprah's two dogs, a pair of almost-matching jet-black cocker spaniels, also scurried out into the waiting area. We sank to our knees, literally, lost in the thankful oblivion of having something to pat and clutch. From their shimmering desks, Oprah's real watchdogs, a pair of strikingly beautiful young women clothed in suitably muted cashmere sweaters and buttery leather pants that hugged their impossibly long legs, eyed us with a cool civility that seemed to suggest, "Just look at that, another couple of white girls gone crazy just five feet and five minutes away."

The door opened again and we were invited into Oprah's office. It is at this point that memory grows untrustworthy. We remember, dimly, shaking hands with Oprah and sitting down in the elegant, expansive room to talk about book club books and authors. It was strangely hard to connect the friendly, simply dressed woman in the chair next to us (wearing no makeup and looking stunning) with the idea of the immaculately polished and devastatingly powerful Oprah who radiates from our television screens and magazine stands. Yet had we no knowledge of that Oprah, we still would have been struck by the absolute force of her presence—you won't be surprised to hear that she exudes an irresistible charisma. Within half a minute we were teetering the barest millimeter from the edge of our seats, leaning in hungrily, eager to be as close to her as we could get.

We had wanted to bring Oprah a gift of some sort, something small but meaningful, and had settled on a pair of hand-painted reading glasses. Ellen handed the glasses to Oprah, explaining, "I tried them on and they were just a bit big on me, and I have a pretty big head, but I thought from seeing you on television that you might have an even bigger head—" Kira lowered her foot purposefully on top of Ellen's under the table—"I mean, not that your head is big or anything; I really like big heads; I've liked people with big heads all my life" (Kira rapidly increased the pressure) "my husband has a really big head, too, and so hopefully they will fit." Oprah laughed easily and said, "You two are gonna have some big-headed babies for sure!" and told a story about trying to find a woman's cowboy hat to fit her in a store in Aspen. As we searched our minds frantically for some way back from this conversational precipice, Oprah's producer, another extraordinarily warm and delightful woman (who no doubt witnesses several such awkward Oprah-induced meltdowns each day) kindly rescued us with a thoughtful question about Denver book clubs.

We still can't believe we got to spend those twenty or so minutes in Oprah's presence, talking about a passion that drives all three of us. No, we didn't recommend any of the "Oprah" books, but we can tell you for a fact that not only does Oprah read each and every book she has shared with her audience but that those she shares are the ones she loves the most. That's why people trust her and buy the books she recommends, and always will, so long as she continues to do so. For us, the most wonderful moment in that meeting unfolded when Kira told a story about working in a bookstore shortly after the original Oprah's Book Club launched. "This middle-aged gentleman came up to me, looking lost and overwhelmed," Kira remembered. "He asked for an Oprah's Book Club book and apologized for not knowing the title. 'It's my first time in a bookstore,' the man admitted shyly. 'It's the first time I've read a book since I was in school.'" Oprah's eyes were shining. "That's the reason I love doing this," she said simply, with a smile. "It's the thing I've loved doing the most, more than anything, I think."

The immediate success of the relaunch of Oprah's Book Club in June of 2003 proves that people want to read books that Oprah likes and recommends. The book club segments will now run three to five times a year and will focus on the classics, in part inspired by Oprah's own dedication to reading great works of the past. Oprah has promised to make the classics "accessible to every woman and man who reads." A membership program has been added to her on-line book club, which now calls itself "the biggest book club in the world." Members of Oprah's club have access to study guides and other information on the selected authors and books. But does "the Oprah effect" continue? Can Oprah really drive huge sales of books we were forced to read in high school? Yes, it would seem so. As the author of the daily trade e-newsletter *Publisher's Lunch* observes, "It's a whole new world when Nielsen

BookScan updates become a weekly headline feature on the Drudge Report!" Weeks after Oprah's recommendation, sales of Steinbeck's *East of Eden*—the first selection for her new classics club—were just behind the staggering advance sales figures of the newest Harry Potter installment.

FROM HIGHBROW TO THE MASSES: TASTEMAKERS IN AMERICA

A reader is not like a critic, who reads for professional judgment. The reader seeks pleasure, enlightenment, self-identification, seduction.
—MALCOLM BRADBURY

Some critics tried to force Oprah into a role she didn't seem to want—that of literary tastemaker. Throughout history, other readers have been more than happy to appease us with their educated reading recommendations and good taste. For instance, in England there are the Literary Guild, the Book Society, and the Left Book Club, just to name a few. Choosing books for the masses is no easy task. The invention of book clubs transformed publishing and reading habits in radical ways.

Book-of-the-Month Club

The Book-of-the-Month-Club (BOMC) has been called a "National Literary Supreme Court." Founded by Harry Scherman in 1926, it is the nation's first mail-order book club, and during its heyday it featured literary experts like Heywood Broun and Christopher Morley as judges who made the book selections. BOMC has made the career of many an author by including a little-known book or first novel; for instance, no one had heard of J. D. Salinger when BOMC chose *Catcher in the Rye* in 1951. One of the intangible benefits of belonging to BOMC is being "in the know"—you can be a housewife in Ipswitch, South Dakota, and still feel connected with the literati of New York by reading the same books.

BOMC put a new twist on things—pay your dues each month and you were promised more than just books, you were promised good taste. BOMC had its hits, and it had its misses, too. Years ago its editors rejected *The Grapes of Wrath, All the King's Men,* and *The Sun Also Rises.* In today's competitive market, BOMC has adapted its selections to reflect more popular authors like Tom Clancy and John Grisham.

Great Books Foundation

When asked to define "great books," a spokesperson for the Great Books Foundation replied, "the best-sellers of all time." Great Books was founded in 1947 by philosopher/educator and coauthor of *How to Read a Book* Mortimer Adler. The mission of Great Books is to make canonical works of literature accessible to anyone and everyone (including young people, through the Junior Great Books program), so people could engage in a "Great Conversation" with the great writers of the past. By "great writers of the past" the founders meant the "dead white males" we're all encouraged to read in school—Homer, Shakespeare, Plato. Great Books pioneered the use of discussion guides, and Great Books teachers are trained in seminars that show them how to engage even the most reticent reader. At its most popular in the late 1950s, Great Books had over fifty thousand members; today it's still going strong with over twenty thousand members.

Readers' Subscription (Later Known as Mid-Century Book Club)

Perhaps the most intriguing experiment in tastemaking for the masses, Readers' Subscription began in a "General Honors" course at Columbia College. The course's instructor, John Erskine, believed the United States lacked Europe's long tradition of tastemaking, and he wanted to do something about it. (A quick side note: Erskine wanted to solve other problems as well. In 1936 he published his book *The Influence of Women, and Its Cure*—and no, he wasn't kidding.) Readers' Subscription was founded by Jacques Barzun, W. H. Auden, and Lionel Trilling, in 1950, growing out of the Columbia course and as a reaction against the "middlebrow" choices of the Book-of-the-Month Club. When it ended in 1963, its membership was over forty thousand. Like BOMC, Readers' Subscription offered a new title every month, at a discount, with each selection introduced by a short essay by one of the editors in a club newsletter. The editors wanted their books to be "edifying, not merely entertaining," and they wanted to address the issue of "greatness" in literature. In other words, they wanted to be highbrow tastemakers.

Other more specialized clubs followed these major players. You may be familiar with the Quality Paperback Book Club, which offers popular titles at a discount. Book clubs—the subscription kind, where you pay your dues and each month or so receive a book in the mail—come in all shapes and sizes. Just do a Google search, and you'll see what we mean. No matter how specific your interest, chances are you can sign up with a service that will deliver the books you want right to your doorstep—you don't even have to choose them. We found over 150 distinct book clubs on everything from African-American literature to zoology. Like romance novels? Try the Rhapsody Book Club. Read a mystery a week? There's the Mystery Guild Book Club. Want to read African-American books with attitude? Check out the Sistah Circle Book Club. If you're a Christian woman, you might want to join the Good Girl Book Club. If you're a Libertarian in New York, there's a book club for you sponsored by the Anarchist Forums. The Graphic Design Book Club selects titles on—you guessed it—graphic design, and the Outdoorsman's Edge Book Club will prepare you for your trek into the wilderness. There's the InsightOut Book Club for gay and lesbian readers, the Taste Book Club for cooks, and the Military Book Club for history buffs. There's even a Children's Braille Book Club. Someone stop us, we could go on for pages and pages and pages! These kinds of book clubs are appealing mostly for their convenience. The more specialized the better—these clubs do the legwork for you, so you don't have to wade through thousands of books to find the one book you want about your pet topic.

RECENT EVENTS

In addition to "The Oprah Effect," we've seen other exciting developments in the book group world over the last several years. In *Bowling Alone: the Collapse and Revival of American Community,* Harvard professor Robert Putnam argues that we're just not spending enough time together. Generational change, electronic entertainment (TV, video games, the Internet), lack of time and money, two-income couples, and urban sprawl are all to blame. This isolation leads to a lack of what Putnam calls "social capital." Book groups provide this social capital—and, as Putnam points out, with an estimated (as far as we know) 750,000 to 950,000 book groups in the United States, book clubs are one of few groups that haven't declined in recent years. Thanks to Oprah's Book Club, book groups today have helped bring books back into people's living rooms, they enjoy great influence in the world of publishing, they're all over the media, and they're appealing to younger and more diverse readers.

One Nation, Undivided: "One City, One Book" Programs

By our last count, forty-one cities have energized their reading communities and initiated "One City, One Book" programs. You've probably heard of this phenomenon, an unusual combination of reading as mass entertainment and community building. In most cases, a library association selects a book and promotes literacy programs aimed at getting the city or town or state to read the book together. "It's very gratifying that people are doing this," admits Nancy Pearl, executive director of the Washington Center for the Book and creator of the first "One City, One Book" program in Seattle in 1998. "But this was never intended to be a civics lesson. This was always intended to be a library program that promoted a deepening engagement that helps people engage in good books."

Seattle started with Russell Banks's novel *The Sweet Hereafter,*

Chicago and many other cities stuck with a safe classic and read Harper Lee's *To Kill a Mockingbird,* Arizona kept it regional and chose Barbara Kingsolver's *Animal Dreams.* The only city to stumble in the implementation of this program is the Capital of Book Gab, yes, that's right, New York City. In spring 2002—when New Yorkers were finally becoming New Yorkers again after 9/11 and arguing fanatically over books—a committee of fifteen librarians, bookstore owners, and educators met to pick the book for "One City, One Book." They couldn't agree and got stuck trying to choose between *Native Speaker* by Chang-Rae Lee and *The Color of Water* by James McBride. Chang-Rae Lee won out, but not before unfriendly words were exchanged, forcing the librarians to leave the group and quit the program.

It wasn't just the planners of the "One City, One Book" programs who were passionate. Like book groups themselves and so much else involving popular reading and issues of taste, the "One City, One Book" program brings out the wicked witty best in its detractors. Before we share one such condemnation, we must give a disclaimer: we think the "One City, One Book" program is great, fantastic, a positive and fun addition to the world of books. However, we couldn't let you get away without reading a bit more from our favorite ornery critic. "I don't like these mass reading bees," Harold Bloom has said unequivocally. "It is rather like the idea that we are all going to pop out and eat Chicken McNuggets or something else horrid at once."

Getting Wired: The Effect of the Internet on Book Groups

There are literally thousands of on-line book clubs out there in the virtual world. We describe in chapter 5 how on-line book groups work and how they differ from off-line groups, and we profile a few on-line groups in chapter 7. We think many on-line book groups are outstanding, but we don't think they will replace living-room book groups anytime soon. When chatting with other readers on a discussion board, we just can't get the immediate, visceral sense of community we get by seeing each other's faces, listening to each other's voices, and sharing a good meal and a glass of wine in each other's homes. That much said, we must acknowledge that the Internet has changed book groups forever. In 1996, when Oprah launched her club, the Internet was beginning to make its way into the family rooms and home offices of America, opening up a world of information right at our fingertips. As the explosion in book groups continued, so did the on-line know-how of book groups members, who increasingly go to the Web instead of to the library to research authors and books. It can be frustrating, at times, to wade through the seemingly endless amount of on-line information out there, but there's no doubt about it: the Internet has given individual readers easy access to the kind of information previously held only in the hands of the experts. Like the book group phenomenon itself, the Internet has had a pluralistic effect: spreading knowledge at the grassroots level, building a sense of community, and expanding readers' minds one at a time.

Book Groups: Past, Present, and Future

In tracing the complex cultural roots of book groups, we discover that in the United States they combine the Puritan urge for consensus ("Did the other members of my group understand the novel the way I did?") and the Emersonian urge for self-improvement ("How can this novel help me understand myself and my world?"). They can be seen as dangerous to society (Germaine de Stael and Anne Hutchinson), and they can be tools used to better society (the Saturday Evening Girls Club, the American Association of University Women, and other literary organizations). For centuries, communities of readers have gathered together to explore the world through books. Sewing circles develop domestic community, salons nurture the intellect, literary clubs enact social change, and social groups challenge the political status quo. What makes book groups so fantastic—so quietly revolutionary—is how they seamlessly combine all these multifaceted aims in a cohesive experience that builds community in a socially fragmented world and focuses the mind in the often overwhelming Information Age.

FOR FURTHER READING

In this chapter we've tried our best to give you a brief overview of the development of book groups. For those readers who want to explore this fascinating history in more depth, we suggest the following articles and books.

Finklestein, David, and Alistair McCleery, eds. *The Book History Reader*. New York: Routledge, 2001.

Hall, David D. *Cultures of Print: Essays in the History of the Book*. Boston: University of Massachusetts Press, 1996.

Harris, Susan K. *The Cultural Work of the Late Nineteenth-Century Hostess: Annie Adams Fields and Mary Gladstone Drew*. New York: Macmillan, 2002.

Hartley, Jenny. *The Reading Groups Book*, 2002–2003 edition. London: Oxford University Press, 2002.

Kale, Steven D. "Women, Salons, and the State in the Aftermath of the French Revolution," *Journal of Women's History* (Winter 2002): 54–82.

Krystal, Arthur, ed. *A Company of Readers: Uncollected Writings of W. H. Auden, Jacques Barzun, and Lionel Trilling from The Reader's Subscription and Mid-Century Book Clubs*. New York: Simon & Schuster, 2001.

Larson, Kate Clifford. "The Saturday Evening Girls: A Progressive Era Library Club and the Intellectual Life of Working Class and Immigrant Girls in Turn-of-the-Century Boston," *Library Quarterly* (April 2001).

Long, Elizabeth. *Book Clubs: Women and the Uses of Reading in Everyday Life*. Chicago: University of Chicago Press, 2003.

Manguel, Alberto. *A History of Reading*. New York: Penguin, 1997.

Max, D. T. "The Oprah Effect," *New York Times*, December 26, 1999.

Radway, Janice. *A Feeling for Books: The Book-of-the-Month Club, Literary Taste, and Middle-Class Desire*. Chapel Hill: University of North Carolina Press, 1999.

Radway, Janice. *Reading the Romance: Women, Patriarchy and Popular Literature*. Chapel Hill: University of North Carolina Press, 1991.

A complete bibliography of the sources we used in our research for this book can be found at www.goodbookslately.com.

For book group support, check out the resources in appendix 3.

2

Read Yourself Wise: The Art of Intrepid Analytical Reading

꠸꠸꠸

'Tis the good reader that makes the good book . . . in every book he finds passages which seem confidences or asides hidden from all else and unmistakably meant for his ear.

—RALPH WALDO EMERSON,
"Society and Solitude"

No two people read the same book.
—EDMUND WILSON

Readers Wonder

"How do people who don't read, you know, read for pleasure, spend their time? How do they manage? How do they make sense of their lives? I know that it sounds judgmental, but I really do wonder. I would shrivel up and die if I couldn't read."

—*MacKenzie, Honolulu, Hawaii*

"The whole point of being in a book group is to see the world through someone else's eyes. That happens in discussion, of course, when you discover just how different your friend's reactions to a certain book are from your own. But it starts in the act of reading itself, when by opening the book you open yourself to another human experience that may be nothing like your own."

—*Joanie, Portland, Oregon*

"[Belonging to a book group] makes you feel less guilty about an activity that society sees as leisure, entertainment, or diversion . . . it gives us an alibi for this kind of guilty pleasure." —*Alberto Manguel,* A History of Reading *(1996)*

As we've seen in the first chapter, book groups have enjoyed a long and frequently lustrous history. At different points during the past centuries they've been at the cutting edge of intellectual movements, lurked in the troubled center of political or social change, provided a refuge for those who are traditionally silent to come forth and speak, or, in one of their current manifestations, operated as the most important and ardently courted force in the book-selling market. Yes, readers, that's you—if you are in a book group, you belong to a devastatingly powerful contingent that can place the formerly unknown author of a literary memoir right next to Nora Roberts or Tom Clancy on the best-seller lists.

For the most part, however, it seems that the majority of successful book groups and book group members have managed to go about the business of reading without undue fuss or fanfare. Just like the amused member of an eighteenth-century prison reading group, who wondered at the town's sudden interest in their "mysterious congress," many present-day book group members have enjoyed the recent resurgence of media fascination—let's just call it a frenzy, shall we—in their activities with a wink and a smile. As one bemused and beleaguered twenty-five-year veteran book group member put it, "In the last couple of years we've been interviewed for six newspaper articles, been courted by four local bookstores, and visited by three professional leaders, all who want to know what we're up to: how we choose books, what we talk about, why we've stayed together for so long. Meanwhile, we're just doing what we've been doing all along—reading some great books, laughing over some not-so-great choices, and looking forward to each other's company."

Book group members around the world, as we will see, remain divided about which is most important—talking about the books or talking to each other. Ultimately it doesn't really matter, so long as the members of any one group are getting the balance of intellectual and social rewards that are important to them. But like any group of people who bond over a shared and passionate interest, book group members have been the target of more than one outsider's dismissal—the skeptic naysayers who claim that a book group is pretty much like a bridge club, or a sewing circle, or Junior League. The claim, that is, that no matter what the alleged purpose for meeting might be, it's really just an excuse for folks (i.e., ladies with loose lips) to get together and gab.

Even if this were true, or is in some cases true, well, frankly, so what? Most of us are grateful for a reason to step outside of the ordinary pattern of everyday life to revel in the company of people whom we like and like to talk with. But the fact of the matter is that almost any book group member will tell you that a book club is not interchangeable with any other organized social gathering. (We mean no offense to any bridge-club or sewing-circle or Junior League member who could make the same argument for his or her own particular passion.) In the case of the book group member, Reading Is the Thing—and, of course, sharing ideas and questions about what you read.

As so many book group enthusiasts have told us, it's important to keep in mind that the book club experience is based on two fairly separate and distinct activities. The first is the personal, private, individual act of reading—your unique reaction to and relationship with a particular book. The second part of the book group dynamic is the group part, the social, the collective, the communal act of discussing the book that you have each read on your own. In a book group, each act complements and energizes the other: the better your discussions as a group, the more alert and attentive you'll grow as a reader, the better your reading, the more insight and creativity you'll have to add to the discussion.

In chapter 4 we'll talk about some of the ways you can sharpen and ignite the discussion part of the book group dynamic. In this chapter, however, we thought we'd share some thoughts and ideas on ways to enhance reading, the fundamental activity at the forefront of a great book group experience. There are numerous tricks of the trade you can sample to improve the discussion part of a book group, but there is also a surprising number of methods and mind-sets you can adopt to improve your reading—some specific to a certain genre (the focus of chapter 3) others useful to any book, regardless of subject matter. You will also find, we hope, that you can turn many of the reading suggestions into discussion questions for any book group selection with relative ease.

ZONING OUT, TUNING IN: PASSIVE AND ACTIVE READING

There are at least two very different ways to read. The first is the passive mode, akin to the way we tend to watch our favorite, mostly mindless TV shows. If you're anything like Kira, you've probably spent countless hours blissfully vegging out in front of delightfully effortless small-screen entertainment (Kira's current major weaknesses include E!'s *True Hollywood Story* and VH1's *I Love the Eighties!*). Likewise, if you're a book person, you very likely have lost yourself in the pleasure of escape reading, sucking down a juicy beach read or maybe that much-loved novel you practically know by heart. A reading escape is one of the best retreats around—it's cheap, it's easy, and, unless you've warped your expectations for real-life relationships by reading too many postmodern French novelists or feisty singles' "chick lit," it's pretty harmless in the bargain.

But reading for a class, or for a book group, or to reach a deeper comprehension of new or challenging material that's important to you, can and should fall into the second category, the active sort of reading, where you push yourself beyond the passive, pure-consumption setting to one of assertive, engaged participation. Arnold Schwarzenegger once pointed out the incredible difference that focused attention could make to bodybuilding. A single, mindful repetition of an exercise—when he concentrated completely on the movement of a particular muscle—yielded an infinitely better result than twenty reps where the future governor of California let his mind wander. We do not use this analogy to imply, of course, that reading should be as hard or painful or germ-infested as a trip to the gym—but rather to imply that active reading can provide the same kind of personal reward when it comes to flexing your mental biceps.

Readers Recommend

"I can't read and retain without a pen," *admits Katri of Chicago, Illinois.* "Sometimes I do go back to look over what I've underlined, but even if I don't, the act of underlining and starring seems to be enough to help me remember a lot when it comes to discussion."

"Post-it notes are my short-term salvation," *says Nancy of Aurora, Colorado.* "I keep a stack by my side and stick them on at random whenever I run across a section in the book that I want to remember or come back to. I've gotten pretty compulsive with my Post-its, so I actually have a color-coded sort of system—green for 'important moment,' pink for 'read out loud and ask for response from group,' and yellow for 'favorite quotes.'"

Calliope of Pasadena, California, is a devoted dog-earist, folding over pages to mark her reactions as well as her place in a book. "Sometimes when I go back I can't figure out right away why I folded down that page, so I have to read it over again. I find that if I spend just ten to fifteen minutes doing this on the afternoon before book club, I can make significant contributions to our discussion."

"Try this easy trick," *recommends Amy, insatiable reader and former bookstore owner, of Vancouver, British Columbia.* "After each chapter or section or story in your book, take a moment to write down three words or phrases (either in the book or on a separate sheet of paper) that will help you remember your initial response to that section's events or characters or language. Do it quickly; don't think about it too much. Bring your 'first reaction' notes to your meeting, and you'll be amazed to discover how much you've captured." *Our advice:* This would probably also work well if you recorded a word or phrase to sum up an overall response to the three components Amy mentions (events, character, writing) for your book as a whole.

"If you read too fast, you need to force yourself to slow down," *says Bob of Portland, Maine.* "That's my problem, so I made a habit of taking a few minutes to think about what I've just read each time I put my book down. I quiz myself by imagining what one question I would want to ask the author if he or she were sitting in my den—even if this question is something as simple as, 'Why did you want to tell this particular story?' Then I imagine what the author's answer might be."

"I keep a reading log," *notes Karmel of Cheyenne, Wyoming*. "It started out as something I did because I felt like even though I read a lot, what I read wasn't sticking with me. At first I tried to write a review or plot synopsis for each book so I would be able to check back for a quick reference. But over time I discovered that what I really liked doing best was to record a couple of quotations and then write about my response based on what was going on at that particular point of my life."

"I like to read the first couple of pages of a book out loud," *reveals Aaron of New York City, a longtime teacher and book group leader*. "Sometimes I go back and read a particularly great paragraph out loud after I've read it silently, just to hear the author's unique choices of words and language. I've found that this helps me slow down and savor a particular writer's talents."

"Make a list of all the major characters in the story or book. Write down a few words beside each name to describe that character's primary motivations—if everyone does this for a particular book, it can be really interesting to share these character descriptions at the meeting," *advises Annie of Falmouth, Massachusetts*.

BASIC ABC'S—THINGS TO LOOK FOR
IN EVERY KIND OF BOOK GROUP BOOK
(WELL, MOST OF THEM, ANYWAY)

"We all want to improve our book group discussion," writes Cynthia of Terre Haute, Indiana, "but it's hard when most of us really like a certain book. Once we've talked about how much we liked a character or a scene or the book as a whole, we run out of things to say and get sidetracked into other topics. But we know that we could do better if we just knew more about good ways to approach book discussion, more things to look for." Cynthia's comment is one we've heard, in some form or another, from hundreds of book group members over these past few years. Despite their often intimidating levels of education, impressively varied backgrounds, and extraordinary skills in their field of expertise, very few of the book group members we've talked to about this stumbling block have spent the past decade sitting around all day learning how to read and think and talk about books. We have. That's more or less the gist of what we always tell readers who ask us, "How do you guys come up with all those questions and ways to look at a book?" Reading and discussing literature for insight and pleasure is a skill like any other, a very specific skill that any interested reader can acquire with some guidance and practice. We've been practicing for a while, while you were busy doing extraneous things like, oh, pursuing your career and raising a family and putting food on the table.

There is absolutely nothing wrong with falling under the heady spell of a great book or with sharing your admiration and awe with your fellow book group members. But, as Cynthia points out, there are limits to just how far you can take a book discussion based on the criteria of liking or disliking something about it. Actually, it's much simpler if you don't like the book at all, or if at least some members don't like it. Most of us find it easier to describe, at pleasurable length, something we find confusing, distasteful, or even offensive. But does this mean that you joined a book group to read baffling, bad, or obnoxious books? That you should be looking forward to the next book that no one could stand reading just because you know the discussion will be lively? Of course not. In the best of all possible book group worlds, you should be reading compelling, provocative, award-worthy stories. And with a minor twist or two in your approach to reading and discussing them, you can enjoy a scandalously exhilarating conversation about even those books that everyone loves, one that can be as intellectually meaty and/or as intensely personal as your members desire. Needless to say, we can't protect you from all the mediocre, tiresome, and annoying books out there—no matter how much we'd like to—nor can we recommend a book that is 100 percent guaranteed to reduce every single member of your group to a stammering supplicant of worshipful devotion. But we can and will try, in these chapters on reading and discussion, to show you some of the things we look for when we're preparing to discuss a book with a group or a class.

In the following chapter, we'll get down to the specifics of enhancing your reading and discussion powers for each of the most popular book group genres. But before we do, we thought it best to provide a refresher course in the basics of literary analysis, for all those readers who, like Erin of Norfolk, Virginia, have expressed a desire to hit the books all over again. "I loved my English classes in high school," Erin wrote, "and I was hoping to find that same level of intellectual intensity in my new book group. But I seem to have forgotten how to go about it."

Even if you have no need or desire to go back to the fundamentals, you may want to look at some of the reading and discussion questions that follow each of the next six sections. You may find just the prompt you need to unpack this month's meaty book for general group consumption.

The Big Six: Essential Ingredients of Reading and Writing

For the past four years, we have been writing discussion guides on many of the titles and authors most treasured by book group readers. As we put together our descriptions and questions for each of these guides, we consider the basic elements that shape the essence of any work of **narrative prose.** As you may or may not remember from your English classes of yore, a narrative is anything—fact or fiction—that tells a story, and prose is simply the kind of writing that isn't poetry—no verses, no perfect rhymes, no consistent rhythms. We look at the six major components of any story: **style, narrator, character, plot, setting,** and **theme.** We encourage readers to focus on the distinctive choices that each writer makes in terms of each of these elements and to consider the ways these choices affect the reader's response to the story. You can safely assume that at least some if not all of these elements will be important factors in any narrative, whether strictly fictional, strictly fact, or somewhere in between. Obviously, certain books will lend themselves more naturally to thinking about specific literary elements than others. So, as a busy reader, you may not have time or inclination to consider each of these factors while reading every book—totally fine. Instead, check out the list below and see if you'd like to brush up on the finer points of any of these basic ingredients that make up a story.

- **What kind of writing and why?** Style, tone, and purpose.
- **Who's speaking?** Narrator and point of view.
- **Who's Involved?** Characters and characterization.
- **What happens in what order?** Structure and plot.
- **Where and when does it happen?** Setting: time, place, specific social climate, cultural values.
- **What's the big idea (or ideas)?** Major ideas and themes.

READER ALERT

At the end of each of the following six sections on style, narrator, character, plot, setting, and theme, you'll find a list of questions to consider as you read any piece of writing. You can also use these questions for discussion purposes, so you may want to keep them handy to help you prepare for your next meeting—perhaps in combination with some of the specific reading/discussion questions for each of the eight most popular kinds of book group books you will find in the next chapter. Not in the mood to organize ahead of time? You can always just bring a copy of this book to your meeting, open to any of the lists of discussion questions in chapter 2 and 3, and fire away.

What Kind of Writing and Why?

One of the first things you will notice as you begin to read a book will be, naturally enough, the writing itself, the thing we can simply call the writer's **STYLE**. Style is something we all innately appreciate and re-spond to—whether in a positive or a negative way—because style is a part of all of our lives; we make literally hundreds of choices every day based on our own personal stylistic preferences. We wake up in a bed-room we've decorated to reflect our style, shower in a bathroom that also represents a stylistic choice, and shampoo our hair with a brand that has been marketed to appeal to a certain sense of stylistic prefer-ence—we seek to be sleek, perky, fluffy, sexy, for example, or maybe to avoid total baldness. And, of course, we are all accustomed to judging the style of others. Even the kindest among us will occasionally spend an uncharitable moment or two wondering how on God's green earth a fellow human being made the conscious decision to decorate his house with those particular Christmas lights or to don that particular pair of shoes. Well, as Mother always said, there's no accounting for taste.

Because each individual author has, theoretically, a completely open field in terms of which words he or she wants to choose and in what or-der to arrange them, any chosen writing style has a lot to say about that author and what he or she hopes to convey. Hence, it is always impor-tant, especially as you are getting into a new book or author, to slow down and consider style as you read.

A writing **style** is made up of several things, and for those of you who lean toward a stylistic preference for knowing the fancy words, here's some of the stylistic factors to consider. First, we have **diction**, which pretty much just means the choice of individual words. Some writers use big ones, others like obscure ones, many prefer plain every-day ones, while still others choose to mimic the colloquialisms of a particular type of speech characteristic of a certain group of people. On the next level we have **syntax**, which is the unique way that a writer puts all those words together in sentences, lines, clauses, or phrases. A writer like Ernest Hemingway is famous for his use of brief, declarative, straightforward sentences—like these from his story *Hills Like White Elephants*:

The woman brought two glasses of beer and two felt pads. She put the felt pads and the beer glasses on the table and looked at the man and the girl. The girl was looking off at the line of hills. They were white in the sun and the country was brown and dry.

Compare this to a selection from Franz Kafka's *Metamorphosis* and you'll see a very different use of diction and syntax:

Under what pretext the doctor and the locksmith had been got rid of on that first morning Gregor could never discover, for since what he had said was not understood by the others it never struck any of them, not even his sister, that he could understand what they said, and so whenever his sister came into his room he had to content himself with hearing her utter only a sigh now and then, and an occasional appeal to the saints.

We can also look at a writer's use of **figurative language,** things such as **similes, metaphors,** and the writer's distinct use of **imagery.** This is simply how the author creates sensory impressions for the reader—how a certain person or thing looks, sounds, feels, tastes, or smells. Colombian Nobel Prize winner Gabriel García Márquez is celebrated for his masterful use of figurative language and evocative imagery, as you can see from this brief sample from the story *A Very Old Man with Enormous Wings*:

The world had been sad since Tuesday. Sea and sky were a single ash-gray thing and the sands of the beach, which on March nights glimmered like a powdered light, had become a stew of mud and rotten shellfish.

From the individual words and the particular combination of all these stylistic choices we can also infer the author's **tone** and **purpose**— style is what's actually down on the page; tone and purpose are what we take away from it. **Tone** is the author's implicit attitude toward the people, places, and events in a story. Whenever anyone speaks to us in real life, we pick up on the deeper meaning of what is said (unless we suffer from Asperger syndrome or any other form of autism) by listening to voice inflections and looking for visual cues. In the same way, we must be sensitive to the author's tone in the story in order to discover his or her **purpose** in telling it. What does the writer want us to see or understand about these people or this event? Should we be sympathetic to a particular character or situation? Why is the description of this particular interaction between these two people important?

That's why we also have to keep a lookout for **irony**—one of the enduring themes in both life and literature is that things, darn it all, are not always what they seem to be. The unexpected complexity that often catches us unawares in life is often a happy inspiration for writers of both fiction and nonfiction, and great authors make the most of these bittersweet little ironies through different narrative devices. One of these is **verbal irony,** which consists of a person saying one thing but meaning the exact opposite, such as when someone might say "Boy, I sure do love getting stuck in traffic!" Verbal irony that is calculated to hurt somebody's feelings is known as **sarcasm:** "You are such a good driver—I love how you always get us stuck in traffic." The next level of irony is often called **situational irony,** which crops up when there is a definite incongruity between what is expected to happen and what actually happens. You leave early for your weekend camping trip to avoid getting stuck in traffic, but so does everyone else. Situational irony abounds in fiction, but it's also a major component to many nonfiction narratives—if you think about the popular "storm" books from a couple of years ago, Sebastian Junger's *Perfect Storm* and Erik Larson's *Isaac's Storm,* both accounts of these terrible hurricanes deal with the all-too-human disinclination to take nature seriously: "Hey, how bad can some wind and rain be? Not going to stop me from raking in the dough!" Last, there's **dramatic irony,** which occurs when an author allows a reader to know more about a situation than a character knows. For example, one of the dramatic ironies of Franz Kafka's *Metamorphosis* lies in hero Gregor Samsa's earnest attempts to look friendly and appealing to his family despite his recent transformation into a gigantic insect. You try to look friendly and appealing when you have turned (either literally or metaphorically) into a giant black shiny beetle with six constantly wriggling legs!

The Skeleton in the Book Group Closet: No One Reads the Book!

You know that book groups have definitely etched a significant mark in our culture's consciousness when the leading ladies of television are participating in their neighborhood book clubs. Yet we can't help noticing that while the writers behind such shows as *The Sopranos* and *The Simpsons* apparently recognize the power and popularity of book groups, their perception of the real purpose of these organizations is not so flattering. As Marge Simpson chirps happily to the Springfield Women's Book Club, "This month, our book is *Bridget Jones's Diary*. So I think it would be nice if we went around the room and each of us say why we didn't read it." Bart's teacher, Mrs. Crabapple, responds in an exhausted moan, "Craaamps." Principal Skinner's aged mother complains testily, "All my friends are dead."

As anyone familiar with *The Simpsons* can attest, the satirical bent of the show is surprisingly egalitarian, so we can't take offense that book group members prove no exception. But this attitude prevails elsewhere. Last spring, for example, we met with a journalist from one of Denver's two major newspapers, a popular columnist who is certainly very well connected with our local book community. During the interview, he asked a pointedly blunt question. "Isn't it true that the deep dark secret behind book groups is that they are all women, and that nobody ever reads the book?"

We exchanged a look as we laughed politely. "It's not exactly a secret that many of them are women," Kira responded practically, "but we're repeatedly impressed by how much and how thoroughly they read." Ellen added, "More and more men are joining these days, so I think you'll see a shift in that balance. In answer to the second part of your question, we can say only that so far we've found no direct correlation between gender and actually reading books versus just using them as coasters."

Maybe this journalist had hoped to get some sort of rise out of us with his question; maybe he was trying to push the interview beyond the "Hey, aren't book groups great?" margin. In any event, his question and our response got us thinking: Does most of the non–book group world believe that the books are just an excuse? Is it because the majority of book group members are women that some outsiders find it easy—imagine, women reading and discussing their ideas! Why, they're going to want to vote next!—to scoff at the premise of intellectual fellowship? What about the increasing number of men joining the book group ranks? Does this give the community more authority somehow, more legitimacy? We decided to ask our readers in the feedback section of *LATELIES*, our monthly on-line newsletter.

"Deep Dark Secret" Adamantly Nixed

Nearly one hundred members from book groups around the country (and others who replied indignantly from Canada, Australia, and Brazil) wrote in to defend the honor of their favorite group activity. While most of these readers agreed that book group membership seemed more appealing to women, they also claimed that—get this crazy thing—they joined a book group in order to read books. "If I just wanted to pretend to read a book every month," Corey asked, "couldn't I just hang out at Starbucks with a copy of *Soap Opera Digest* concealed inside my volume of Proust?" Kula joked, "That's one of those comments that you hate to dignify with a response, but I will anyway. I'm sure that some people join book clubs to force themselves to read more, but if that doesn't work, it's not so challenging to back out and turn on the Discovery Channel instead."

Corrine was able to dismiss both charges with devastating testimony to the contrary. "What? Nonsense! Our group, Booklovers Ink, has had members of both sexes from the beginning. We have provocative discussions, shun best-sellers, and favor the classics, returning repeatedly to Nabokov, Ishiguro, Faulkner, and Balzac. We have a brilliant mentor who is a true classicist, and we send out a newsletter and discussion questions ahead of time each month. Few college survey courses could offer such a reading perspective. That guy should be forced to read Grisham for an entire month as punishment. Or join our book club—he doesn't know what he's missing!"

Most of the members who responded to the charge of book groups as an example of feminine pretension run amok were not so surprised by the accusation, even as they eagerly repudiated it. Leah argues, "For those not in a book group, it's just an excuse to drink wine and gossip. Anyone in a group knows differently. The first question that someone in another group will ask you is, 'What are you reading?' The next is, 'Did you like book X?' What about books W, Y, or Z?' After five years with a group I am amazed at what incredibly busy women are reading, researching, and discussing in such depth." Corinne claims that "everyone in my household knows that book group is a very important evening for me, and they know the amount of work I put in to get ready for the discussion, as does every member of my group." Lynn Pusillo is one of the few members who wrote in to admit to a less-than-literary chapter in her book club's history. "Many years ago we had too many people in our book club who came to socialize, and who frequently hadn't read the book at all. Once we decided to create a good list of questions for each meeting, these members shaped up, or left, and we got much more serious."

So much for the myth that book group membership is merely an excuse to cackle like hens—although some cackling is permitted. But what about those daring men who persist in participating in what is regarded by many to be a woman's work? Randall is one of these bold pioneers, a member of both a men's group that discusses works by African-American writers and a "mixed" group that he joined with his girlfriend. "Women are just more comfortable with the process of evaluating and trying to understand people, with sharing their personal reactions. In my men's group, we read almost entirely nonfiction; we talk about things that really happened and debate their significance in terms of the real world. In the couples' group we read fiction, and it took me a while to appreciate that this kind of discussion is just as valuable. It's just not the way that men usually talk to each other." And it's not just the way men talk with each other that's different, it's *where*. In our experience working with men's groups, we've noticed that many, if not most, men's groups do not meet in each other's living rooms. No, they meet in bars or restaurants. Is it the public space that appeals to men? The football game playing on the TV behind the bar? The pool table beckoning when the discussion drags? Mark, member of a Denver men's book group, gives one explanation: "We don't really want to host," he said honestly, "so when we go to a restaurant—as long as we can hear each other speak—it's perfect. We don't have to cook, and we don't have to clean." Bob, a Methodist pastor and founder of an impressive number of successful church book groups, has a similar outlook on men's participation. "Men are conditioned to talk in a very different way than women, and they bond through shared interests or activities, not by talking about their feelings. It's slightly different in a church because the emphasis is on awareness and acceptance." But Bob estimates that the ratio of women to men in his church book groups may still favor the ladies by about two to one. Sally says that while her group currently has no male members, they would gladly encourage their participation. "Men are welcome in our group; we just don't have any interested, apparently. We meet at the public library and advertise on the bulletin board, so it's open to all. Please join us for an evening and give it a try!"

So now that you know a little something about **style, tone,** and **purpose,** here are some general questions that you can ask yourself as you read almost any book that tells a story, or that you can turn into discussion questions for your next meeting.

QUESTIONS OF STYLE FOR READING AND DISCUSSION

- What word or words would you use to describe this writer's style?
- What about any particular words or phrases—anything unusual to your ear or eye? Why is that? Have you run across any great descriptive imagery, distinctive expressions, or startling bits of dialogue that you'd want to share with your group?
- Is there anything in the narrative style of the book you're reading right now that stands out undeniably for you? That is considerably different from the kinds of things that you are used to reading?
- Does anything in this author's style remind you of any other author or writing you've encountered in the past? Can you make favorable or unfavorable comparisons?
- If you can, identify a word or phrase to describe a style and/or tone that would be the exact opposite of those you find in the book you're currently reading. Imagine your book written in that very opposite style—how would it change the book's meaning, purpose, or flavor?
- Is the author's style specifically linked to some of the themes or major ideas in the book in some way? How does that work or not work?
- Think about the author's or narrator's voice in what you've read so far in your book—how would you describe the tone or purpose? Does the narrator present the main characters in a sympathetic way? Is the writer's purpose to amuse, to scare, to teach a particular lesson about the human character or experience? Does the writer attempt to offer a scathing social commentary of any particular group of people or single type of person?
- Which other members of your book group would be most likely to appreciate or criticize this writer's style?

Who's Speaking?

As you read carefully to consider the elements of style, you're also going to come across somebody generally known as the **narrator**, who is writing from a certain **POINT OF VIEW**. It's always vital to remember that the **narrator** and the **author** are not necessarily the same person—the narrator could be expressing opinions that are not those of the author or presenting events in a way that is not quite true to fact. The narrator is the voice that is telling the story, and the writer's decision to create a particular narrator speaking from a particular **point of view** is a highly significant one. Think about a couple of these decisions in terms of a book group favorite: What if Harper Lee had decided to write *To Kill a Mockingbird* from Jem's or Atticus's point of view instead of Scout's? What if Lee had decided to use a **third-person** narrator instead of a first-person's, Scout's "I," voice? What if Lee had decided to write from the point of view of a less intelligent, less observant little girl or from that of an older and more sophisticated young lady?

There are seven basic points of view that indicate a particular narrative choice. Of course, within a single book they can be mixed up in a variety of ways. And certain types of writing lend themselves most naturally to a single point-of-view choice—a memoir will be most likely written in the first person, while a nonfiction account of a particular person, time, place, or event will probably be written in the third person, often in the objective mode. But fiction is pretty much wide open—the writer can approach a story from any perspective he or she finds the most engaging.

First let's look at the possible first-person narrators, all of whom speak in the "I" voice (or, very occasionally, in the "we") and who are themselves characters in the story:

1. **First-Person Narrator Major:** A major character in the story uses the "I" voice, such as Scout in *To Kill a Mockingbird*. Sometimes we encounter multiple first-person narrators, as in the novel *House of Sand and Fog*—Andre Dubus III switches

back and forth between the first-person perspectives of his two main characters as a way to build the tension and divide our sympathies.

2. **First-Person Narrator Minor:** A minor character in the story uses the "I" voice, an observer to the action, such as Gatsby's neighbor Nick in *The Great Gatsby*.

3. **First-Person Narrator Collective:** a group of characters in the story use the "we" voice, such as the adolescent neighborhood boys of Jeffrey Eugenides's *Virgin Suicides*.

Next you've got your third-person narrators, who use "he," "she," "they," and "it" to tell the story, and who are not characters within it.

4. **Third-Person Narrator Omniscient:** Narrator can take us inside minds and perspectives of all the characters, so we, like the narrator, are all-knowing. Ann Patchett uses this expansive point of view to create sympathy for multiple characters in *Bel Canto*.

5. **Third-Person Narrator Limited Omniscient:** Narrator can take us inside only one or two characters, so we see action only from the main characters' perspective.

6. **Third-Person Narrator Objective:** Narrator does not see into the mind of any character. Reports action and dialogue without telling us directly what the characters think and feel. Shirley Jackson uses this technique to chilling effect in "The Lottery."

Last, and most unusually, you'll occasionally run into the seventh possible narrator choice, a **second-person** narrator, when the story is told in the "you" voice. One example that leaps to mind is Mary Karr's memoir *Cherry,* in which that second-person voice creates a sense of both immediacy and distance for the reader.

The major reason for identifying and thinking about the point of view of a story is to figure out where the author stands in relation to the people, places, and events he or she is describing. We tend to have the most sympathy for the characters whose perspective we share, and the most distrust for those whose thoughts and feelings we do not—it's no accident, for example, that Reverend Price is the only member of the Price family who doesn't get to narrate a chapter of Barbara King-solver's *Poisonwood Bible*. Even if we have sympathy for a first-person "I" narrator, we must question his or her ability to report and interpret accurately. Narrators can be **unreliable** for a variety of reasons: they might lack self-knowledge, or they might have a particular desire or ambition that blinds them to certain realities, or they might be inno-cent and inexperienced—a **naïve narrator**, such as Mark Twain's Huck Finn or J. D. Salinger's Holden Caulfield.

Now that you've freshened up on narrator and point of view, here's a question or two you might want to ask yourself about the book that is currently at your bedside or in your bag.

QUESTIONS OF NARRATOR AND PERSPECTIVE
FOR READING AND DISCUSSION

- Identify the narrative point or points of view. Why do you think the author decided that this single or multiple perspective was the best choice to tell this particular story?
- Imagine that the author had chosen to present the story from a different point of view—maybe told the story in first person in-stead of third person, for example, or from the perspective of a different character or person, or from multiple perspectives—how would that change the story significantly?
- How close do you get to any of the characters or to the story? Would you say that the narrative perspective encourages an atti-tude of emotional intimacy or observer's distance?
- Whom do you find to be the most sympathetic, intriguing, or re-pellent characters? Does narrative perspective play a part in this for you?
- Do you think that the narrator (or any one of the narrators in a story that makes use of multiple perspectives) is a reliable narra-tor? Do you think that the author closely identifies with the narra-tor or narrators? Or is it clear to you that the author maintains

some kind of ironic distance from the narrator or the narrative voice?

- Do you like this narrator? Is the narrator sympathetic? Do you trust the narrator's account of specific events and/or people and his or her interpretation of them? If the story is told by multiple narrators, do you side more with one than another?
- Do you have any personal preference for a certain type of point of view? Does your book group, as a whole, tend to have any preference for a particular type of perspective: single, multiple, first-person, third-person?

Who's Involved?

For many of us, **CHARACTER** is the most crucial of all literary variables, the leading factor that determines whether we like, love, or hate a particular book. Some readers demand sympathetic characters; others are delighted by intriguing characters, even if they are personally loathsome. In most cases, however, we are fascinated by the way an author creates a unique and complex character, and by the choices a character makes for or against personal change. It's important to note that we can still talk about character in terms of most nonfiction books, such as memoir or history. Even when an author is depicting real people who lived outside the pages of the book, he or she is still making a number of choices in terms of how to describe or define any one individual person.

Let's think about the power of an intriguing character in terms of two familiar British classics, Charles Dickens's *Christmas Carol* and Robert Louis Stevenson's *Treasure Island*. Scrooge and Long John Silver are both fairly unpleasant old men: greedy, self-serving, malicious, antisocial, and, to top it off, physically unappealing specimens to boot. The difference lies in the way that each author decides to develop the character. Scrooge starts out as an unsympathetic character but makes an incredible journey of personal growth in the space of a single evening, with the help of four ghostly assistants. This, of course, is exactly why the story continues to seduce each new generation of fans—if someone as nasty and ugly and, let's face it, old as Scooge can turn into Tiny Tim's new best beloved Big Brother overnight, then surely there's hope for the rest of us, too, isn't there? Scrooge is a **dynamic character** because he changes and develops as the story progresses. By contrast, Long John Silver starts his life in the novel as a warmly sympathetic character, a rascally lovable old sea dog pickled in irreverent brime. Both he and the narrator are playing a little game with their enthusiastic audience, and it's up to brave lad Jim to uncover the menacing truth that lurks beneath Long John's mischievous banter. By the end of the novel, Long John Silver hasn't really changed one bit; he is a **static character**. Unlike Scrooge, he makes no eleventh-hour sprint for a more spiritually fulfilling life, yet most readers of two centuries and counting have loved him the better for it. If Scrooge represents the human longing to turn one's life around, Long John represents the equally human (if less noble) desire to rebel against tiresome adult responsibilities and morals, to grab all the gold for ourselves and set sail for the high seas.

Novelist E. M. Forster coined a term or two to describe the extent to which a certain character is developed and made convincing. Scrooge and Long John Silver are both examples of what we can call a **round character,** one who possesses a certain depth and complexity, who is multidimensional, who can surprise or puzzle us. By contrast, a **flat character** would be one who embodies one or two ideas or traits that can easily be described in a few words. Bob Cratchitt of *A Christmas Carol* and the doctor of *Treasure Island* are both essentially flat characters: we can count on Bob to be poor but disgustingly loyal and nice, just like we can count on the doctor to be tediously efficient and officious. Flat characters tend to be fairly one-dimensional. They do not exist to serve as personifications of psychological complexity, but rather to serve as models of a certain kind of behavior or way of thinking. Some flat characters are immediately recognizable as **stock characters;** we are all familiar with these stereotyped beings from television, movies, and popular fiction such as romances or thrillers. Stock characters are types, not individuals; they come prepackaged with a certain set of associations and prejudices, so we don't have to do any work to understand them: the dumb blonde, the wise old woman, the sadistic boss, the rock-chinned hero, and the nutty sidekick are just a few examples. A preponderance of flat or stock characters can indicate a certain failure of imagination or inspiration on the part of the author, but a good writer can use such simple folk as worthy foils to the more convoluted and conflicting motivations of the well-developed characters.

Also worth noting, if you're not familiar with them already, are the descriptive words that define the most central kinds of characters, the **protagonist** and the **antagonist.** Keep in mind that the protagonist, the main character, is not necessarily the same thing as a **hero** or **heroine,** nor is the antagonist necessarily a **villain.** Hero-ism or heroine-ism implies courage, valor, and, of course, heroics, but the main character of a story may not exhibit these traits. In fact, a certain kind of protagonist may be more accurately dubbed an **antihero**—he or she may be weak, confused, even pathetic. If the antihero learns anything at all during the course of his or her story, it may be that he or she is alone in a pointless existence devoid of God or any other benign and sensible presence—Yossarian from Joseph Heller's *Catch-22* is a classic example. Likewise, a villain is associated with evil and malevolence, and the protagonist's antagonist or antagonists may not actually be out to destroy him or her in any purposeful way.

As you focus on some of the most compelling (or boring, or disgusting) characters in the book you have been reading, here are some of the things you can ponder:

QUESTIONS OF CHARACTER FOR READING AND DISCUSSION

- Who is your favorite character so far? Do you like character because he or she reminds you of yourself (or someone you know) in any way or, conversely, possesses qualities you do not? Can you sympathize with his or her situation or actions? Or is this a person that you would dislike in real life but love as a character because he or she is convincing and compelling?
- Do you sympathize with the main character or characters? Is the narrator more sympathetic to certain characters than to others? Is

there any character that you like more or less than the narrator seems to?

- How much self-knowledge does each or any of the main characters possess? Does self-knowledge make this character or characters more appealing or more frustrating?
- Would you call any of the main characters a dynamic character, that is, someone who has changed and developed during the story? If so, does this change seem lasting and profound or only temporary or superficial? Which characters remain static, seem the least inclined to alter their beliefs or behavior?
- Which characters in the story are round (complex) and which are flat (simple, one-dimensional)? Do you wish that the author had chosen to "flesh out" any of the characters?
- Are the characters, either as a cast or as individuals, convincing? Are their actions plausible, realistic? Do you understand their motivations? Do any characters stand out as either unconvincing or ultimately mysterious?
- Compare certain characters based on their similar roles, either personal or professional. You could compare one mother to another, for example, and evaluate each mom's parenting style or expectations for her offspring. In the same way, you could compare the fathers of the story; or the children; or the siblings; or the husbands, wives, lovers, etc. You could compare characters based on a similar social role—either official or unofficial—how do two characters compare as leaders, or lawmakers, or peacekeepers, for example, or as rebels or instigators?
- Consider any minor characters who appear infrequently or act on the sidelines. Why, do you think, the author chose to include these characters? How does their presence contribute to the main plot or to our understanding of the major characters?
- Which characters in the book will the other members of your discussion group think are the most admirable, compelling, convincing, or unforgivable?

What Happens in What Order?

Every story, even the one you told about why you were late to work this morning, has a **PLOT.** Plot is simply the author's arrangement of incidents in a story, the way the author controls the order of events. A good writer knows how to attract, persuade, and surprise the audience by very specific choices in the presentation of events.

The most common and straightforward way to tell a story is **chronologically,** that is, begin at the beginning and end at the end. Many writers, of course, choose to move back and forth between different time periods, in order to lead up to a final surprising moment of revelation—think of Jonathan Safran Foer's *Everything is Illuminated* or Joanna Scott's *Make Believe;* both novels make great use of **nonlinear** narrative to lead up to that final kaboom. Then there's the old favorite technique of **flashback,** a strategy that allows the writer to nip back to certain scenes or events to throw some light on a current event. When a story starts **in media res** or "in the middle of things," the reader is thrown directly into the heat of the action. We can still find traces of this epic tradition in contemporary fiction in novels such as Dan Brown's *The Da Vinci Code* or Mark Haddon's *The Curious Incident of the Dog in the Night-Time,* both of which open with the discovery of a highly unusual murder. Sometimes it's not so easy to determine what has happened when: if you're reading the work of a writer such as William Faulkner, Virginia Woolf, or Michael Cunningham (specifically, his 1999 novel *The Hours*), you'll be confronting a **stream of consciousness** technique, as the writer attempts to duplicate the actual working process of the human brain, present observations and past memories all banging up against each other.

Regardless of how the writer chooses to organize the sequence of events, there are three basic plot points that you are likely to run across in almost any story. Generally, at some point near the beginning of a story, you're going to get some **exposition,** the background info that a reader needs to make sense of what's going on between the characters. Once the author has given you some sense of context for the characters and the action, it's time for a **complication** to get the story moving, some new person or event that intensifies or changes an existing situation. In Myla Goldberg's novel *Bee Season,* for example, the previously mediocre student Eliza wins the grade-school spelling bee and discovers an unsettling bond with her father as he devotes his life to her singular talent. If you're lucky enough to be reading a true page-turner, the conflict and suspense will build steadily and dramatically to a point of **climax,** the ultimate moment of greatest emotional tension for both you and the main character or characters—Eliza nearly loses her mind as she attempts to reunite her family by performing the permutations suggested by the Kabbalistic mystic Abulafia. At the end of the story, the plot will come to some sort of **resolution,** but more sophisticated books, like Goldberg's, will allow readers to draw their own conclusions about the meaning of the last pages and the story as a whole.

For the book group reader, the value of knowing something about plot and standard plot patterns is that it can help you appreciate the way that the most innovative writers toy and mess with our expectations of what's going to happen. The best book group books are usually those that feature some tricks and turns in the course of action, leading us to speculation and discussion of character and meaning, rather than placating us with simplistic answers. Book group readers are also most likely to be intrigued by stories that feature **internal conflict** as well as **external**—it's always intriguing to watch a character struggling against the demons of his or her own mind as well as those antagonists in the physical or social world.

QUESTIONS OF PLOT AND STRUCTURE FOR READING AND DISCUSSION

- How would you describe the basic plot structure? Is it mostly chronological, sequential, or is there a certain amount of skipping back and forth between past and present?
- How does the ordering of events influence the story? Why, do you think, the author chose this particular presentation of events? Can you imagine how the story would suffer or benefit from a different organization?

- What are the main points of conflict in the story? When are they revealed? Can you identify the major internal and external conflicts for the main character or characters?
- How much does this writer depend on suspense and surprises? Does the use of suspense or surprise work effectively in the story? Do any of the surprises seem contrived or unconvincing?
- Does or will this story have some kind of concrete resolution? Did the ending seem to fit in with the rest of the spirit of the story— that is, do you buy it?

Where and When Does It Happen?

Next, if you happen to be so inclined, you can start looking for and identifying some of the elements of the story that make up a little something that we know as **THE SETTING.** The major elements of any narrative setting are three: **time** (obviously), **place** (no kidding), and, perhaps less immediately glaring, the specific **social environment** in which the characters are romping. This last can be a little more difficult to pinpoint, but it's the most important when it comes to understanding the context and in thinking about the specific points of conflict for any character in any story. Occasionally, of course, you run into that unusual story in which setting is neither specific nor essential—it's entirely possible to imagine a story that consists of nothing more than two characters speaking to each other about a problem between them—a *Waiting for Godot* type of thing—but this is very rare.

In most good stories, setting does more than lay a placemat for the main meal of the narrative. Setting can be vital in establishing the **mood** or **atmosphere** of a story—try to imagine Harry Potter without Hogwarts, or Anne of Green Gables living in central Brooklyn, or the Headless Horseman tearing through your local strip mall. The skilled use of a particular dramatic setting can be especially effective when a talented author uses it to establish one kind of expectation and then rattles us by unrolling a very unexpected scroll of events. We tend to think of houses, playgrounds, suburbs, and schools (at least, we did before Columbine) as safe and stable, even boring places, so it's all the

more unnerving when such locations are the scene of any kind of sheer zaniness, uncontrolled chaos, creeping terror, dumbstruck love, battles to the death, you name it.

You won't get far in thinking about the central meanings or main ideas of a story unless you are ready and willing to consider the distinct social environment of the time and place in which it is set. Unless you appreciate the rigidly stratified grid of fifteenth-century Delft that provides the backdrop for Tracy Chevalier's *Girl with a Pearl Earring,* you'll overlook many of the deeper implications of the relationship between Vermeer and Griet. If you think of nothing else when you think about setting, you have to think about the specific **cultural values** of any group of people in a story—their collective ideals, fears, desires, ambitions. This social group can be a big one, such as a town, a class, a race, a nationality, or it might be very small—the intimate world of a family or the imaginary world shared by two creative friends. You have to ask yourself, What is most important to these people? Who has the power to determine or change what is most important? How does the main character, or characters, fit in with this society or struggle against it? How important are these cultural values to the main character? Try applying some of these questions to your current book of choice.

QUESTIONS OF SETTING FOR READING
AND DISCUSSION

- Can you identify the specific **time, place,** and **social atmosphere** of this story?
- How vital is this particular location and period to this particular story: could the story have played out, more or less the same, in another place and time?
- How does the author's description of the physical surroundings contribute to the mood and meanings of the story?
- Think about points of change. Does a familiar or comfortable setting become hostile, disturbing, or suddenly transformed for any of the main characters?
- Can you identify one or more of the social issues or problems that the main character or characters will face in this particular social

world? Where does the protagonist fit in among his or her most immediate social groups? Are the protagonist's goals, fears, or ideals consistent with the group of people who surround him or her?

- As you continue to read, try to define the main points of conflict for the novel's central characters. How many of these conflicts are related to the character's place or position in a larger social context?
- Who is in power in this particular setting, and who is not? What attempts do the powerless make to achieve some kind of personal independence?

What's the Big Idea (or Ideas)?

Last but not least, we come to the main thing that we look for in a story: meaning. Every story is told for some reason or another and has at the very least one meaning, even if that meaning is that there is no meaning, no rhyme or reason, to some facet of human existence. Yes, readers, we're talking about **THEME** here, a word that for many of us may have some negative associations. If you were unfortunate enough to have to write what used to be called "themes" in an English class, or if you suffered (or are currently suffering) under the misguided tutelage of a teacher who demanded that you answer questions like "What is the universal theme of *Moby-Dick*? What is the major theme of *Hamlet*?" and if that same misguided pedagogue insisted that there was only *one right answer* to such questions, then you may groan inwardly at the very idea of identifying central themes of a narrative work.

But fear not. First of all, a theme, after all, is just another word for a central or major idea of a story. Second, as you know all too well by now, most stories have more than one major idea going on. Third, any book group book worth its salt is going to be **ambiguous** in a certain way—a bad thing when you were struggling through literature exams at school but a great thing when you have the freedom and encouragement of a book group to explore your ideas about the book and the world. This means that you can interpret the main points or particular meanings of a specific person, place, event, action, speech, or dynamic in a story in more than one way, so long as the story supports such a reading.

Most of our most intriguing and provocative authors, those who write the fascinating, ambiguous, morally complex stories that make for the best book group reading, are not so interested in providing a single easy answer to a tough human problem. Rather, they create characters, relationships, events, and stories in such a style and manner as to encourage us to question some of our most fundamental human desires and problems. Often they will make use of certain reccurring **symbols, images,** or **motifs** to attract our attention to a particular issue, phenomenon, or paradox. While there is no single method or precise formula that is guaranteed to whip you to the center of a story's major themes, there are some helpful strategies and queries that can help you determine for yourself what ideas or issues the author is trying to illuminate for your consideration. You may want to look at one or more of the major elements to any story that we've been discussing in this chapter—style, point of view, plot, character, and setting, because a good writer will use all these factors to his or her advantage in exploring major ideas. Here're a few that may get you started:

QUESTIONS OF THEME FOR
READING AND DISCUSSION

- Pay attention to any and all titles and headings: of the book itself, of chapters, or of sections. These may very well provide a clue to major ideas, concerns, and questions that the author is trying to address. Do you see any patterns emerging?
- Consider the author's writing style—does the style seem to hint or allude to some of the important meanings in the book? Look for tone and purpose as well—which events or characters are presented with the most detail or the most sympathy?
- Is the narrator a reliable one? If she, or he, is telling her own story, how much do you think the narrator understands about the events going on around her, or him? If the narrator is an unreliable or naïve one, why do you think that the author used this narrator to present the events of this story? What purpose might this serve?
- Focus on the protagonist and other main characters. Have any of the main characters changed significantly during the story? Have

any reached any important insights due to the events or actions that have taken place? Sometimes the characters that surround the protagonist can give you a great clue about the significance of a particular idea or decision—so ask yourself what parallels you see in their situations.

- Is the plot straightforward? Or is the timeline of events in any way nonchronological? Does the order in which the author presents information affect the way you interpret the point of the story?

- Look for recurring images, symbols, events, situations, objects, even words. What points does the narrator keep coming back to? What people or events refuse to die, that is, refuse to lie quiet or remain still?

- How does the setting of the story contribute to the major ideas and issues that the story raises? How does the specific cultural and social environment contribute to the conflict in the story? Do factors such as age, race, gender, class, politics, or religious belief play a significant role in the outcome?

- Compare the ways different kinds of people deal with the major points of conflict in the story. Can you argue that a certain person or kind of person has some success in rising above conflict, which is denied to the others? Is there a character who might epitomize failure in overcoming obstacles?

- Take a pen and quickly write down simple words or phrases that you would use to describe the major concerns or points of contention in the story—make this fast and informal; don't stop to censor yourself.

- Can you identify a possible **synecdoche** for this story? *Synecdoche* simply means "a part for a whole," a single sentence, image, situation, quotation, or even a character that could stand for the point of the story as a whole. Many of us might remember such lines from Voltaire's *Candide* as "the best of all possible worlds," or "cultivate your garden"—either of these phrases could serve as a synecdoche to the larger meaning of the novel.

3

For Every Book a Season and a Question: Customized Considerations for the Eight Most Popular Genres

In the last chapter, we looked at some of the things you can think about as you read any story, some of the literary elements that you might want to consider as you prepare for a book group discussion of any kind of book. Now it's time to get specific. Most likely you're going to have the best luck sharpening those reading-and-meeting claws if you can think about these strategies in terms of a particular kind of book.

If you've read a book or two in your time, you've probably noticed that you have some definite ideas about what kinds of writing really do it for you. Ellen's husband, David, is an aficionado of the kind of books whose very titles, he points out, "make most people start to bleed out their ears, metaphorically speaking." When he hits his local bookstore, David heads straight for what we have affectionately termed "the Long and Boring Section," returning gleefully with such stimulating selections as *The Age of Federalism* and *The Wealth and Poverty of Nations.* If you share some of David's inexplicably arcane tastes or shoulder the unfortunate burden of having such an erudite reader in your life, you may want to check out the aptly named "Long and Bor-ing" page on our Web site at www.goodbookslately.com. David and friends will be recommending such juicy gems as *Thirty Years of the Federal Reserve* for all you infinitely patient, excruciatingly curious, and obscurely practical knowledge vultures out there.

It's a special kind of reader who joyfully whiles away the hours of his or her free time in pursuit of such admittedly worthy information. The authors of this current companion are not so inclined; nor are we specialists, in any sense of the word, in reading history, political science, mystery, science fiction, or poetry. So in this chapter we will confine ourselves to providing suggestions for reading and discussing the eight types of books that we know best, which are also the eight kinds that "general interest" book group readers tend to read most or all of the time. First, we'll look at the strictly fictional categories:

- **The Classic Literary Novel**
- **The Contemporary Literary Novel**
- **The Short Story Collection**
- **Popular Paperbacks**

Second, we'll look at what are usually termed "nonfiction" categories (as we will see, the boundaries that separate fact from fiction can get pretty messy):

- **The Memoir/Autobiography**
- **Creative Essay/Creative Nonfiction**
- **Strict Nonfiction: Historical Story**

Finally, we will also devote a few tips to handling that potentially most difficult of all book group reading categories:

- **The Book I Hated and Sort of Hated You for Choosing**

READER ALERT

At the end of each of the eight book group book categories, you'll find a list of questions to consider for reading and discussing any book that belongs to the particular genre. Think of each set of customized questions as a supplement to the more general questions listed at the end of each section in chapter 2. You may wind up tinkering with some questions in order to refine them for a specific book (you can do this either before or during your meeting—try both and see which works best).

Reading the Novel: What Is "Literary Fiction"?

Readers Confess

"I know that our book group reads mostly what people call 'literary' novels, but I guess I don't know exactly what that means, how to describe or define that word."

"We have some debate in the group over the good stuff, the hard stuff. Some of us like to read stories that are really challenging, really 'literary,' but others go for 'literary-lite.'"

"What is it that makes certain kinds of stories 'literature'? Is that the same as 'literary fiction'?"

In her seminal study of book groups in Britain, *Reading Groups* (Oxford Press, 2002) author Jenny Hartley puts to bed the myth that reading groups wallow in mediocrity, revel in "middlebrow" book selections. From the enthusiastic responses of hundreds of participants who completed detailed questionnaires, contacted Hartley by phone and E-mail, and invited her to join their groups for a meeting, Hartley learned that when it comes to reading-group choices, "the bulk of the titles are what booksellers call literary fiction." Citing favorite reading group authors such as Ian McEwan, Margaret Atwood, and Toni Morrison, Hartley concludes that despite what some elitist reading-group detractors dismissed as the mindless fetishism of middle-class mundane drivel—yes, friends, there are such strange and deeply unsettled malcontents—"middlebrow is not a helpful label to describe this reading." Amen to that, Ms. Hartley!

As we have learned in the past three years working with American book groups, things are pretty much the same on this side of the Atlantic. The vast majority of book group readers who responded to our survey named "literary fiction" as their most popular and frequent reading choice and/or named authors who belong to this celebrated group as their longtime favorites. Thanks to the stupendous efforts and phenomenal success of Oprah's Book Club, any North American reader who happens to wander into an average-sized airport bookstore can now choose from a variety of literary titles. Just think about it: nowadays you can pick up a novel by Joyce Carol Oates or Jane Smiley as you scramble through the United terminal at O'Hare. Flash back five or six years ago, and you were pretty much stuck with Stephen King, Tom Clancy, or Mary Higgins Clark (or, if you scanned the self-help shelf, maybe something in the realm of *Chicken Soup for the Unwed Teenage Mother's Soul*). Not that we ourselves haven't savored the delights of such consistently entertaining storytellers on numerous occasions, but sometimes you want something a little less, well, consistent. Something that can surprise you, captivate you, challenge your expectations as it makes you wonder about this crazy thing we call life—that sort of thing.

These are the kinds of books that book group readers have been devouring and discussing for years (even if they couldn't buy them in airports). In fact, these are the sorts of books that discussion groups have been enjoying steadily since the origins of book groups themselves. But what, exactly, is "literary fiction"? And how can thinking a little bit more about the foggy nature of the "literary novel" help you polish your reading and discussion techniques when it comes to this omnipresent book group centerpiece?

We've been asked many times by many journalists what kinds of books work well for book groups. If we offer the pat answer "literary fiction," we have learned that we may be asked to explain what this is or, worse, what "literature" is. Only fair, of course, seeing as we've set ourselves up as experts. Experts are supposed to have expertise, you see. Well, we're proud to say that we stole our definition of "literature" from a bunch of kids. The best one we've ever run up against was volunteered by a mostly novice group of freshman English students at the University of Denver.

In one of her Introduction to Literature classes, Ellen asked her students to compare two pieces of writing on the joys of married love, one from a popular Harlequin Romance author and the other from a short story by Gail Godwin called "A Sorrowful Woman." The Harlequin Romance, the class decided, tidied up its loose ends neatly and offered a set of pat and easy answers to the uneasy troubles of domestic love. The lovely and cultured heroine of the story has been terribly afraid to tell her incredibly successful and appropriately ruggedly handsome husband that she is unable to bear children. Will he still love her? Will he look upon her as a barren and useless burden? The answer, surprise, surprise, is a resounding "No!" He is sympathetically moved by her tragic infertility and reduced to manly tears in contemplating the weight of the fearful secret she has carried all these years! He loves her for her plucky courage, moral fiber, and, of course, her bountifully breasted but tiny-butted size-four figure! They will adopt a trio of equally plucky Third World orphans and take them to baseball games! All is bliss. Now we know. By contrast, the Godwin story presents a portrait of a woman who already has everything that the Harlequin heroine feared she might not. The attractive woman of "The Good Wife" has a lovely home, a lovely husband, and a lovely child, each more shiny, adorable, and nurturing than the next. But for some strange reason, she is not happy. Why not? What does she long for? What is she afraid of?

As the freshmen students of Ellen's class debated these matters, they came up with a long and messy list of possible culprits and potential sources. "See, that's the difference between the two stories," one student complained. "The Harlequin story gives you all the answers. But the Godwin story just makes us ask more and more questions." His classmates agreed and concluded that maybe that was the element that separates "popular" fiction from what we call "literary" fiction. Thanks guys, we owe you one, again.

Old School: Reading the "Classic" Literary Novel

What IS a Classic?

Literary novels come in two varieties: the Hot New and the Beloved Old. All right, that's simplifying things just a bit. There's also that limbo region where hot new novels go to ferment quietly until, if they are very, very good, and/or very, very lucky, they will become classics, stories for the ages. Let's take a look at that classifying process. What is it that makes a literary novel a classic? Is it time? Is it quality? Is it authorial intent? Or simply the reader's decision?

Readers Wonder

"What exactly do you consider a literary classic?" asks Angela of La Jolla, California. "My book group has long been burdened by the idea that we ought to be reading more 'classics,' the sort of books many of us managed to avoid reading in high school or college. But how old does a book have to be to be a classic?"

"Are Wallace Stegner's Angle of Repose or Harper Lee's To Kill a Mockingbird classics?" Jaime of Omaha, Nebraska, asks. "If they are, if books from the second half of the twentieth century can be included in that category, then our book group is indeed reading literary classics."

"It's not a classic unless the author is dead, am I right?" asks Martina of Skokie, Illinois.

Excellent questions, all. For those of you blissfully unconcerned about or happily satisfied with the possible responses to such a dilemma, please skip ahead to the next section. We're imagining that at least some of our readers might be curious about this matter, however, because this question of "what is a classic?" has come up again and again as we visit with book group after book group. We're sure that none of our savvy readers will be surprised to learn that there is, of course, more than one school of thought when it comes to answering this query. Certain experts (classics professors, mostly) claim that nothing that comes after the Romans can be considered a classic. Other professors draw the line at American literature—arguing that no American writer can be considered "classical," because all American writing is based on the borrowed tropes and texts of much older European cultures. A slim majority of professors of literature would probably tend to define a "classic" as anything that was written prior to the twentieth century, while many others would make an argument for anything preceding World War I. Yet most would probably agree that literary classics are works that have stood the test of time and will continue to speak to readers and audiences for many, many years to come—even if we're all forced to read e-books in whatever version of the bathtub will torment our great-great-grandchildren in the distant, murky future.

So much for the academic viewpoint. Now, what does a "classic" mean for the rest of us?

Readers Define

"A classic is anything that might be included in the reading curriculum at the high school or college level—anything from the Greek plays to such American authors as Faulkner or James Baldwin."   *—Zach, Seattle, Washington*

"We like to pick up on classics-in-the-making. Books that may not yet be taught in schools, but which future scholars, historians, and readers will look back to as a way of understanding life in the later part of the twentieth century, the beginning of the twenty-first. Wallace Stegner's *Angle of Repose,* written in the 1970s, will still be around in a hundred years. So will the work of Nadine Gordimer, and J. M. Coetzee out of South Africa. Margaret Atwood's stuff, especially her earlier work, is already a classic, as far as we're concerned."   *—Karen, Montreal, Quebec*

When you think of literary classics, in this case classic novels, do you tend to agree with Zach or Karen?

It's an interesting question and one you may enjoy debating with your book group at the start of a discussion of an allegedly "classic" story. As far as we're concerned, Zach and Karen are both right. It all comes back to that quality test-of-time issue for us. The reason we read certain books in school is because somebody decided that these works had something to show and teach us—both about the universal human mess that spreads across the ages and about a specific culture during a specific time. That somebody might have been somebody very learned and literate, who possessed some considerable "classic-making" leverage. Take the example of Herman Melville's *Moby-Dick,* for instance. When Melville first published his leviathan tome in the mid-1800s, the novel was not an immediate smashing success, to put it mildly. In fact, frankly, nobody was particularly impressed—both critics and readers thought it was fanciful and ponderous—or, in today's terms, weird and long. It wasn't until the late 1920s that a group of British scholars got together and discovered that hey, there might actually be something to this "Call me Ishmael" thing. But a literary work might also become a classic because a whole bunch of ordinary somebodies like it so much that it becomes a part of a culture, a sort of institution in society. Charles Dickens originally published most of his novels in a serial (magazine) form, a chapter or two each week or month. These episodic installments were wildly popular with the general reading public—which, of course, wasn't as general as it is today because not as many people could read. But those who could gulped down each installment and hungered for the next in much the same way as modern television viewers eagerly consume and await the next episode of *Six Feet Under* or the latest *Law & Order* franchise. It's worth noting, too, that even the illustrious Shakespeare was once a sort of David E. Kelley of his time; even very poor people could sometimes save a penny to watch his plays from the pit, the "standing room only" section devoid of seats and littered with nut shells and rotting fruit.

Such works, whether endorsed on high or down low, eventually became part of **the canon,** which is a word that describes the collection of books experts have decided are worthy of our prolonged attention. Another reason that many books and authors stand out from the pack and last for the long haul is sheer shocking originality. While a reputed author of yore may seem old hat by the standards of our sleek modern skulls, you can bet that he or she wrote about a previously unmentionable topic, or in a previously unimaginable fashion, that took the readers of his or her day by surprise and even made some of them very, very nervous. So if we go by these standards, even books that are only thirty years old, or twenty, perhaps in some cases even less, can be considered "new classics" at the very least. For the hard core among you, however, you can always stick by Martina's litmus test of death: if the author's dead and we're still reading his or her work, yes, it's most likely a classic.

QUESTIONS ON CLASSICS FOR READING AND DISCUSSION

Start with STYLE: **What kind of writing and why?**

- DON'T FORGET to read a page or two of this classic novel out loud, somewhere near the beginning of your meeting. This is particularly vital if you are reading a much older story that most likely will be written in an old-fashioned or unfamiliar style, perhaps using some once-hip words or phrases that the modern reader may not be hip to in this day and age.
- Is the writing style "dated" in any way—that is, do you notice words, expressions, or turns of phrase that indicate that this book is not a product of the current time?

Move to NARRATOR AND POINT OF VIEW: **Who's speaking?**

- Does the narrator openly acknowledge or comment on the social issues and problems of this specific time? Or is the narrator more interested in telling a story that is somehow "timeless"?

Focus on the CHARACTERS: **Who's Involved?**

- Can you argue that any of the main characters are simply a product of their time and place? Do the characters seem "old-fashioned" to you in any way?

Check out the PLOT: **What happens in what order?**

- Is the presentation of the plot strictly chronological? Do you notice or remember any plot devices that seem contrived or old-fashioned?
- Consider the main sources of conflict (external and internal) in a classic story—are any of these people or problems the product of a specific time and place, that is, not likely to trouble characters in a more contemporary novel?

Think about the SETTING: **Where and when does it happen?**

- Is the cultural environment of the classic novel mostly the product of its time, its day, or does it possess certain universal or enduring qualities that keep these particular social concerns relevant?

Don't forget THEMES: **What's the big idea (or ideas)?**

- Are the main ideas and central concerns of the novel ones that continue to intrigue or trouble us today?
- How would you explain the "staying power" of this novel? What does it have to say about this particular place and time, and the people who lived during this time? Why has it lasted, and will it continue to last into the next century?
- What is your personal definition of a "classic"? Do you agree or side with any of the definitions offered by the readers and critics we've quoted?

New School: Reading the Contemporary Literary Novel

What IS the Contemporary Literary Novel?

If you are in a book group, chances are this is the kind of book your members tend to read the most. As we discussed above, both adjectives that describe this kind of novel are somewhat open to interpretation. For some readers, contemporary is anything written in the last fifty years, for others, "contemporary" means something that hit the shelves in the last five. The term "literary" can be equally up for debate, depending on what your definition of "literature" may be. In our minds, a great literary novel will meet and surpass the four following criteria:

1. In each case the author's writing style is confident, distinctive, original, and provocative.
2. The author has something unique to say about a unique group of well-defined, complex characters.
3. The subject matter and storyline are interesting, compelling, and surprising—no easy formulas, no pat endings that wrap everything up with a bow.
4. Finally, and most important, these authors have crafted characters, events, and stories that are **ambiguous**—open to more than one kind of interpretation that encourage discussion and debate. These novels provoke us to ask questions rather than satisfy us with easy answers.

Why This Contemporary Novel? Why Now?

What sorts of things should you be looking for as you read a contemporary literary novel? In many ways, this isn't too different from the literary elements that you would try to identify and think about as you read a "classic" work—the main difference, of course, is that a contemporary novel, by definition, is one that is written with a contemporary audience in mind—the author's main intended audience are the people who are currently sharing the world with the writer.

This, of course, would also have been true for any writer who wrote at any point in the past, but we are not his or her contemporaries, so we will read an older work with a new or different cultural point of reference.

Another question to consider is just how you came to be reading this particular contemporary novel. Case in point: a few years ago, an author named Anita Diamant wrote a little book she called *The Red Tent*, a novel that imagines the lives of the women in the Old Testament's first family—Isaac's personal harem. The only problem was that at first nobody cared too much—the novel didn't sell particularly well. But Anita Diamant had a great story to tell, and she wasn't going to let it whimper away without some kind of bang. She got out there and pounded the pavement, hitting a large number of Jewish community centers, synagogues, and affiliated book groups, offering to meet with any group that wished to discuss her book. Before the book group world (or, for that matter, Diamant's deeply thankful publishers) knew what had hit them, a bristling best-seller was born.

With all the contemporary literary novels out there competing for your attention (literary novels are THE most popular genre for most book groups), you might want to think about how the particular one you're reading and discussing now has earned or won its front-and-center position—how did this book or author make it from the lower dusty shelves of eventual obscurity to the discerning hands and laps of your members? Why did you select this novel or think that you would be interested in reading it?

READER ALERT

> **If you're interested in reading-and-discussion questions for the contemporary novel, we advise that you skip back now to the questions at the end of each section in chapter 2 at this point. We have only a question or two to add as you consider this category:**

- You are reading a contemporary novel, but is the setting contemporary? How important was the setting in terms of influencing you or your group to read a particular contemporary novel?
- Compare the private experience of reading this novel with the public one of discussing it in a book club. Was one experience superior to or more enjoyable than the other? Or is this one of the rare books that triumphs in both spheres—that is a pleasure to read and also provides lots to talk about?
- Is this contemporary novel one you would enthusiastically recommend to other book groups? Why or why not?
- Is this an "important" novel? This is a word that book-jacket blurb writers toss out a lot, but is it one you can use to describe this book?

Reading the Short Story Collection

Readers Confide

"We tried one short story collection in [our] book club, and I felt sort of cheated, because we only discussed one of the stories." —*Kennedy, Madison, Wisconsin*

"We don't read short story collections because we agree that we all like more time to get to know the main characters and to connect to one big story instead of several little ones." —*Better, Sun Valley, Idaho*

"It's hard to talk about short stories, because you don't have that much time in a book group to get to each one. Also, you may not know how to talk about any of the stories as part of the whole picture. Also, I guess, because we're just not used to it." —*Roger, Dayton, Ohio*

"We are that weird anomaly, a reading group that actually reads as many short story works as we do novels or memoirs. That's probably because a lot of our members are English teachers, so we're used to discussing short stories from anthologies. We really enjoy it because you can focus very carefully on specifics—not like talking about a novel where so much of the writing gets lost."

—Marianne, Kansas City, Missouri

Time for a Change?

It's definitely true that many book groups shy away from short story collections, usually for reasons that resemble one or more of those stated above. If your members will be perfectly happy should they never look a short story in the eye for the duration of your book group career, then, by all means, feel free to pass. On the other hand, you may find that including the occasional short story collection is the perfect way to shake things up a bit. The short story form demands a certain level of skill, focus, and attention from both writer and reader the novel does not—that is, the writer must construct an original story, believable characters, and a framework for major themes in a very limited number of words and pages, while the reader must proceed slowly and carefully if she is to pick up on all the clues of meaning. Unlike many novels, all good short stories are to the point; they waste no time on extraneous plot lines. If you are a reader who has only a limited time each evening when you sit down to grab a few precious minutes with a book, you can get lost in a sprawling novel. By contrast, most of the time you can finish an entire short story in a single reclining and move on to the next one the next free minute you have to read. It's usually pretty easy to identify the major players and most important moments in a short story, in a way you can't always do so quickly when it comes to a big fat novel. True, you may not have any better idea what this player or moment *means*, but you can at least identify him, her, or it with relative ease.

Focus on the Few, Expand to the Whole

"I like reading short stories, but we've had trouble talking about them in the book group. Should the idea be to discuss all or most of the stories in a collection? Is each discussion of each story a 'separate' kind of thing?"

—Molly, Coos Bay, Oregon

Good question, Molly! We've struggled quite a bit with this one in our own maiden voyages of leading a class or a book group through a short story collection. Here's what we've found works best. Instead of trying to give equal talk time to all or most of the stories in the collection, **focus on three (four, if you're particularly ambitious) stories in detail.** Take a vote at the beginning of the meeting to determine which three or four your group wants to discuss in depth. Treat each story kind of like a poem or the lyrics to a favorite mysterious song— that is, stop from time to time to look closely at individual words, lines, and sections. As you begin talking about each of your three top choices, you will, of course, want to read an opening page or paragraph out loud to refresh your memory, to get warmed up to this particular cast of characters and sources of conflict, and to consider how much the author's style, perspective, and tone vary from story to story.

As you discuss each story in detail, feel free to make comparisons to other stories in the collection, even the ones you are not "featuring" in discussion. Think of the short story discussion as a two-part process. First, you'll want to consider things such as style, point of view, character, plot, setting, and theme in terms of each story. Toward the end of your meeting, focus on any **common elements** of situation, conflict, or meaning that seem to pervade or shape the collection as a whole.

QUESTIONS ON SHORT STORIES FOR READING AND DISCUSSION
Start with STYLE: **What kind of writing and why?**

- How would you describe the writing style you see in these three stories? Is the style—use of certain kinds of words, certain types of sentence structures—much the same in the three stories, or do you notice some significant differences? Try reading a few sentences from each story out loud if you're having trouble.
- Can you pinpoint a particular tone for any of the three stories, or for all three? How does the author or narrator in each case seem

to feel about the subjects he or she describes? What does the author or narrator want us to realize about them?

Move to NARRATOR AND POINT OF VIEW: **Who's speaking?**

- Identify the narrative point of view in each of the three stories. What similarities or differences do you see in the narrative point of view of each of the stories you are discussing?
- How would you describe the narrator of each of the stories (sympathetic, naïve, unreliable, prejudiced, perceptive)? Does the narrator seem to possess a certain amount of self-awareness? Or are any of the narrators less observant, less sophisticated, less sensitive than he or she imagines?
- Does the narrative point of view change from one of the main characters to another in some way, and what, exactly, causes that change?

Focus on the CHARACTERS: **Who's Involved?**

- What traits, situations, or problems do any of the characters from the three stories have in common, if anything?
- Which characters experience a change or a new realization, and which stay basically unchanged? What kind of changes or realizations seem to be the most important for the characters in these stories?

Check out the PLOT: **What happens in what order?**

- Do you notice any similar elements or issues or points of conflict in the opening plot of these three stories?
- Look at the way the writer builds suspense or conflict in each story, and also (very importantly) how each story ends. What kind of resolution do we get to any of the problems in the stories? Which stories share similar kinds of problems and resolutions?

Think about the SETTING: **Where and when does it happen?**

- Can you identify the setting of each of these three stories? What is the time and place of each? How would you describe the cultural or social environment of each story's main characters?
- In terms of specific cultural issues or social concerns, what do the three stories have in common? Do the characters share any similar cultural situations or worries?
- How do the characters fit into the larger social world of each of the three stories? Are they insiders or outsiders? Do any of the main characters seek to change their place or position in society?

Don't forget THEMES: **What's the big idea (or ideas)?**

- Can you identify some similarities in the settings, issues, conflicts, and characters of these stories? Does it seem that some common themes or central ideas are beginning to emerge? What sort of desires or dilemmas hold the collection together?
- Don't forget to look back at the titles of each of the stories in a collection—does the title help you establish a particular meaning or meanings for each story? Or does the story help you understand the importance of the title?
- Is this short story collection one you would recommend to other book groups that are seeking to break into the short story mode, just for a change? How does this collection compare, favorably or unfavorably, to any others you may have read?
- Did you notice any difference between today's short story discussion and the way your group typically talks about bigger narratives, such as novels or memoirs?

Reading Popular Fiction: Yes, You Can!

Readers Protest

"Some of the books that come with reading guides are hilarious—I mean, who are they trying to kid? Like any reading group is going to waste their precious reading and meeting time talking about something so simple!"   —*Carol, Cincinnati, Ohio*

"Anyone who has actually been in a book club knows the tougher books also make for the best discussions."   —*Ginger, Baton Rouge, Florida*

"We finally stopped trying to pretend we were more sophisticated than we actually are—sometimes we do challenge ourselves with 'hard' novels, but we also treat ourselves to the latest paperbacks on the best-seller lists. Thank you, Kelly Ripa!"
—*Joyce, Reno, Navada*

Can Smart Groups Have Fun Discussing "Easy" Books?

The majority of book groups tend to get their kicks from the literary as opposed to the popular novel. This makes sense because a lot of very popular fiction isn't terribly complex or ambiguous. A lot of popular fiction depends on certain reccurring patterns, plots, characters, and points of conflict—a good way to determine if a story fits a formula is to imagine plugging in a different set of characters or a different setting; if the basic story would remain pretty much the same, you've got an old familiar standby on your hands. Not all popular fiction is formulaic, of course, but most of it makes a relatively small demand on the reader. You may not know who done it or why or how, but you can be fairly sure you'll get all the answers at the end. You generally have a good idea of who and what you're rooting for and/or against, and you're confident that the girl or the detective will get her guy at some point. But does that mean you couldn't have a good discussion about the work of one of the world's favorite authors, such as Anne Rivers Siddons, Maeve Binchy, or, of course, J. K. Rowling? You could indeed, but you may have to work a little harder. You will have to read for content as well as pleasure, to keep a lookout for specific cultural messages and values that the book celebrates and deplores. You can become an amateur cultural anthropologist for a day and think about what makes the particular people in the particular society of the novel move and tick.

In college sociology, film, cultural studies, and literature classrooms, students are taught to read all kinds of popular cultural mediums for meanings and messages. With some practice, you can "read" a magazine ad or a television commercial for certain implicit shared cultural values and ideals, and this can be really interesting if you can look at a similar piece of advertising from another culture or time period to make some comparisons. For example, think about looking at two American ads for women's lingerie, one from Victoria's Secret of today and another from Maidenform of the 1950s. Reading the copy and looking at the images, you would notice that our ideas of what is sexy, what is feminine, what is comfortable, and what is desirable have changed over the years.

You can do the same sort of exercise while reading a popular novel. It's important to remember that many of today's literary "classics" were once the popular favorites of their day, granted, the particularly clever and compelling popular favorites. Today we read the work of Charles Dickens in school and in book groups; we can study his novels for clues about the culture, conflicts, and concerns of Dickens's England. We can look for reccurring themes and symbols in his stories; we can discuss his deft and delightful modes of characterization. Just because something is popular, or was popular, does not mean it can't be good, clever, or worth our time.

One good way to start doing this is to pretend you are a reader from, say, the twenty-fourth century, or from a totally different cultural background, or even from another planet, if you're into that kind of thing. Discuss this novel as if you were a brand-new immigrant to, or a devoted scholar of, the particular social and cultural world that this book represents. If you were reading a Maeve Binchy novel, for example, you'd want to ask yourself questions about the day-to-day life of the characters in the tiny rural towns of 1960s Ireland that her books almost always feature. Or perhaps you are reading a mystery novel set in turn-of-the-last-century Britain, so you'll keep an eye on the way that your author represents the people and important cultural values of that time and place.

What sort of questions might you ask yourself if you were reading a popular novel for a book group? How would you tweak our basic questions about style, point of view, character, plot, setting, and theme? Imagine these prompts in terms of a popular novel that you have recently read or are familiar with.

QUESTIONS ON POPULAR FICTION FOR READING AND DISCUSSION
Start with STYLE: **What kind of writing and why?**

- Writers who are fortunate enough to be very popular often express themselves in a more simple and straightforward manner, but you can still pick up on some specific inclinations in their style and tone. Read a page or two out loud to yourself, and pay attention to any words, phrases, expressions, or sentences that stand out. How does this writer manipulate style to grab your attention quickly and hold it?
- What about the balance of dialogue and descriptive passages? Does the author depend more on one than the other to move the plot, impart information, or win our sympathies?

Focus on the CHARACTERS: **Who's involved?**

- Which of the main characters are "round" characters, that is, complex, fully drawn, capable of surprising us? Are any of the characters "stock" characters, that is, they represent more of a type of person, a caricature, than they do a specific individual?
- Does this story have a hero or heroine, a villain or a villainess? Do any of the good or the bad guys "change sides," either in the mind of the reader or on the page?

Check out the PLOT: **What happens in what order?**

- Is the plot formulaic in any way? Could you sum up the plot in a few sentences?
- How much does the author depend on suspense and surprise to make the story compelling? Does the author manage to surprise you?

Think about the SETTING: **Where and when does it happen?**

- How important are the time, place, and specific cultural environment to this story? Is this a story that could just as well be set someplace else?
- What social values or cultural desires does this novel support or ridicule? In the world that this novel represents, how does the ideal man or woman behave? What battles must he or she fight? How does the ideal professional (cop, detective, scientist, wizard, etc.) behave?

Don't forget THEMES: **What's the big idea (or ideas)?**

- Why do you think that this novel or this author have been so successful? What human fears and desires does it address? What cultural values does it support or reject?
- Can you sum up the major theme or idea of this novel in a few words?
- Why does this novel fit into the category of popular fiction, in your estimation?
- Does this novel belong to a subgroup of popular fiction that you are familiar with, such as romance, mystery, adventure story, three-hankie weeper? If so, how does it measure up to your favorites in this subgenre?
- Do you think "popular" is synonymous with "easy to read"? Do these two things always go together? If a book is "easy to read," is it also, in your opinion, going to be "hard to talk about"?

Personal Stories: Reading the Memoir or Autobiography

Readers Inquire

"Memoirs are included in the Autobiography section of my local Barnes & Noble. Does that mean that memoirs and autobiography are basically two words for the same thing, or is a memoir sort of like a short biography? Why are some stories 'a memoir' and others 'the memoirs of' so and so?" —*Matthew, Houston, Texas*

"Can you talk about themes or characters in a memoir? Or does that not work in a nonfiction story?" —*Kara, Trinidad, Colorado*

Now we move on to the first of our nonfiction categories, the personal story, also known as the memoir or the autobiography. Although memoir and autobiography are quite similar in content and purpose, a **memoir** tends to emphasize the people and events that the author has known or witnessed, while an **autobiography** is more likely to focus primarily on the inner life and significant actions of its author. Generally, an autobiography attempts to cover the course of an entire life (or life so far), while a memoir usually focuses on a specific period of time or subject in the writer's experience, such as Susanna Kaysen's *Girl, Interrupted*, which chronicles the time she spent in a mental institution in the 1970s. The choice between using **a memoir** versus **the memoirs** of a life is a personal one—whatever the author and publisher like best in that case. We will discuss our reading recommendations in terms of memoir, since memoir is generally more popular with book groups, but you can think about these points and questions in terms of any work in which an author is recounting the story or stories of his or her own life.

The A-List: If These Books Were Celebs, They'd Get into the Best Parties

Books . . . are like lobster shells, we surround ourselves with 'em, then we grow out of 'em and leave 'em behind, as evidence of our earlier stages of development.

—DOROTHY SAYERS

In July 2002 independent booksellers across the country were asked to choose the best books for book groups, and the results were published in the newsletter Book Sense 76. You probably won't be surprised to learn that Barbara Kingsolver's über book group book *The Poisonwood Bible* topped the list. Here are the others:

- *The Red Tent* by Anita Diamant
- *Girl with a Pearl Earring* by Tracy Chevalier
- *House of Sand and Fog* by Andre Dubus III
- *Memoirs of a Geisha* by Arthur Golden
- *The Sparrow* by Mary Doria Russell
- *The Hours* by Michael Cunningham
- *The Angle of Repose* by Wallace Stegner
- *To Kill a Mockingbird* by Harper Lee
- *Plainsong* by Kent Haruf

So, what do you think? Any surprises? Any books or authors you think should have been included? We wanted to hear it straight from the horse's mouth, so we conducted our own survey and asked book group members to choose the top-five best book group books of all time. Here's what we discovered.

In some ways our list looks a lot like the Book Sense list: *The Poison-*

wood Bible, Girl with a Pearl Earring, The Angle of Repose, The Red Tent, and *The Hours* all made the top ten list. One book that doesn't appear on the Book Sense list but that got lots of votes in our survey is *One Thousand White Women* by Jim Fergus. Yep, it was pretty popular on both sides of the fence, so to speak, earning our award for Most Ambiguously Nominated book group book. *One Thousand White Women* got equal votes for both favorite *and* least favorite book group book. Here's what a few readers had to say:

"We loved *One Thousand White Women* by Jim Fergus. It was readable, with great characters, and inspired great discussion." —*Nancy, Redondo Beach, California*

"*One Thousand White Women* was a favorite because of its unusual story line based on a minor truth. Strong locale. Strong female protagonist. Written from female point of view by a man." —*Susan, Greenwood Village, Colorado*

"*One Thousand White Women* bombed. The entire group thought it was poorly written and not well researched from a historical point of view. We thought everything about it was awful—except for the person who recommended it."

—*Bobbe, Denver, Colorado*

Always a crowd pleaser, historical fiction was nominated in droves— one of the most popular was *Ahab's Wife or, The Star-Gazer* by Sena Jeter Naslund.

"*Ahab's Wife* was a favorite in our group because we love historical fiction. I was absolutely entranced by the beautiful language, structure of metaphors, etc., in this incredible book!! I will NEVER forget it. I cried when I finished, because I didn't want to leave it." —*Carol, Englewood, Colorado*

And now a drum roll, please. The book that captured our readers' minds and hearts, the one that drove them to write paragraph after paragraph of effusive praise, the book that tops our A-list of the best book group books of all time (or at least of the 2002 season) is . . . *Bel Canto* by Ann Patchett.

"*Bel Canto* by Ann Patchett is so rich with characters, we could have discussed it for hours and hours and hours." —*Kim, Denver, Colorado*

"Although I'd like my own book to be chosen, I have to recommend Ann Patchett's *Bel Canto*. This book is the reason I read books—it is funny and horrifying and sweet and insightful. It is hopeful and sad and heartbreaking and wise. I kept looking at the book jacket, thinking: how can Patchett know these things and not be one hundred years old? I loved the book. Maybe I haven't made that clear. Thank you, Ann Patchett, for being such an astute observer of human nature. Every now and then you read something and when you finish, you know you'll never be the same for having read it. This is a book like that—geesh—it's just plain wonderful. Thank you for letting me get this off my chest."

—*Alison Clement,* author of Pretty Is as Pretty Does

As a genre, memoir is enjoying a particularly rich and pervasive popularity these days. If we look over the lists of best-selling books, bookseller picks, and reader's favorites from the last few years, we can find many much-loved memoirs topping the charts. In fact, considering the memoir's widespread appeal—both to the discerning readers and the host of talented new authors who are expanding and, so to speak, rewriting the book on memoir—we could say that the form is in the midst of a creative renaissance. But, of course, the memoir, as a literary creation, has inspired authors to pick up their pens and readers to turn the pages for several decades, even centuries, long before *Angela's Ashes* or *Running with Scissors* arrived on the scene. Most scholars credit sixteenth-century French philosopher Michel de Montaigne with creating the first version of the form. Montaigne's *Essays* represents a seminal point in the history of memoir because he decided to stick himself right in the middle of his musings. His decision to insert his personal perspective and experiences to shed light on his philosophical and cultural ponderings represented a drastic break from the gentleman's norm at the time, which demanded a distanced, impersonal presentation of thought. As we address the unique literary demands of reading the memoir, we must also keep in mind the particular challenges for the memoirist who creates it because constructing a memorable memoir is not just a simple matter of writing about yourself in any old way. Memoir is more, much more, than a solipsistic exercise; in fact, you could argue that memoir is a brave, bold move in an age-old great humanist tradition—that of trying to define what it means to be human in a certain place at a given moment in time.

On that noble note, let's think about some of those reading conundrums that are specific to memoir. For example, when you talk about the people an author presents in a memoir, including the author him- or herself, can you refer to them as characters? If a memoirist chooses to highlight certain events of his past, while speeding past others with little or no comment, can we assume these events were obviously of no importance to the story of the particular experience he or she is trying to relate? Is the author of a memoir, by definition or nature, the most reliable narrator and interpreter of his or her own life? The flip answers to these questions are Yes, No, and Gee That's a Tough One, Let's Say Not Always, but let's look at these queries in a bit more detail. The reason you can still think of the real people that an author describes in a memoir as **characters** is because they are, in a literary sense. The memoirist is choosing particular characteristics and quotations to highlight certain aspects of their personalities or to explain their significance to the events he or she is describing. The author is also creating **dialogue** for his characters—let's face it, most of us don't remember word for word what our fathers said to us even last week. The same idea works in terms of thinking about the **plot** of a memoir, that is, the author focuses on situations and events that are important within the specific subject of his story. Most memoirs are about some unusually intriguing aspect of the memoirist's experience, so the writer will filter out any account or circumstance that he feels is not applicable to the main gist of the story—but the memoirist may also choose not to tell the reader about certain realities that he is just not willing or ready to share. In this sense, an author may not always be the most reliable **narrator** and interpreter of his own life—it's entirely possible that he may be too close to the material or not as self-aware as he thinks himself to be. If we can use fictional terms to describe memoir, can we still include memoir in our **nonfiction** category? Well, we can, but we can't say that memoir is strictly nonfiction. Instead, it represents a stylized account of real-life people, things, and events that share many of the main literary components of literature.

Why Are You So Special?

Anyone who sits down to write her memoir, and who expects to get it published, and who hopes to have a bunch of people read it, should first stop to consider the daunting question that Patricia of Middleton, Ohio, so succinctly presents:

> Why should I care? I mean, that's the big question that some of these memoirists seem to have failed to consider. Why should I, the average reader, care about you, about the life of an ordinary person, who may not be famous, accomplished, or even notorious? What about your life was so damn special that you thought the world was hanging breathless waiting to hear? Don't get me wrong—I love memoirs, in fact, they're my favorite book group reading. But I only love the ones in which the author makes me care deeply about his or her life, that give me a glimpse inside another person's world that is so very different from my own.

As the memoir continues to grow in both popularity and creativity, more and more aspiring authors are leaping aboard the *Angela's Ashes* boat, hoping to turn the raw material of their disappointing lives into literary fame and fortune. Unfortunately, not all memoirists had a childhood as rich in potential memoir fodder as did Frank McCourt. Some other memoirists suffer from the opposite problem—their past experiences make Frank McCourt's bitter childhood look like your average visit to Hobby Lobby, but no matter how woeful or weird or wayward your youth, you need a powerful pen to turn that angst into a great memoir. And it's not just that you have to be able to write well, to create interesting sentences and evocative images, you also have to be able to tell a story that will captivate your reader, that will make her, like Patricia, care about your life. Recently, for example, we were reading a memoir that purports to celebrate the author's extraordinarily promiscuous history. Okay, check off item A: the author *has* enjoyed some very unusual experiences—it's not all of us who can say that we've been penetrated anally over a hundred times per orgy we attend. You may not want to read about his kind of thing, but most of us would agree that it's certainly out of the ordinary. We can also check off criteria B in this case: the author can turn a decent phrase, and her writing is clean (in style if not in content) and clear and to the point, mostly devoid of annoying rhetorical flourishes. However, in our opinion, the "compelling story" factor, the "C" quotient, is totally missing. There's a certain shock value in the first few pages of the memoir, but even our sneakiest peeks at the naughtiest sex become tedious if we are forced to keep peeking over and over—anyone who's tried to read a complete work of the Marquis de Sade will know this only too well.

QUESTIONS ON MEMOIR FOR READING
AND DISCUSSION
Start with STYLE: **What kind of writing and why?**

- What does the author's style say about him as a person? What expectations do you have for this memoir based on your initial experience of the style?
- How would you describe the tone and purpose of the memoir? How does the memoirist's style influence your response to the events he describes? Does the style seem to support and invigorate the story, or does it seem forced or artificial at some points?

Move to the NARRATOR AND POINT OF VIEW: **Who's speaking?**

- How much distance is there between the author who is writing and the stories she is telling? That is, how much time has passed between the events described and the point at which they are written down?
- How would you describe the way that the memoir's author represents herself? What sort of picture do you get of this person from her own descriptions? Do you think the author "as narrator" tends to over- or underemphasize any personality or character traits in her self-presentation? Is the memoir narrator's voice "sympathetic"—that is, do you identify with or like this person?
- Pretend that you have the power to ask this author to choose three words, of any kind, to define or identify herself. What do you imagine those three words might be? Why these three particular words? What do you find in the memoir to back this up?

Focus on the CHARACTERS: **Who's involved?**

- Who is the single most important person in the writer's life, either in the past or the present, judging by the stories in this particular memoir? Is his relationship with this person a good one? How would you describe this relationship? What has this person taught the memoir's narrator about himself?
- How does the author feel about each of the major "characters" that he introduces? Is there a difference between the way that the older author feels about these people than he did during the former time and past experiences that he describes?
- Do you think the author judges any of the people who play a part in his life unfairly? Or do you feel that the author has let anyone off the hook too easily?

Check out the PLOT: **What happens in what order?**

- Just like any other book, a memoir has to start at some specific point in time or in thought. Consider the memoir's first lines, first paragraphs perhaps. Why, do you think, the author chose to begin her memoir in the specific manner that she did? What is the first story or memory that she tells, and why is this important to opening up the memoir as a whole?

- Who or what is the memoir narrator's greatest enemy? Her most challenging obstacle? Is this nemesis a tangible person, place, or thing, or is it something more metaphysical, such as self-doubt, time, religion, love, etc.? How does the memoir's narrator attempt to survive, overcome, or come to terms with this obstacle? Is she successful in your opinion?

- If you have finished a memoir, how would you describe the ending? Why, do you think, the author chose to end her memoir in the particular way or place that she did? Do you find out what happens in the "end" of this particular story from the author's life? Are you satisfied by this conclusion?

Think about the SETTING: **Where and when does it happen?**

- Consider the author's attitude toward his own place or significance in a larger scheme of things: does the memoirist identify himself with any larger social groups, organizations, institutions, or ideals? How important do these larger social forces become in shaping the events of this memoir?

- Would you classify this author as a rebel? As an outsider? Does he attempt to subvert or circumvent some of the dominant social norms of his immediate surroundings? If so, how successful is this person (according to his own account) in finding or creating a new set of rules to live by?

Don't forget THEMES: **What's the big idea (or ideas)?**

- Do you think this is an "important" memoir—that is, one that has something unique or special to say? Do you think that it challenges or redefines our traditional understanding of memoir as a genre? Do you think that it will stand the test of time? Why or why not?

- If you had to guess what the author of your current memoir would say about her source of inspiration, what would it be? Do you think the author did justice to this source in the memoir? Why or why not?

- Is the memoirist a good writer of her own life? A good storyteller? Does she manage to turn the raw material of experience into a compelling tale?

- Do you notice any obvious "gaps" in the story? Any points where the author seems to have left out or glossed over important information?

- What might the author classify as some of the major themes of her life? Do you notice any themes, or any significant patterns, that the author seems to overlook or downplay?

Other Personal Stories: Reading Memoir's Cousins, the Essay Collection, Creative Nonfiction, Travel Writing

What is creative nonfiction? If the literal meaning is the correct one, then I am one of the great creative nonfiction storytellers of our time.

—*Candice, Fargo, North Dakota*

Now we move to what is admittedly a bit of a catch-all category. We're talking here about writing that tells a personal story or stories, narratives that explore ideas and events that the author has observed, experienced, or heard about. Why, then, are these kinds of stories not considered memoirs? The best way to answer this is to look at some examples. David Sedaris is a noted humorous essayist and speaker; he tells some screamingly funny stories in his aptly titled work *Me Talk Pretty One Day*. But this book isn't strictly a memoir. It's a collection of **essays** on a variety of experiences, Sedaris's accounts of family, friends, lovers, and moments of personal humiliation. Most memoirs generally stick to a centralized subject or thematic experience, while Sedaris's stories are more loosely grouped and spread out over time. If a memoir explores a particular experience or theme, then why isn't Bill Bryson's *Walk in the Woods* a memoir, strictly speaking? After all, this story is all about Bryson's questionably sane decision to hike the entire Appalachian Trail of the eastern seaboard and features his many witty observations on nature, outdoor experience, and twentieth-century people trying to act like Davy Crockett (and failing miserably). Well, it's mostly because Bryson's work is more appropriately grouped in the **travel writing** category—he has written numerous books on his experiences in both familiar and foreign lands, focusing on his experience as a tourist. Last, we can look at another example of a memoir cousin in this grab-bag category, which is a work of **creative nonfiction** by author Jo Ann Beard, *The Boys of My Youth*. Creative nonfiction is one of those troublesome terms that is tough to define by exact parameters, but in essence the phrase suggests the intentional melding of fact and fiction. In Beard's book, for example, the author describes a long-ago morning when her mother and her aunt go fishing, pregnant with Jo Ann and her cousin. This account may be based on family lore, but Beard imagines a detailed scene she couldn't have witnessed, creating a story and images out of her own fertile musings.

Things to Keep in Mind When Discussing a "Fuzzy" Category

First off, you want to keep in mind that it might be a little bit fuzzy. If it's a work of armchair travel, for instance, you know sort of where you're at, so to speak. You may have read some travel writing, so you know what travel writing is generally like. If it's a book of essays, such as David Sedaris writes so wonderfully, for example, then things start to get just a wee bit foggier. You may have read some personal essays before, like in college, perhaps, but chances are they weren't exactly like Sedaris's unique manipulation of the form. And what if you're reading something mysteriously called "creative nonfiction"? The first thing you'll want to do if you are reading a book that seems to belong to some unfamiliar or nebulous category is to try to determine the name and nature of this narrative:

- What is the best category title for this work?
- What are your criteria for determining whether or not a book belongs in this category? Have you read or encountered other works that might fit into this category?
- If the category itself is not one you are familiar with, this may be a good thing to do a little on-line research about—try to find an expert's definition of this category and present it to the group. Use this definition as a starting point for your discussion—ask yourself how well or how closely the author conforms to this framework—or whether she turns it on its heels (which can be a good thing).

READER ALERT

You can use many of the questions from the Memoir section above to discuss most autobiographical stories that may not belong strictly in that category. But below are some additional possibilities.

QUESTIONS ON PERSONAL STORIES FOR READING
AND DISCUSSION
Start with STYLE: **What kind of writing and why?**

- How would you describe the style of each of these writers? Can you identify a purpose for each of these writing examples—to entertain, to inform, to explore, to critique? How do the style and the format of the writing work together?

Move to the NARRATOR AND POINT OF VIEW: **Who's speaking?**

- How would you describe the narrator of the story from what you've read thus far? How do you think she would describe herself?

Focus on the CHARACTERS: **Who's involved?**

- Is the narrator the main character of the story or stories? Who are the other major characters in this drama or comedy? Which characters does the author treat with the most sympathy or disdain?

Check out the PLOT: **What happens in what order?**

- What specific point of a personal life does this story or stories chronicle? Can you identify a story, a section, or a chapter within this book that seems to represent a climax of sorts for the narrative?

Think about the SETTING: **Where and when does it happen?**

- How is the setting of this story or stories significant to the author? Why, do you think, he chose to write about his personal experiences in this time and place? How does the author represent the cultural norms and values of this setting? Does the author or narrator seem to "fit into" this space?

Don't forget THEMES: **What's the big idea (or ideas)?**

- Can you identify some recurring themes in this story or stories? What unifying elements—questions, concerns, challenges—hold this work together?

Reading Nonfiction: History, Biography, Sociology, and Cultural Studies

"Our group has read some nonfiction," *reports Camden of Albany, New York,* "but we prefer fiction, because there's so much more room for imagination and inter- pretation."

Well, yes, yes and no. Camden does, of course, have a good point—it *is* harder to "read things into" a work of history or cultural study or pop- ular sociology—but not as hard when you get in the habit of treating a nonfictional account like any other story, that is, colored and tempered and shaped by the hands of a very specific individual who has an agenda of sorts, just like any other writer. Consider the opposite point of view:

"I think nonfiction titles make for better discussion. It's always easier to talk about real-life issues and situations rather than trying to critique the author's writing. Dis- cussing nonfiction usually leads us into some interesting debates on current issues or moral ethics, encourages us to engage in philosophical debates, and allows us to ask, 'What would you do in this situation?' " *says Lynne, Blacklick, Ohio.*

As we mentioned above, we are not experts, of any sort, on how to read a serious work of history or historical scholarship. The main reason for this is that we haven't had much practice working with book groups that read nonfiction. The majority of groups we've encountered tend to stick to fiction or memoir. Sharice Templeton from Cleveland, Ohio, speaks for many of her book club brethren on this topic: "We're com- fortable with the idea of analyzing and debating the aspects of a story. That's the best time in a book group—when everyone has wildly differ- ent opinions and interpretations of a single character or moment. With nonfiction, the question is how to have a good debate over facts. If we don't have much detailed prior knowledge of the topic, how are we go- ing to bring our own interpretations to the book?" Not every book group reader feels the same, of course. We have met and talked to many members of both strictly nonfiction book groups and of groups who read on both sides of the fact/fiction fence. Most of you won't be surprised to hear that we have yet to meet a "nonfiction only" group that isn't also a "men only" or "men mostly" book group. "We read political and military history, for the most part, with some sports and humor thrown in once in a while," says Kurt of Grand Rapids, Michigan. "We would be happy to have a woman join the group, or at least we say that we would, but it isn't really an issue since none of the women we know has ever expressed an interest." Kylie of Denver, Colorado, is in a couples book group and reports that her group reads both fiction and nonfiction, but that "we each get to pick one book for the year, and it is true that the histories and biographies are usually chosen by a male member, not always, but usually. Although I chose the new JFK biography for this year, and we're all really excited to read it." Well, all that said, we're going to try to give you some advice on some basic techniques to read a work of strict nonfiction to the best of our abilities.

Can We Separate Fact from Fiction?

When you are considering a work of nonfiction—a biography of JFK, or a historical account of a Civil War campaign, or a popsociology study of book group culture, let's just say—can you still read it for the literary elements (style, narrator, character, plot, setting, and themes) that we have discussed? Yes, as a matter of fact, you can, to a certain extent. The author is still telling a story; the book is still a work of **narrative prose**. The author still writes in a certain distinct style, for a particular purpose. She must choose a narrative point of view, or points of view, generally that of an objective third-person narrator. She will construct characters, of a kind, by deciding to include certain quotations, events, and actions from the life of that real-life person. The author has to choose a chronology for her story—which events will she present in which order? She will recreate specific historical settings, attempt to recreate a particular social climate for the reader. Even the writer of nonfiction will focus on a particular thesis, a specific idea or conclusion about the overall meaning or significance of a certain person's life, or a particular cultural/historical event.

Start with STYLE: **What kind of writing and why?**

- How would you describe the style of this work? Is the writing such that you quickly gain interest in and knowledge of this subject or people? Does the writing compel you to keep going?

Move to the NARRATOR AND POINT OF VIEW: **Who's speaking?**

- Most nonfiction studies are written from the third-person objective point of view. However, "objective" is as objective does, that is, you can still guess the author's sympathies or antipathies to the people and events that he is describing. How would you describe the author's attitude toward his subject?

Focus on the CHARACTERS: **Who's involved?**

- In addition to considering how the author portrays his main subjects, you can also look at the way the author chooses to characterize the supporting members of his historical cast. Who are the heroes or the villains of the work?

Check out the PLOT: **What happens in what order?**

- What are the main points of conflict, barriers, or obstacles for the subjects of this work? Does the author do a good job of choosing and sorting real events in order to create an interesting account or story?

Think about the SETTING: **Where and when does it happen?**

- Is the author successful in making this particular time and place come alive for the reader? What does the author think is *most* important or significant for you to know about the social world and cultural climate that these people lived in?

Don't forget THEMES: **What's the big idea (or ideas)?**

- Why did the author choose to write about this time or these people? What did she hope to discover and illustrate about the subject? If you have read other books on this subject, how do you think this work of scholarship compares?
- Can you identify a major theme or purpose of this work? What does the author hope to prove about the subject? Does the author refute any commonly held beliefs about this subject or contradict any experts who have written previous work on this topic?
- What did you find most meaningful or surprising about this subject? What interesting facts or perspectives will you take away from this book?
- Will you be interested to read or learn more about this subject or author?

Reading the Book That I Hated (And Sort of Hated You for Choosing)

One of our members is still trying to live down choosing *The Bridges of Madison County* for the book group. I'm probably the most guilty for teasing her about it— but did she ever deserve it! —*Anonymous*

Now we come to the last and, for many of us, the most difficult category of reading. How can you commit to active reading of a book you seriously dislike? That annoys, frustrates, bores, or depresses you to the point of hopeless ennui? That is riddled with unintentional humor or ridiculous pathos? That is, frankly, a shameful waste of your time? The answer, regretfully, is "not easily." However, if you can practice a little positive reframing (a handy psychological concept), you can rationalize this negative experience to your advantage. All it takes is a little patience—for both the book and the member who chose it, and the determination to improve your reading skills even in the case of something that just isn't your cup of tea. And, to be fair, we should add that despite the vitriolic opinion of the anonymous reader above, a major reason that *Bridges of Madison County* became a best-seller was because so many, many book group readers supported it ardently. Curious which books the readers who answered our survey mentioned most often as the soul-sucking culprits? You may be surprised when you flip to our special feature in chapter 4, "Report from the Front Line."

Too many of us are guilty of emotional extremism when it comes to reading or talking about books—we know and say we love a particular story or hate another one, but we may not be able to verbalize succinctly just *why* we adore or detest it. Determining the why can be very useful in both cases, both for the positive and the negative. Most of us are familiar with what can happen when every member of a book group loves this month's book: a warm but not very scintillating discussion. On the opposite end of the scale, in the event that almost everyone hates a particular book (except, perhaps, the unlucky member who chose it), you can potentially run up against an uncomfortable wall of cranky bitterness. But if you're willing to put your bitterness aside, you *can* read the lame-duck book group book for maximum critical enjoyment, and you can bring all your powers of disappointed perception to a glass-shattering pitch of pithy insights during your discussion.

We can't give you an example of this kind of book because different readers are going to hate different things. It's hard to admit and sad to think about, but we must confront the melancholy possibility that some among you might even hate one or more of the "great for book group books" we recommend in chapter 9, or on *www.goodbookslately.com*, and might even, well, *resent* us for choosing. For the moment, picture yourself asking these kinds of questions as you read and discuss the book you have most recently despised.

QUESTIONS ON THE BOOK YOU HATED
FOR READING AND DISCUSSION
Start with STYLE: **What kind of writing and why?**

- How do you feel about the author's style? Is this style partly to blame for why you don't like this book? What about the style didn't you like? Are the sentences too long and convoluted and hard to follow? Or too short and simplistic? Are there too many unnecessarily long descriptions? Or not enough description to ground you? Was the dialogue unoriginal or stilted?

Move to the NARRATOR AND POINT OF VIEW: **Who's speaking?**

- Consider the narrator or narrative point of view of the book that you hated. Was the narrator part of the problem? Did the author shift between too many different points of view, or stay too long with one boring one, to keep your attention and your interest? Could you sympathize with or relate to the narrator?

Focus on the CHARACTERS: **Who's involved?**

- How do you feel about the main characters of this book? Are they complex, interesting, developed, dynamic? Does the author fail to make these characters compelling as specific individuals?
- Did you like or relate to any of the main characters? Was your lack of sympathy or interest in one or more of the main characters the reason you couldn't stand the book?

Check out the PLOT: **What happens in what order?**

- When did you start to dislike this story? How quickly did that happen?
- How would you rate the plot of this story? Is the plot part of the problem—that is, were you annoyed that the plot seemed unrealistic, or were you disgusted by the ending?

- In your opinion, was this story worth telling at all, or did the author just do a bad job telling it?

Think about the SETTING: **Where and when does it happen?**

- Were you initially attracted to or initially put off by the setting of this story? Were you interested in reading a story set in this time and place?
- What sort of job does the author do in giving you a realistic or convincing picture of the social world in which this story is set?

Don't forget THEMES: **What's the big idea (or ideas)?**

- Can you identify any of the major themes or central ideas of this book? Are these themes or ideas worth exploring in general, failing because the author did a terrible job exploring them in a new and interesting way?

4

Talk Up a Storm: The Thrill of Electric, Eclectic Book Group Discussion

The pleasure of reading is doubled when one lives with another who shares the same books.

—KATHERINE MANSFIELD, *LETTERS*

Readers Weigh In

"Ah, the joy of a good buzz—there's nothing like it. I'm talking, of course, about the buzz of rapid-fire book argument that my husband can hear all the way down the hall when we all get so excited and opinionated and passionate in talking about the book that we are all shouting at each other across the room!"

—*Karen, Greenville, South Carolina*

"My good friend, who's kind of an intellectual snob, used to say that she didn't get the whole book group thing—I guess she thought that book groups are just an excuse for women to get together and gossip, not to really take a book seriously. Well, I invited her to one of our meetings—we were discussing Annie Proulx's *Shipping News*—and she was pretty surprised to discover that several members debated all kinds of things about it that she hadn't even noticed. Needless to say, she wanted to join, but we already have a waiting list!"

—*Maggie, Davenport, Iowa*

Here's one of the most amazing book group discussion stories that we have ever heard. It's from Dorothy of Denver, Colorado, an incredibly avid reader and a member of a neighborhood book group for the past seven years. The nine members of Dorothy's book group expect a certain level of thoughtful, enthusiastic participation from each other when they meet, which is why they just weren't sure what to make of Marion (not her real name). "This woman never missed a single meeting," recalls Dorothy, "she was there every single month. But she never said anything, I mean anything, about any of the books we read, except to ask a question or two, nor did she ever volunteer any opinions on what to read next." Things went on like this for years, until one surprising month Marion spoke up about the book in question. And spoke again, and again, and again, making many pithy and interesting and insightful comments. "We were really happy," says Dorothy. "We figured that it had just taken her a while to get comfortable or that maybe in the past she just didn't want to admit that she hadn't had time to finish the books." The members of Dorothy's group eagerly awaited the next meeting to see what Marion would do. She showed up promptly as usual but then remained utterly quiet for the rest of the discussion. The next month, and the next, Marion remained staunchly faithful but steadily silent, leaving the rest of the members of the group to wonder about that one freak aberration of Marion's literary participation. And so things continued on as usual, until the month when another member, Grace, a schoolteacher, asked the group to read a Nancy Drew mystery for next time. "Well, of course we thought this was pretty strange," Dorothy remembers, "but we all agreed to it." Dorothy says she isn't sure what the members were expecting to happen when they gathered in Grace's living room, but none of them were prepared for what did. As they finished their coffee and began to talk about the book, Marion dropped her bombshell. "This is a great meeting for me," she confessed, "because this is the first book I have ever read in my entire life."

And so Dorothy's group learned that one of their number had not only made it through high school without learning to read, but that she had wanted so badly to take part in the fellowship and discussion—based on something that she could not do—that she had shown up for every book group meeting for the better part of a decade just to be in the same room with a conversation she could not share. The one time she had been able to participate in the discussion, she had managed to get hold of the book on tape from the library, even though, of course, she didn't have a library card, nor was she able to choose the tape from the shelf for herself. Dorothy didn't tell us why or how Marion had made the decision to reveal her shameful secret to Grace, but it seems that when she did, Grace began to teach her to read, leading to that incredibly proud moment Dorothy's book group was lucky enough to witness.

This story, incredible as it is, highlights the most vital nugget of book group activity that every loyal book group member in the world holds in common. Reading a good book is a great thing, but talking about that book with other eager readers can be an even greater thing. Especially when all of the readers are armed, ready, and willing to unload a powerful round of dynamic discussion.

So, how do you get ready to talk about a book? How can you guarantee yourself the best possible shot at a riveting debate each and every time? That's what we'll be considering in this chapter, with a little help from our book group friends across the continent.

In the next three sections, we'll look at what you can do before, during, and after each or any book group meeting to launch a great discussion campaign. We hope you'll forgive us the military metaphors—we had some fun with them!

GATHER YE AMMO WHILE YE MAY: PREPPING FOR BATTLE (BEFORE BOOK GROUP)

Experienced book group readers know a dynamic discussion depends on a little prep time ahead. Yes, ideally, you do have to read the book, of course, but you can do even more than that, if you want. With a very little extra effort, each loyal member of your group can make a simple but significant contribution to the triumph of the company effort.

Oh Captain, My Captain: Choose a Leader

What will you do when your book group is captured by aliens or guerrillas who make the imperious demand, "Take me to your leader"? Since Mulder and Scully are no longer available, and George W. might be busy, why not pass the buck to the leader of your book group?

You don't have a leader, you say? Well, that's fine, but you had better appoint one before next month's meeting—just to be prepared in the unlikely event that you are accosted by extraterrestrials and someone needs to take command, or in the very likely event that your book group discussion will flow much, much more smoothly if you have a leader in charge. This leader does *not* have to be a professional leader by any means; in fact, it's usually easier to select someone from your group. The leader does not have to be the same leader each month—most book groups depend on some system of rotating leadership.

Why is it good to have a leader?

Because most group discussions of five or more people, whether in the classroom, the committee room, or your living room, work best if someone specific is at the wheel, in some capacity. It's up to this person to keep things moving and people on track to make sure everyone gets her turn to speak and to wrap up the discussion to a satisfying conclusion.

Is that what a book group leader does?

That depends. In most groups, the leader will open the discussion with a prepared question or two, keep an eye out to intervene (in a friendly, diplomatic manner) if the discussion goes haywire, grinds to a halt, or if several members all begin talking at once. Some leaders, of course, are more formal or forceful in these efforts than others—that's just a matter of personal style for both the individual and the group. The leader may be the one to gather and present some kind of background information on the book, or that may be someone else's job.

"We go down our list alphabetically. Member A will host the group, Member B will lead the group, and member C will find and provide some background material on the author. Next month, Member B will host, Member C will lead, and Member D will do research, and so on."

—*Bonnie, Freeport, Maine*

How do you decide who will lead?

"The host or hostess is always the leader in my book club. That way there's no confusion, and it can be easier to prepare and take charge in your own house."

—*Peter, Chicago, Illinois*

"The hostess never has to lead in our book group—she has enough to do already, getting food and drink for us all. Each member is responsible for hosting and leading exactly six months apart—so there's not too much pressure on anybody."

—*Tobie, Indianapolis, Indiana*

"We don't ever choose an official leader, because one of two people in our group usually kind of takes charge. This is fine with the rest of us because both these women are really nice and very diplomatic when it comes to making sure that we all get our turn. They also both know how to ask good, leading questions."

—*Sammy, Pueblo, Colorado*

These are three possible ways to do things, but you can experiment to find what works best for you. If you choose a rotating leadership, keep in mind that some shy or reserved members of your group may not want to occupy such a vocal role. You may decide this is fine and find another way for them to contribute, perhaps in digging up some background information on the book. Or you might just remind those bashful readers that hey, it's an extrovert's world, so tough it out, baby, it'll be good for you. The important thing is to know or decide ahead of time who will be in charge—either formally or informally—so the member, or members, has time to make any necessary preparations.

Report for Camp: Read Carefully

If you want to spur your book group on to even greater analytical heights, don't take reading lying down. No, wait, that's not the right aphorism. It's fine to read while you're lying down, unless doing so makes you prone to narcolepsy. By now, you know yourself and your reading habits pretty well, so take advantage of this knowledge. Give yourself enough time to read this month's entire book group book, at the pace that you like the best, in a manner so that you will (ideally) enjoy, appreciate, and retain much of what you read. If you give your most concentrated and mostly undivided attention to your book group book, you'll be giving yourself the chance to make some provocative reading discoveries that you can drop in the collective lap of your group.

There are a variety of techniques you may want to try to help you remember and retrieve the key points you hope to bring up in discussion (you can see a complete list of these in the "Readers Recommend" section on page 35 of chapter 2), but one of the simplest and most effective is to reread the first and last chapters once you've finished the book. Do this sometime in the twenty-four hours prior to your meeting, and you'll be even more impressed by the sheer ingenuity of your fresh insights.

Report from the Front Line: What Are Book Groups Reading?

Good Books Lately interviewed and surveyed readers from diverse book groups across the United States (and a few groups from the United Kingdom and Australia) to discover what book groups are reading (or not reading) and why. Some answers we expected; others we didn't. Here are some of the most significant, surprising, and interesting results.

Yes, I Definitely DO Want to Read That Book

- We asked our respondents to consider the most important factors to their group in deciding that they definitely *do* or definitely *don't* want to read a particular book. The top five cited reasons for wanting to read a book were
    1. "Book is well-written or stylistically unique"—79 percent
    2. "Book has strong characters—distinctive or sympathetic"—74 percent
    3. "Book by well-liked author"—71 percent
    4. "Book is a literary prize-winner"—68 percent
    5. "Story about foreign or unknown locale/culture"—65 percent
- Eighty-three point three percent of book groups read mostly general or "literary" (nongenre) fiction.
- Twenty fiction authors most frequently mentioned were Toni Morrison, Isabel Allende, Barbara Kingsolver, Wallace Stegner, Charles Frazier, Amy Tan, Tracy Chevalier, Alice Sebold, Anita Diamant, Joyce Carol Oates, Yann Martel, J. M. Coetzee, Sena Jeter Naslund, Andre Dubus III, Myla Goldberg, Ian McEwan, Carol Shields, Michael Cunningham, Adriana Trigiani, and Arthur Golden.

- Thirty-nine percent of book groups who read nonfiction read mostly memoirs and autobiographies.
- Ten nonfiction titles most frequently mentioned were Bill Bryson's *Walk in the Woods,* Jonathan Harr's *Civil Action,* Frank McCourt's *Angela's Ashes,* Alexandra Fuller's *Don't Let's Go to the Dogs To-night,* Laura Hillenbrand's *Seabiscuit,* David McCullough's *John Adams,* Katharine Graham's *Personal History,* Mitch Albom's *Tuesday's with Morrie,* Jill Ker Conway's *Road from Coorain,* and Thomas Friedman's *Lexus and the Olive Tree.*

No, I Definitely DON'T Want to Read That Book

- The most commonly cited factors for *not* wanting to read a book were
  1. "Book by author you haven't liked in the past"—50 percent
  2. "Story about dysfunctional family (i.e., sexual abuse)"—26 percent
  3. "Work in translation—international fiction/nonfiction"—21 percent
- When asked "Are there any books, or any particular authors, that your book group simply will *not* read," 47 percent of book group readers said "yes." Danielle Steele has the dubious honor of being the most frequently named author book groups would like to avoid.
- Although many book groups specialize in genre fiction (or dabble in it from time to time for a change of pace), the least favorite kinds of books were "mass market" fiction, science fiction, fantasy, horror, mystery, and romance.

Maybe, I'm Feeling Kinda NEUTRAL About That Book

- A whopping 79 percent of our survey respondents were neutral about "hot" new books, with only 15 percent admitting that they "definitely *do*" want to read buzzworthy titles.

- Similarly, when deciding what to read, 82 percent were neutral about best-seller status and 79 percent were neutral about books featured on TV (*Good Morning America, The Today Show, The Oprah Winfrey Show,* etc.).
- We were surprised to learn that while historical fiction is a favorite genre among book groups, 68 percent felt neutral about choosing a "story that teaches you about 'real' people and 'real' situations" and 64 percent felt neutral about choosing a "story set in a real or imagined historical past."
- Our readers were split 50–50 about books that feature a "story about really depressing events, i.e., children dying."
- Some books featured in Oprah's Book Club were mentioned as well, often for being "too depressing."

What We Were Surprised to Learn

- Because many groups tell us that book length is an issue, we were surprised to learn that 79 percent of our readers were "neutral" about choosing a "book that's on the long side" and only 21 percent said that they would definitely *not* want to read books over 350 pages.
- We hear that book group members want a book that will keep them up at night, but the votes are almost split on this one. Forty-seven percent say that they definitely want to read a book that has a "page-turning story—very readable, compelling" and 50 percent told us that they were neutral about this seemingly most important literary characteristic.
- In our twenty-first century "self-help nation," it's good to know that while 18 percent of our readers definitely want to read a "story that helps you learn more about yourself" or a "story that's related to your own life experience," a dramatic 55 percent prefer a "story that helps you learn about other people."

- Interestingly, three books repeatedly made both the "most favorite" and the "least favorite" book lists, earning them first, second, and third prize for Most Ambiguously Nominated Book: *One Thousand White Women* by Jim Fergus, *The Sparrow* by Mary Doria Russell, and *The Corrections* by Jonathan Franzen.

Do Your Field Research: Take Notable Notes

At this point you might be thinking: "Take notes? Hey, I'm in a book group to enjoy reading, not to assign myself extra homework." True enough. But taking notable notes doesn't mean you have to whip out your pencil and your legal pad, unless you like pencils and legal pads. If you own the book you are reading for book group and are not planning to "regift" it, go ahead and take those notes right in the margins or ends of chapters. Your method matters not, but you do need to think about how you are going to remember the characters, events, and ideas that got your mental gears creaking as you read, so you can be sure to share at least one of them with your group. Find a way to help your group get to the discussion points that are important to you—many others will likely share your curiosity or conviction about certain people or elements and will be grateful that you took a moment to refresh your memory.

Send Out Your Scouts: Hunt Down Author, Subject Info, Reading Guides

In the old days, all an author had to do to win our affections was write a good book, find a good publisher, or self-publish. It's not quite so easy in these competitive times. With more and more books being published each year, creating more and more choices for that all-important book group market, most authors and publishers are going the extra mile to create material for book groupies to sink our teeth into. Publishers and authors have created Web sites for easy access to information on authors and books, are writing reading guides to fuel and inspire book group discussions, and generally are ready and willing to do whatever they can to earn your book group patronage for their titles. There are also now several handy book group Web sites—including, ahem! a rather good one at www.goodbookslately.com—you can use to find pretty much any kind of author or subject or book information that you'll need. Look in appendix 3, "Book Group Resources" to find a comprehensive list of these useful tools for talk.

Most book groups we've talked to agree that having some background information to share with the group is an invaluable way to provide new perspectives and keep things rolling. It's always fun, for example, to see what an author has to say about his own work because so often the reader reads the book and interprets meaning in quite a different way than the author himself. Which is great, because it teaches you that your group can and should argue with the author's idea of what is most important about a book.

Who should be responsible for tracking down this information?

That depends on your group. Here're three different methods for your consideration.

"It's best if a specific person is in charge each month—either the hostess, or the leader, or maybe an 'elected' research geek for the month or the six months or the year. That way you'll be sure to have it." —Ellie, Baltimore, Maryland

---

"In our group, the person who chose the book (we each get one pick a year) is also responsible for finding information about the author or the book to bring to the group." —Jan, St. Louis, Missouri

---

"We don't have an 'official' member whose job it is to find information on an author or book, but luckily, there is one member who always seems to enjoy this job—me!

So long as you have a Martha in your group, someone who actually enjoys finding info on the Internet, you can always count on getting good reviews and opinions about the book."
—*Martha, Providence, Rhode Island*

When should the members of the group receive background material?

In our opinion it's nice if book group members have a chance to read some or all of the book before they start looking at what other people—the author, the publisher, or the critics—have to say about it. But you can handle this in whatever manner an individual or a group likes best. In our Good Books Lately book group (made up of our staff and advisors), certain people, like Kira, always collect some on-line links to author or critical resources and e-mail them to us ahead of time, so we can look at them or print them out whenever we want. She also keeps a couple of extra copies at her house, so that certain other forgetful people can look at them during the meeting, if not before (sometimes, being Kira, she laminates them).

Plan Your Attack: Three Is the Magic Number

Pssst. We have a secret. We probably shouldn't be telling you this because we won't sell too many copies of this book, but there is one, we repeat, one ridiculously easy thing you can do to nab a nifty discussion in the bag, each and every time. Are you ready? Okay, here it is. Ask each member to come up with and write down three discussion questions or prompts for the book before they come to the meeting.

What should these questions be about? Anything, so long as they address something in the book you're discussing. Encourage your members to ask questions or raise points about the characters, events, themes, or ideas in the book—any elements that they are curious about and may also be a subject of interest and debate for the group. As you read, keep an eye out for provocative, complex, and ambiguous people and moments. Let your own convictions and questions lead you to create a debate point or a discussion query for the group. The discussion prompt might be a simple request for information about someone or something in the book: "Are we supposed to read Jann Martel's *Life of Pi* as a metaphor for life in general?" Or, it could be phrased in the form of a debate statement, leaving room for argument: "I think the tiger and the sharks in *Life of Pi* represent two aspects of Pi's consciousness. What do you guys think?" Your question could also be more general, something like: "This book reminded me of several parablelike stories that were popular fifty years ago, like *Animal Farm* and *Lord of the Flies.* Did anyone else think of older books like that?" Or even more general: "Which character do you sympathize with the most or dislike the most in the novel?" Or, "Were you surprised by the ending of this book?"

The main idea is to come up with discussion questions or prompts that are controversial—in a good way—meaning that different members may have wildly different responses to them. If you've chosen the right sort of book group book, the story will be riddled with material that demands a variety of interpretations. If you're having any trouble coming up with these three questions, get a little outside help. Maybe you'll want to look at the "Questions for Reading and Discussion" you can find at the end of each section in chapters 2 and 3. Write down your three questions and make sure to bring them with you.

LAUNCH YOUR CAMPAIGN:
FIGHT THE GOOD FIGHT
(DURING YOUR MEETING)

Now that you've gotten all smart and everything, you're ready to knock the proverbial stuffing out of this month's book. You're ready to head to your meeting and give that book the working over of its entire shelf life.

Eat, Drink, and Be Merry: For Tomorrow We May Talk

In the immortal words of the Artist Formerly Known as the Artist Formerly Known as Prince: "Don't worry. I won't hurt you. I only came to have some fun!" We can't tell you how many groups we've visited that apologized for being too social. Never apologize for that! If you can enjoy great company and have a stimulating intellectual discussion in the same evening, you are officially ahead of 97 percent of the world for the day. Your social time should last exactly as long as you want it to: if you meet for two hours, and you spend thirty minutes talking about the book and ninety minutes just talking, and everyone is happy about that balance, then good for you. If you spend thirty minutes chatting about anything and everything, and ninety minutes discussing only the book, then you are equally fortunate. In order to catch up with your friends, warm up to members you may not know as well, and get fired up to talk about the book, you need that time for unstructured social interaction. The only real bit of advice we have to give you about how to divide your social and your discussion time is to *divide* them. Avoid mixing the two as much as is possible or is reasonable. Don't start quizzing members about the book as soon as they walk through the door, and don't let the conversation wander off sporadically to the fantastic sale at Nordstrom once you start seriously talking about the book.

Establish a general time division between social and book talk with your group, and stick to it. This way both kinds of conversation will be satisfying and rewarding, and people who come a bit more for one than the other will know they'll get their chance.

We used to have a real problem with this, until we agreed that the first forty-five minutes of the meeting would be devoted to catching up, but that the last ninety minutes would be devoted to discussing the book. Now the more socially minded people show up promptly at seven for wine and fun, leaving unobtrusively when they've had enough book talk. The more serious members often don't show till seven-thirty and stay for the long haul.   —*Kim, Denver, Colorado*

Salute the Captain: Let the Leader Take Charge

If the appointed leader of tonight's book group meeting stands up, rubs her hands together, cackles evilly, and shouts, "You're all mine now!

Mine, mine, mine!" you may want to leave at this point. You should definitely put some serious consideration into choosing someone else for the job. Here are some guidelines on what to expect from your intrepid discussion leader, whomever she may be. Once you have chosen a leader for the meeting, let this person:

- Help the hostess (unless she is the same person) get everyone settled in the discussion space.
- Call the meeting to order: make or ask others to make any official or social announcements regarding book group business, and get the discussion rolling with a great starting question.
- Keep the discussion on track and make sure everyone who wants to speak gets her turn.

The leader can do this last in a very informal and unobtrusive way, simply by gently nudging the conversation back to the book or by deciding the order in which three vocally enthusiastic members should speak. Your leader is not a teacher or a lecturer, really more of a mediator, a referee.

Make this fun for all. As you may remember from school, half the joy of getting to be a team captain, board monitor, or traffic-light attendant is if you get to hold or wear something cool as an emblem of power. If your group is up to it, you can get as ridiculous as you want with this. Design a special and silly "captain's hat" for the leader of the month to wear, or make a "wand of power" out of random household items for the leader to hold straight in the air when she needs to call for silence or when she is choosing a certain member to speak. We've visited with book groups that have a great time with this sort of thing, but if the very idea of such childish goofiness offends your sense of dignity, then by all means, pass. Perhaps you can use this suggestion to find ways of your own to keep your discussion both playful and purposeful.

Play to Your Strengths: Identify Any
Knowledgeable Insiders

At the starting point of your meeting, you may want to take a moment to acknowledge and welcome the contributions of any member who has some personal experience or practical knowledge related to the subject of the book. Maybe you're reading T. C. Boyle's *Tortilla Curtain* and Darrell used to live in that exact part of Southern California, or maybe Anna has something pertinent to say about the immigrant experience, having moved to the United States from Venezuela four years ago. Maybe you're reading Margaret Atwood's *Alias Grace* and Carmen has read all of Atwood's novels, or Jane, a psychiatrist in non–book group life, can offer some interesting tidbits about the study of mental illness at the turn of the century.

You don't need to pounce on these members and ask them to present a lecture then and there. Instead, you can say something like, "When we get to the right time to talk about it, I will be excited to hear what Kirby has to say about Barbara Kingsolver's representation of life in the Congo, since he spent a year there in the Peace Corps." Or the leader could say, "Debbie reminded me just before we sat down that Barb's dad was a Baptist minister—we'll have to see when we get there if Barb wants to tell us how convincing she found Kingsolver's portrayal of growing up with a preacher for a dad!" This is a nice idea, both because it encourages these members to add to your understanding of a certain work of literature or a certain cultural perspective, and because it makes people feel good to be sought out as experts, of a kind. The one caveat to this suggestion is that you don't want to encourage any famously tangential member to take off on an unrelated story about his travels around the world. It's fine, in fact, good, to bring in personal stories to shed light on meanings and interpretations of the book, but, for the most part, stick to using them as a way for other members to gain new appreciations and insights that are related to the story in some form or another.

Rally the Troops: Each Member Reports

Here's another discussion technique we at Good Books Lately use each and every single time we sit down to facilitate a book group. We lifted this one off a history professor at Northwestern, a delightful soul whose prodigious gray belly always protruded from between the buttons on his shirt, but who nonetheless ruled supreme in the seminar room—a veritable master at sucking each and every student into a passionate discussion of even the most initially uninspiring topics, such as the endless wars waged by and against kings named Henry or George. Dr. Buttons (not his real name) had a variety of discussion cards up his sleeve, and one of the most consistently effective was his round-robin roll call at the start of every class. Bouncing on his toes with excitement, he would ask each student to name one person, event, or issue that he wanted to make *certain* that the class would address. "I know each of you is burning with so many questions about the Tudors," he would gasp happily, "but to be fair, I'm going to have to ask you to choose just *one*. Each of you will name the *one* question or issue that we simply have to talk about! I'll write each of your ideas on the board, and then we'll check them off as we go through." For some strange reason, this worked eerily well. In the face of Dr. Buttons's buoyant enthusiasm for his subject, you were ashamed to admit, even to yourself, that you didn't give a rat's rear end about any European dynasty and were dying to go home and watch *All My Children*. And before you knew it, you got a little interested in those pesky Tudors, despite your best intentions.

You can borrow a page from the good doctor's book and try this at your next book group, with a couple of adjustments. Get yourself something big to write on that everyone can see—a poster-sized paper taped up on the wall, for instance, or a poster board propped up against a chair or table. Choose someone, maybe your hostess or leader, to write down a word or phrase for each person's vital discussion issue, something basic to remind you of the big idea. Then go around the room and ask each person to contribute one aspect of the book or story that they must discuss—character or concept, positive, negative, or neutral. A *Poisonwood Bible* discussion board, for example, might look something like this:

> African vs. American characters
> Is Kingsolver unfair to Rachel?
> Eyes in the Trees
> Real vs. Fake Mission—Reverend Price?
> Double meaning of words, Adah's palindromes
> Second half too long?
> Snake in the Grass—Betrayal
> Culture shock—greatest changes

Keep the discussion board up where everyone can see it and pick a good place to start. You can discuss these topics in whatever order flows naturally. Each time you notice that you've hit a new one, give the person who chose it a chance to expand on her question or observation. Ask one member to keep an eye on the clock and call time once you have only fifteen or twenty minutes of discussion time remaining before the end of the meeting. The discussion-board secretary can then check off each of the topics that you've already hit upon and see if there are any big or burning issues still a-festering unaddressed.

Attack at Dawn (or Dusk): Onward Literary Soldiers

If someone in your group has made the effort to provide information on the author or book, or to procure a reading guide, make sure you take full advantage of that heroic sacrifice. If this ardent researcher has made copies of background info or discussion questions to pass out to everyone in the room, take a moment to read an author bio, a pithy critical comment, or an intriguing question out loud. If she hasn't made copies for all of you, then you have no choice but to stone her with coasters, after which she may be permitted to read the author's bio to the room. If you want to make a discussion board as well, you can do this either before or after the researcher's brief, yes, *brief* (two to three minute) report.

Sound the Reville: Read the First Paragraph or Page Out Loud

If you ignore all the other recommendations in this book, or all the other suggestions in this section (except, of course, the Magic Three—you can't forget the Magic Three), here's one step you can't afford and shouldn't want to skip. There is a big difference, somehow, between the way you process an author's words as you read silently to yourself and the way you will hear and appreciate these words if someone reads them out loud to the group. One ideal way to begin talking about any book is to begin by talking about the author's **style**—what kinds of words the author chooses and how he or she arranges them on the page (for a quick overview of the components of style, turn to the **Style** section in chapter 2). And the best way to latch on to any author's style is to take a moment to read the first couple of paragraphs or pages out loud. Whether you're doing the reading out loud or the listening, you'll notice more tiny but important little things about that author's style in that brief section than you may have observed while wolfing down the entire book at home. "Our facilitator asked a member to read the opening two pages of Kent Haruf's *Plainsong*," remembers Heidi of Omaha, Nebraska, "and as she did, a hush fell over the room. We had all noticed his unusual style when we were reading, of course, but hearing them read aloud made us feel the power that those simple sentences commanded." Take a minute to do this somewhere near the start of your discussion, and you will not regret it; we promise.

Fight the Battle, Not the War: Break Down Big Questions

Your group is starting out on the questions in a reading guide, and you come to this beauty at the top of the page: "What are the political, cultural, philosophical, and family relationship issues at work in this novel?" Okay! Are you ready? One, two, three . . . Go! Believe it or not, incredulous readers, this is an actual discussion question from one of the less distinguished publisher's reading guide—no doubt the work of an overloaded marketing intern, poor sod. What the heck are you gonna do with this one?

Using a little of your own considerable discussion savvy, you could just toss this question right out the window. Instead, start with something smaller, like a discussion of the motivations of each of the main characters. Or, you could take this elephant—no, mastodon—of a question and break it down into more accessible parts.

Pretend you were dealing with the elephant question above in terms of Alice Sebold's *Lovely Bones*. One simple way you could start would be to focus on the book chronologically, in terms of the three basic plot elements you'll find in most stories, which work something like this. In the opening pages or sections you'll usually find some sort of **exposition,** descriptions that give you information on the **status quo** of the characters and their basic situations. The status quo is interrupted by some sort of change, which creates tension or **conflict,** the new circumstances that force the story of the book to get moving. Last, in the end, the events of the story will wind up in some sort of **resolution,** which may be happy, sad, or inconclusive. Too often certain book group members make the mistake of trying to discuss the end of the book before they take time to go over the beginning and the middle. It's useful to understand something about the way things start out in a story if you're going to have a meaningful discussion about change and transformation.

So your basic plotline looks something like this:

Status quo (exposition)—conflict (tension)—resolution (ending)

If you think about it in terms of Alice Sebold's *Lovely Bones*, for example, it would work like this:

Status quo (exposition): Description of Susie Salmon's family life before her death.

Conflict (tension): Description of Susie's murder and different family members' reactions and responses.

Resolution (ending): Description of the ways Susie and her family members come to terms with Susie's murder and stop living so much in the past.

Now, start to break down the big question into smaller parts. There are many ways you could do this, and no one right way. Just keep this handy discussion mantra in mind: **Break down complex ideas, build up to major themes, and save the biggest questions for last.** After all, you won't have much luck analyzing the essence of an elephant if you don't first stop to ponder a few of his individual characteristics. Here's an example of how this might work:

Start with the Status Quo

Family relationships: Discuss the family dynamics of the Salmon family before Susie's murder. How would you describe each of the member's relationship to Susie?

Cultural (social) issues: How would you describe the social or cultural world that Susie lived in before her death? Is Susie comfortable in her two main social realms, family and school?

Philosophic (thematic) issues: Are the people in Susie's world as wary about violence toward children as we are today?

Proceed with Conflict

Family relationships: How does Susie's murder change the relationship between her parents and her remaining siblings? Which family member does Susie spend the most time watching from heaven, and why?

Cultural issues: How do the authorities and the community at large respond to Susie's disappearance? What kinds of things does Susie now notice about the people and friends of her neighborhood?

Philosophic (thematic) issues: Discuss Susie's version of heaven. How does her heaven compare to the world she left behind? What does Susie miss the most about her life on earth?

Conclude with Resolution

Family relationships: Which, if any, of Susie's family members seem to have come to terms with her death by the end of the novel?

Cultural issues: The world of Sebold's novel is divided between the culture of the living and the culture of the dead—what happens when characters from these two worlds exchange places? In terms of our own cultural values, why, do you think, Sebold's novel has been so successful?

Philosophic (thematic) issues: Has Susie found a kind of peace by the end of the novel? How is her heaven starting to change?

Fight to the Finish: Stick with One Topic at a Time

All right, we know we said that if you disregard all the other advice in this section besides the Magic Three and the Reading Aloud, we would accept it and move on, but there is just one more crucial discussion practice that can truly transform any book group meeting. We've heard from many book groups we've facilitated that the most significant contribution we made to the discussion was our mostly polite traffic control—we try to stay with one topic, one character, one event at a time, until we feel like the majority of members have had the chance to address that topic to their satisfaction. "Our group is an especially clever and talkative one, I think," says Anne of Evergreen, Colorado, "but that can sometimes be a problem—we have too many people too eager to dive into too many different points of the book. One person's comment about a character leads another person to ask the same question about a different character, and once we bounce on that second character another member will ask, 'What did you think about what he did at the end?' And so forth." So here's our advice to Anne and all book group members who feel frustrated by a certain lack of focus in the discussion process. Talk to your group about how you'd like to aim for a more organized dissection of your books. Acknowledge that, of course, it's hard because there are so many things to talk about in an interesting book and because each member will find slightly different points to ponder. If each member does get to contribute a point at the beginning of the meeting, and if you record these points in Dr. Buttons's style, it will help your group to remember and to address a contribution from everybody. But ask your members to assist the leader in keeping the discussion from splintering off into multiple directions.

The Gatekeeper Experiment: A Diplomatic Solution

Here's an interesting twist on the leadership premise we've heard about from several book groups in the recent months. The idea, according to Karen of Anaheim, California, is to find a member to act as the "gatekeeper." "It's the leader's job in our group to come up with the questions and to ask them, and to make sure each person gets her chance to speak," says Karen, "but we realized that we were still running off into too many ideas at once. So we appointed a gatekeeper, and her job is simply to remind us to stay with one thing at a time. The leader starts the question and decides who will speak in what order, and the gatekeeper maintains the course. Let's say that we've just begun discussing Character A, and a member starts talking about Character B. The gatekeeper will say, 'Let's make sure to keep that in mind when we get to Character B.' It works because we've picked three really conscientious and nice people to rotate as gatekeepers, and we all agree that our discussions have become so much more solid and in-depth."

Bring in the Big Guns: Release the Magic Three

Hark! What's that? It's quiet all of a sudden, too quiet. If a discussion falls flat in the forest, and no one's there to save it, will it make a noise? You bet it will, and it will be the noise of people coughing, or shifting, or refilling their wineglasses and looking at their watches. Your discussion has been proceeding merrily along, when all of a sudden you find yourself with nothing to say. . . .

Now's the time to ask your members to whip out their three dynamic discussion questions once again. Perhaps everyone volunteered one of their questions to get you started on your "most important" discussion board, but chances are you haven't touched on all three of the heavies for each member in your group. Take a moment to allow someone or everyone the opportunity to find a great discussion prompt from his or her list. First one to shout it out gets the book-talk ball rolling again, in whatever direction he or she chooses.

Ear to the Ground: When to Lead, When to Listen

"One of my best friends from book club is a wonderful person in general but an absolutely terrible listener. Most of the time, when you talk to her, you can tell that she is just barely listening to what you're saying; the whole time you're speaking she's just thinking about what she'll say next and waiting impatiently for you to finish so she can say it. This became a real problem in book group, and she was the only one who didn't know it—other members didn't like being interrupted so often, or that she would suddenly change the entire topic of discussion if she had something to say about something else. Frankly, the discussion goes best when she's absent."

—*Karenna, Grand Rapids, Michigan*

"Don't be in such a rush to contribute a pithy comment that you fail to appreciate the insights of others. Do what I say, not what I do. I try to practice what I preach, but sometimes I get so excited that I have trouble restraining myself. The whole time that other members are talking I'm just waiting for the moment when I can wow the group with my amazing perceptions. I am bound and determined to get that thought in as soon as I can, even if the conversation has taken a totally new direction."

—*Jeremiah, Trenton, New Jersey*

Sometimes the advice you get early in life is the best—as Mrs. Sealy, ruler and despotic overlord of morning kindergarten in Andover, Massachusetts, always told Ellen at storytime, "Eyes center, mouths shut, ears open, and hands to yourself!" Grant the same respect and attention to your fellow members as you would if Mrs. Sealy were there to freeze you with her icy glare. Check in with yourself to see that you are practicing as much active listening as you are active talking. Pay attention to exactly what is being said, then let your comment build on what has come before. Most book group members are inherently skilled at this, but we've all observed some exceptions.

Rehash the War: How to Enjoy Yourself Even More Next Time!

Are you one of those unfortunate people who often think of the perfect thing to say or do after your chance is over? Let's say you arrive at your meeting dying to talk about this month's book, but you leave troubled by some nagging disappointment. Maybe you feel like the group didn't really touch on the most important or interesting stuff about the book, or maybe you think too much time was wasted on a very minor or trivial point. Maybe you wish that your group could get as serious about the book as they can about Cassie's spinach guacamole dip or that you had remembered to ask everyone why one character's hair turned green and the author treated it like it was no big thing. Well, as we all know by now, hindsight is twenty-twenty, but it is possible to turn your hindsight into foresight. If you are truly dissatisfied by something that did or didn't happen in a recent book group meeting, take a few minutes to think about some of these questions for yourself:

- What, exactly, is the source of disappointment for me?
- Can I figure out who or what caused this problem—do I share responsibility?
- Would other members have seen this as a problem, or is it just a problem for me?
- Is this problem an ongoing one, or was this just an isolated case?
- What would I have liked to see happen instead?
- Is there any way I can make a personal effort to make things different next time?

- Is there any way I can make a general, friendly recommendation to the group to improve some aspect of our discussion?
- Is there someone in the group I can call or e-mail to get support or maybe just to talk about the issue that didn't get addressed?

TALK TROUBLESHOOTING:
ANSWERS TO FREQUENTLY ASKED
DISCUSSION DILEMMAS

Q: *What's the best way to get a lively discussion started? My group does okay once we get going, but we're slow out of the gate.*
—*Laurie, Montreal, Quebec, Canada*

A: Tamara of Tucson has a great trick to share for this one. "Before the meeting starts, we write the names of each of the participating members and all of the novel's main characters (up to ten or twelve) on little scraps of paper and dump each pile into two different hats. Then a random member gets to choose a name out of each hat, and the member selected has to come up with a discussion question about this character. After which those two names, real and fictional, are put aside, and we move on to a new member and new character if we need to do so to keep things going. We tried this once on a whim and we had so much fun with it that we still bring the hats out for a spin every few months." (If hats and slips aren't your thing, try one of the discussion starters you'll find in the first half of this chapter.)

Q: *Sometimes our conversation is going great, but then we hit a snag—nothing like dead air to make you feel uncomfortable! The longer we can't find anything good to say about the book, the harder it is to think of something. How do you bring a dead discussion back to life?*
—*Dara, Eugene, Oregon*

A: We love this answer from Ruth of Denver, Colorado, who admits that she is a proverbial book group troublemaker. "If we run into a slow spot, I just make some really ignorant or obtuse comment about the book—something that other members are *guaranteed* to disagree with. Pretty soon they're all fighting it out and having lots of fun. By now they've started to figure out when I'm doing this—the trick is to say it with a straight face and confident conviction." For more ideas on how to beat a dead horse back to life, see "Plan Your Attack" on page 114 of this chapter.

Q: *I think I'm going to have to quit the book club unless we can figure out a way to keep our meetings from turning into group therapy (or, worse, group bitch) sessions every other meeting. This might sound cold, but I joined a book club to have interesting discussions about what I read, not to hear about Sharon's depression or Sarah's divorce. Any ideas on how to find a better balance between personal experiences and book discussions?*

—Kendall, Sacramento, California

A: "You have two choices," says Mandy of Jackson, Mississippi. "Either find a new book club to join, or convince everyone in your current book club to do things your way." Mandy has herself a point there. The first thing you'll want to ask yourself is if you are the only member who wishes things could be a little more analytical and a little less personal. You might find out by talking to another member whom you like and trust. If you get the idea that pretty much everyone else in the club is perfectly happy with the present therapeutic format, make plans to find a new one or start one of your own (see chapter 5, "A Group of One's Own"). But if it seems like at least half of the other members of your group might be inclined to swing the other way, you could enlist their help to install a new regime. Ask a warm and well-liked member to be your spokesperson at the start of the next meeting. He or she can say something like, "I wanted to ask you all if we could try something different tonight. It seems like some of us would like to talk a little more about just the book, and some of us would like more time to share the personal experiences that the book makes us think about. Maybe tonight we could try to spend the first forty-five minutes discussing mostly the book, and the last forty-five we could talk mostly about the things in our own lives that are related to the book." Then see what happens. Keep things loose and relaxed: if someone starts to tell a "personal" story during "book" time, listen attentively and then use that story to nudge the discussion back to an element of the book itself. "What Denice was saying about her son reminded me that I wanted to ask everyone if you were surprised by Robert's treatment of his son at the end of the novel." If this doesn't help to alter the balance between the personal and the analytical over time, you are back to Option A.

Q: *Help! Our group is being held hostage by one extremely negative and bossy member. None of us know what to do about this, but she is really starting to poison the atmosphere of our meetings. She interrupts other members when they are talking, or, worse, just sighs loudly and rolls her eyes when someone says something she doesn't agree with. Sometimes it seems as if she only likes a book if the rest of us dislike it or hates one just because we enjoyed it. Which would be fine, except that she is so critical, verging on insulting, about other people's opinions. What can we do, other than pretend to dissolve the club and meet again without telling her?*

—Kyra, Omaha, Nebraska

A: "You should pretend to dissolve the club and then meet again without telling her," says Charlie of a mountain town in Colorado, which she asks to keep nameless. "That's pretty much what we had to do to get rid of one of our members—we were too chickenshit to tell her off, but everyone was sick of her constant, loud, negative energy. There're only six members in our group, so it wasn't too hard—several of us 'decided' that we were too busy that year to commit to a book group, and so we agreed to give it a 'rest.' Two months later the 'rest' was over for everyone except for her. Our spouses were sworn to secrecy, and almost two years went by before I ran into her in the grocery store and she asked if the book group was ready to get back together again." Well, Charlie's solution is certainly one way to go, but you might want to try a few other methods before you resort to subterfuge. One thing to keep in mind is that so very often people of an unusually critical or commanding mind-set aren't really aware of their power to wound—in fact, this kind of behavior often masks a terrible insecurity of some kind. Sometimes these discussion doomsayers think that they are simply "helping" other people to face unpleasant realities. You may need to find a way to let your book group crab know that other members may be interpreting her comments in a way she didn't intend.

Ask a courageous, confident, diplomatic member of your group to talk to her about her book group behavior in an informal setting outside of the club. This member could invite her out for coffee and drop a very broad hint during a casual chat. Keep in mind that critical people are quite often (if secretly) even more critical of themselves, so the book group diplomat should stick to the two great rules of productive, constructive criticism: use "I" statements instead of "you" accusations and offer a specific example instead of making broad generalizations. Instead of saying, "You are always so critical and nasty in book club, and you are really pissing people off," try something like, "I thought Charlie looked kind of hurt and upset after you disagreed with her about the theme of *Corelli's Mandolin* last week at book club. Do you think she might have taken your argument as a personal attack?" If this one-on-one intervention doesn't do the trick to soften your problem member's blows, you can move on to your second plan of attack. Have the leader, or hostess, or whoever is opening the meeting, make an announcement that several members in the group have asked for a little more loving care from the group as a whole. "Some of our shyer members have said that it's hard for them to contribute when they are interrupted or criticized when they do. Can we agree that we will all do our best to avoid interruption or personal attack?" If your club crab takes this as a personal hint, good. If she is offended in any way by the new group rule, let her know she is free to join a different group—pity the poor souls who inherit her!

Q: *We have tried using reading guides to encourage thoughtful discussion, but the results are so mixed. Some of the guides work pretty well, but in others the questions are totally unhelpful. Aren't most of these guides written by the authors themselves? How can some authors be such bad interpreters of their own work?*

—Dylan, Tacoma, Washington

A: If authors did write most or all of the reading guides for their own books, or even for another author's books, the discussion questions would be mostly very good. Probably not unanimously good, for, in all honesty, an author is *not* always the best interpreter of her own work, especially if the author is still relatively close to the material. Many times savvy readers or experienced critics can see issues, attributes, or problems in a work an author cannot see. However, as publisher reading guides go, you are generally safer if you can find one that is the work of an author, writer, or teacher—you'll probably find more interesting questions presented in a more sensible order. The majority of the publisher reading guides, in fact, are produced by the marketing departments. Considering that many marketing folks haven't received much training on teaching books, or leading people through book discussions, it's actually pretty wonderful how many of the reading guides are really quite good. But the quality of questions will vary from guide to guide, depending on who wrote it and how much time she was granted to prepare it.

It is true that certain publishing houses have spent a great deal of money and energy improving their book group programs. Vintage, for instance, has had one of the very best for many years, and you won't find a shabby reading guide in their collection. Ballantine includes guides in the back of all potentially book group–friendly paperbacks, which you can't beat if you're looking for something quick and immediate. For a complete list of all the publishers and places that you can go to for reading guides, check out appendix 3, "Book Group Resources." Of course, we hope you'll consider our line of reading guides, the Read*Smart*Guide® series, as well—you can check out the list of available guides at the back of this book or on our Web site at www.goodbookslately.com.

Q: *What should we do about three of our members who never, well, almost never, seem to finish the book? As a result, the rest of us have to avoid talking about the ending of the novel, so we don't ruin it for them.* —Lee Ann, Rochester, New York

A: "Announce to your book group that from now on your meetings will be run like the reality TV show *Survivor*. All those who have read the book and come prepared to discuss it in its entirety have won the immunity challenge and are safe from extinction. All those who don't read the whole book can be voted off the island—in this case, your book group. The only way they can get back in the door is by providing a list of great discussion questions for next month's book or by bringing some really top-quality cookies, appetizers, or libations. All right, you probably can't run a book group like *Survivor*, but think how much it could improve *every* aspect of your reading, meetings, and discussion if you could. Maybe you could just *threaten* to run your book group like *Survivor!*"

—Fredrika, Birmingham, Alabama

There you have it, Lee Ann. It's all about the immunity idol. But if you aren't willing to model your social behavior on the fine examples provided by reality programming, let's try for a more workable answer to your question. We have heard from many book group readers and leaders who maintain that anyone who doesn't read or finish the book should not bother to show up for the meeting—totally kosher so long as everyone in the group agrees. However, in general we don't think it's a good idea to make any of your members feel unwelcome at a certain meeting. Everyone has a crazy month from time to time, and some people are just slower readers than others. Even if you are willing to bend that "Don't Read, Don't Come" rule, there is no reason to punish those in the group who did get to the end of your book. If you want to make the effort not to discuss the end of the book until the end of the meeting (a good rule of thumb anyway), those who didn't finish can feel free to leave if they don't want to find out what happens. You can also make a rule that anyone who didn't read the book (or a good portion of the book) is not allowed to make comments about *anything* they haven't read yet. They are welcome—in fact, warmly encouraged—to attend the meeting, and they can ask questions, and they can make comments about the part that they did read, even if it was just the title. There's nothing mean or nasty about having reasonable expectations for your group—you want to encourage your members to read carefully, think critically, and see the job through to the end whenever possible.

Q: *One of my friends has had a professional leader take over her book group. This seems to be working well for them, but I don't like the idea of letting an outsider take the reins every single time. Can we find a book group leader to lead our group just once, for something different, and, if so, how do we find that leader?*
—*Tyler, Durham, North Carolina*

A: See? That's what happens when you let strange people come into your home. They just waltz right in, eat your grub, and insist on running the whole show!

It may be that your friend's group has made arrangements to hire one of the book group leaders who commit to a group for a longer period of time, such as a year. But the vast majority of professional leaders (usually folks with a background in teaching or bookselling) are pretty flexible, so it shouldn't be too hard to find someone in your area to visit your group just once for a complicated book or a special occasion. In our own case, for example, yes, we do work with some book groups that ask us to facilitate the meeting every month, or to choose their entire year's worth of books, or to provide Read*Smart*Guides® for every meeting, or some combination of the above. But the majority of the groups we work with ask for only occasional assistance—we meet with them once or twice a year, we provide reading guides for a couple of the tougher books, we give them recommendations for what they may want to read in the future.

In addition to hiring a professional leader to facilitate or lead your group, you can also think about contacting an author to meet with your group to discuss his or her own work. Usually the author will do this for free, so long as everyone in the group agrees to buy a copy of the book. Many book group readers are surprised to learn just how easy it is to get authors to come to their meetings—trust us, most authors *love* meeting with book groups! Not only is this a great way to promote their books and boost their sales, but they get to meet with an enthusiastic audience of savvy readers. You may also be surprised to discover that you can get quite well-known and prestigious authors to come to your home. Publishers and authors are both waking up to the power of the book group audience, and lots of big author tours now include stops at several book groups as well as the best bookstores in town. In order to find either a leader or author to meet with your group, please see the "Leaders and Authors for Hire" section of our Web site or check out the complete list of "Book Group Resources" at the end of this book.

Q: *The woman who helps us choose books from our local bookstore said that every group should have an established leader. Is this true?*   *—Jocelyn, Atlanta, Georgia*

A: Ellen of Denver, Colorado, replies, "Yes, you must always have a leader for everything you do in any kind of group—otherwise, society would break down, Western civilization would crumble, and we'd all go back to roasting slabs of meat on sticks and being eaten by wolves." Hmmm, I don't know if I trust this Ellen of Denver person—let's see some credentials!

Unless the woman at your bookstore is insisting that she be the one to lead your group each and every time (in which case you should ask to see her credentials), she does have a point. You can read more about it in the section above, "Oh Captain, My Captain," and it is a good idea to have somebody at least roughly in charge of leading each discussion. How "established" that leader might be is up to you. The point is that a group discussion of any kind does tend to flow and flourish better if someone specific is at the wheel—mediator may be the best title for this person. Choose one of your members for the task each time. It's up to this person to open the discussion with a good question or prompt, to nudge the discussion back to the book if talk starts heading south, and to intervene politely if too many people start talking at once. This leader should also be prepared to castigate, shame, and punish any two members who are gossiping idly while another member is trying to talk because this is VERY RUDE. Or she can just give them the evil eye.

Q: *Our group is a mix of talkers and listeners—actually, I could even say loudmouths and chair warmers—a certain four or five members dominate the discussion almost entirely, while another four or five never open their mouths. Is there any way to make things more even?* —*Cameron, Sarasota, Florida*

A: Book group member Tara of Missoula, Montana, has a reasonable suggestion for this one. "Unfortunately, you can't make people behave in a way that is completely foreign to them. You can, however, set some public limits and encourage some personal goals. We had a major imbalance like this in my book group and have found a couple of ways to change it for the better. The first thing we did was to try to control the big talkers—I was one of them, although I didn't know it at first! We gave the hostess a major leadership role—it was her job to choose who could speak first when a bunch of us started in at once. When a certain person had already spoken several times, the leader would say something like 'If you could hold that thought for a minute, Sandy, I think that Jenny has something to say about this first.' She kept doing this again and again, very politely, very warmly, and after a while the talkers got the idea. Meanwhile, we made an extra effort to encourage the quieter members both on and off the court. So often I'd talk to a member who'd have great things to say about a book either before or after the official meeting, and I'd say, 'That's so true! I wish that you would bring that up at the meeting—you have such great ideas, and I would love to hear more of them. I bet everyone else would, too.' When the traditionally silent members would offer a comment or question during the discussion, we'd be very supportive, compliment the point, and make sure to find a way to keep the discussion on or around it for a few minutes."

Q: *What's the best way to end a discussion or meeting on a satisfying note? We seem to consistently have trouble with this.* —*Carly, Lexington, Kentucky*

A: One good way to conclude (in addition to finishing all remaining scraps of food and booze) is to end with "big picture"-type questions.

In general, as you talk about any literary work, it's a good idea to follow, in a loose way, a certain order of discussion points:

- Begin with the beginning of the book—the introduction of certain characters, themes, and situations.
- During the main part of your discussion, you will be talking about the development of many specific characters, themes, and situations.
- At the end of the discussion, you will, of course, want to talk about the ending of the work—whether it surprised you, satisfied you, or left you hanging in some way. You will also want to use this time to talk about some of the book's major concerns, themes, and ideas—the whole "why" of the book, its purpose, its driving motivations.

In order to have a set of "big picture" questions handy and unmolested by the last quarter of your discussion (the final twenty or thirty minutes), you can do a couple of things. First, ask your group to keep an ear out as you talk about the rest of the book for the kinds of general or thematic questions that seem to address the "big picture" of the work as a whole. The point is to identify prominent ideas, central themes, or general questions about the book and to save them for your final rally. Ask a "big picture" secretary to take some notes and make a list of these kinds of discussion issues as they come up, then later to make use of this list in your final quarter. This "save the biggest and best for last" policy will help you do two things: first, you'll be discussing the book in the best possible order, giving people the chance to think about (or to rethink) certain smaller, specific instances in order to work up to discussing some version of the monolith question: "What's this all about?" Second, you'll have guaranteed that you'll finish off the meeting on a powerful note.

5

A Group of One's Own:
Creating a Stupendous, Tremendous,
One-of-a-Kind Book Group

Books are drawing members of the "me" generation out of their urban solitude and into intimate discussion groups. From recent college graduates to people a generation older, these readers are confounding the conventional wisdom that video has replaced vellum.

—*NEW YORK TIMES*, MARCH 1989, LIFESTYLE SECTION

ALL THE COOL PEOPLE ARE DOING IT: ESTABLISHING YOUR BOOK GROUP'S MISSION

Our book club is a circle of friends using books to weave their stories within a story, among laughter, friendship, and shared experience.

—*Member of Tom Price Book Club in Western Australia*

You might assume that most book group members joined or created their group with a clear sense of *why* they wanted to do so. Many do. Nonetheless, our experience has suggested that some readers form book groups and go about their business without a clear discussion of their hopes, their goals, their mission. It's easy to get lost in the details of organizing the group and to forget why exactly you're doing it in the first place. Don't let this happen to you! Establishing some kind of shared expectation—whether it's formal and written or informal and verbal—with other members of your group is the most important thing you can do to build understanding and ensure success. If you're just getting started, this is a natural first step. If your group has been together awhile, it's still a good idea to revisit this question regularly: "Are we all getting what we'd hoped out of this experience?"

Hopes, Goals, Mission

Now this may sound a bit corny, but we promise it works. Take out a piece of paper. Describe, as best you can, the moment when you decided you wanted to be in a book group. Trace that impulse back to its earliest roots. Was it from listening to a friend talk about how much she adored her group? Was it after reading about book groups in the newspaper? Did Oprah have anything to do with it? Next, try to capture whatever it is you hope to get out of being in a book group. Whatever your reasons—however silly or small or serious or gigantic—write them down. Now distill what you've written into just a few words. Voila! You've discovered your mission. Now what do you do with this information?

Although there are as many different book groups as there are book group members (which means the possibilities could potentially be endless), we've identified some basic profiles to help you get started. We've collected some informal "mission statements" from members of various book groups, with the idea that one of them will strike a chord with you and help guide you as you create your own. Following these brief testimonials, more in-depth information about book group types—including the pros and cons of each—will give you some direction as you decide who might join, what to read, and where and when to meet.

"We Just Want an Informal, Fun Chat" Book Group

Readers Weigh In

"Our shared mission is to choose a book, read it, and think about it on a deeper level than we might have previously. And to have lots of FUN!!!"

—*Antoinette, Camperdown, New South Wales, Australia*

"Our understanding (we wanted NO rules) is that we are all OPEN to any suggested title that is presented. We come to an agreement in a most amicable fashion on the reading choices—whatever they may be. We simply want to keep reading, discussing, and enjoying each other's company." —*Stephanie, Hays, Kansas*

"We want to discuss good books and be able to discuss our thoughts without being criticized." —*Susan, Little River, South Carolina*

The casual book group described by Antoinette, Stephanie, and Susan is probably the most common. But just because they're relaxed doesn't mean they don't have lively discussions and a rewarding intellectual experience. In groups of this type, the overall tone of most meetings is light and the discussions are often informal, blending the personal and the literary in a cozy way.

"We Want to Be Part of the Community" Book Group

Readers Weigh In

"I had no idea where to start, so I went to the local public library. I joined a group there, and even though we're not really friends outside of the book club, I feel like I'm part of a really nice group of people." —*Jane, Montreal, Quebec, Canada*

"I just moved to the area, and I didn't really know anyone. I wanted to find other like-minded people. I guess that at first, even more than the book, I was excited about meeting people."
—*Shawna, Seattle, Washington*

"I started my book group with our pastor to enhance our congregation's sense of community and to give us a new way to spend time together."
—*Jim, Des Moines, Iowa*

If what you want is that mutual sense of communion, look no further than your local community center. If you're like Shawna, a book group may be the perfect way for you to get to know people in a new place. Local religious organizations often offer book groups to their members as well. Try your local library, bookstore, or café—these are great places to meet like-minded readers. If they don't have an in-house group, they'll often have a public posting area where book groups can advertise.

"We're a Serious-Minded, Literary" Book Group

Readers Weigh In

"Our goal is to read a wide variety of books each year—one classic, one biography, one nonfiction, one mystery, etc. One month we also have a read-a-book/see-the-movie get-together, usually reading and watching a classic."
—*Ellen, Eden Prairie, Minnesota*

"We're a bunch of retired teachers. What can I say? We like to learn—that's why we're together. We take our group seriously. It's like an extension of college—I always feel energized after we meet."
—*Will, Los Angeles, California*

"I know of other groups that are much more relaxed. But we're doing what we want. We read challenging books and we research the authors, get reviews, etc. We always have an assigned leader to steer the discussion. *Everyone* reads the book. It's not a rule, just an expectation. We're here for the book."
—*Allison, Brooklyn, New York*

As Allison points out, this kind of book group is all about the book. Well, not *all* about the book—there's some casual conversation thrown in occasionally. If what you want is deep, critical, well-read, informed literary discussions, make sure you surround yourself with readers who feel the same way.

"We're All Family and Friends" Book Group

Readers Weigh In

"Our main purpose is to read and discuss new books, but our other purpose, equally important, is to be friends with each other and support each other."

—*Carrie, Belleville, Illinois*

"I started our mother-daughter book group when Helene was nine, and we've been going strong for four years. It gives us the kind of quality time together we might not have otherwise."

—*Nancy, Akron, Ohio*

Remember those "Reading is FUNdamental" posters? These groups take that motto to heart. They know sometimes the best way to bring people together is not through Thanksgiving dinner but through sharing a good read with those nearest and dearest. Like Carrie and Nancy, if you want your book group to deepen and extend existing relationships, look no further than your family and friends. You'll need to consider who to invite, and this may depend on or influence the kind of books you read together.

"We Work Together and Read Together" Book Group

Readers Weigh In

"Two of us at work talk about our favorite authors at times. We check to see if we've read anything new or exciting lately. So we just started talking about the possibilities of establishing a book club at lunch over several weeks. Two of us decided to put it out in an E-mail and see who responded and was interested. We meet during our lunchtime, and sometimes others 'wander' in the lunchroom and stay to talk or listen."

—*Elaine, Denver, Colorado*

"I'm an executive manager at a midsize software design firm. I realized that I didn't know some of my coworkers very well, I only saw them in meetings. I decided that a business discussion group would give us a chance to read the newest business books and get to know one another better at the same time."

—*Max, Beaverton, Oregon*

Business book groups are increasing in popularity and can take several forms. One, like Elaine's group, is a casual group formed by coworkers to discuss the kinds of books they already read for pleasure. Other groups, like Max's, read and discuss business books to enhance their professional knowledge (good for the company) and to improve teamwork through book discussions (also good for the company). If your company is amenable, make use of all the infrastructure already present— newsletters, e-mail listservs, bulletin boards, monthly meetings—to get your group started.

"We're Coed," "We're All Women," or "We're All Men" Book Group

Readers Weigh In

"Our book group grew out of an artists' group. We're all women, and we read only women authors. Book group gives us a great sense of empowerment."

—*Bev, Taos, New Mexico*

"Our book group arose from a discussion that two friends and I had about our interests in reading and our speculation about the possibilities of finding others in our gay men's community who might also be willing to join a monthly book discussion group."

—*Louis, Colorado Springs, Colorado*

"Our book club started with just the wives, but then our husbands were jealous, so we invited them to join us. Now there are six couples—you should see how we argue about books! Sometimes it gets really heated, but it's all in good fun."

—*Margaret, Dallas, Texas*

As you know, most book groups are made up of women. Some, like Bev's, do this intentionally; for most, it's just the way things happen. But men's groups and coed groups (including groups for content couples and for swingin' singles) are becoming more and more common. Whether you cross the gender line or not, the makeup of your group will affect the kinds of books you read and the kinds of discussions you enjoy. Likewise, if the gender makeup of your group is important in how you understand your mission, you'll probably find that your reading choices will reflect that gender dynamic in some way.

"We're Wired and Online" Book Group

Readers Weigh In

"On-line groups are very easy to fit into your schedule, and fun to do, and you meet great people, and you can join more than one because they are so easy to handle and fit into your schedule. And you don't always have to read the book if you didn't want to or couldn't and can still sit in on discussions and we usually have more than one book a month so people can choose one over the other or both if they want, and it gets more people reading something each month."

—*Marianna, Monroe, Michigan*

"My sisters (and our children) have, over the years, spread across the United States. We talk to each other daily by E-mail and started talking about books that we were reading. The idea came naturally to start reading the same book at the same time and then discuss it in a chat room! After collecting suggestions and ideas from everyone—I made a schedule of readings for the next three months, and we are now reading."

—*Rose, Sterling, Colorado*

Marianna brings up a good point: on-line groups don't require the same kind of space and scheduling that off-line groups do. This gives you freedom to participate whenever and wherever you please, which is great. Don't assume that you have to be faceless strangers: Rose started an on-line family book group made up of her sisters and their children, and we've heard of on-line groups getting together in person years after meeting on the Internet.

WHOSE BOOK GROUP IS IT ANYWAY?: FINDING AN EXISTING BOOK GROUP OR GATHERING READERS TO START YOUR OWN

First of all, before you break out the "to-do" list and begin sorting out the details of building a book group from scratch, consider this: creating a book group is a lot of work. It's incredibly rewarding, of course, and once the groundwork is done, the chores can be shared among all the members of your group, but initially, there's a lot to be done. Are you up for it?

If not, don't feel bad! Consider finding an existing group to join. This is a good idea for those of you who have never been to a book group and may want to get your feet wet. Consider some of these issues as you look for an existing book group or as you think about the people you'd like to invite to join your own group.

Family and Friends

Don't overlook the obvious! Do you have a friend or a family member who's in a book group? Ask if you can attend a meeting as a guest, to see how they do things. If you find a group to visit, make sure you read the book and come prepared to discuss it. That way, if the group is open to having new members and turns out to be a good fit, you'll have a chance to see how they organize their discussions before you make a commitment. Don't overlook your children! If you have kids between the ages of nine and thirteen, gather some like-minded families for a parent-child book group. You'll never regret it.

If you decide to be in a book group made up of family and close friends, consider these pros and cons:

The Pros

If you're meeting with people you're close to, chances are you'll be comfortable, and that's good. Feeling safe may make it easier to open up, which makes discussion livelier. Plus, you'll be surprised at all the stuff you'll learn about people you thought you knew so well, just by talking about a character or two.

The Cons

One of the greatest gifts the book group experience can give us is the chance to see the book—and the world—through new eyes. The more homogenous the group (and ironically, sometimes, the better you know one another) the less likely you are to have this perspective-shifting experience. Also, some book group discussions challenge us to think about—and talk about—really sensitive, personal topics. While you might think at first that it would be easier to do this with friends and family, sometimes it's just the opposite. Sometimes you may feel freer to reveal things about yourself to people whose only connection to you is through a book group.

Neighbors and Coworkers

Many, many long-standing and happily bonded book groups started with a group of neighbors or coworkers. If you'd like to gather your neighbors, tear down that proverbial fence and begin your group with a block party! If gathering with folks at work appeals to you, decide if you're going to be a regular, normal book group or a professional book group. If it's a career-enhancing group you're after, see if you can organize with your company's help and resources.

If you decide to be in a book group made up of neighbors and coworkers, consider these pros and cons:

The Pros

Neighbors and coworkers can sometimes provide that perfect combination of comfort level and diversity that makes for a great book group experience. Chances are, you'll know these people well enough to say what's on your mind, but you won't know them so well to be able to guess what they're going to say before they say it. When you gather them around you—the people you see every day, but only for a quick "good morning"—you help build a sense of community that can enrich your life in unexpected ways. Business book groups often break down that nasty hierarchy that may keep you and your coworkers apart.

The Cons

What was that proverb again? Good fences make good neighbors, you say? Well, there is the possibility that something will occur in book group that will complicate your until now placid relationship with a neighbor or coworker. Then again, tensions could build while mowing the lawn or copying a company memo, so why not take a chance? But especially if you work in a highly politicized office, you may want to go to the powers that be, so your book group is officially sanctioned.

Bookstores, Libraries, Cafés

Some bookstores, libraries, and cafés offer drop-in groups, so you can attend when you're in the mood or when you're interested in a specific book—perfect for commitmentphobes and really busy people. Talk to your friendly local librarian, booksellers, or coffee *barista*—chances are, you'll discover there's someone to help people like you. Check out public posting areas for book club "want" ads, or, if you're looking to attract members, try posting your own flyer.

If you decide to be in a book group formed with the help of a bookstore, library, or café, consider these pros and cons:

The Pros

The nice thing about these groups is that often they're ready-made in all different shapes and sizes. If you're a die-hard mystery or romance reader, if you want a nonfiction group, or if you want a group made up of writers, this may be the way to go. Most likely, you'll be in a group of people with diverse backgrounds and perspectives, so your discussion experience is sure to be a learning experience. Plus, since you'll get to know one another primarily through the books you read, you'll share a unique literary bond.

The Cons

We won't hide the truth. One cold, snowy night in January of 1995, Kira created (and then facilitated for the first three months) over two dozen book groups at Tattered Cover Book Store in Denver, Colorado. Of those groups, only three (that we know of) are still around. Sometimes these groups gel, and sometimes they don't. The three that have stayed together—for eight years now—benefited from common reading interests, a shared commitment to the group, and a clear sense of what each person wanted out of the group. That's the negative side-effect of gathering complete strangers for a project that requires consensus. Our advice in this situation: be extra sure you have an understanding of your mission with the members of your group.

Religious and Community Centers

Many religious and community centers have drop-in groups you can join. If not, approach someone in charge of community relations and see if the organization will help you get the word out. Initially, at least, you may want to connect your reading with whatever association you have in common, but don't feel limited by this connection.

If you decide to be in a book group formed with the help of a religious or community center, consider these pros and cons:

The Pros

If you decide to join or to draw members from one of these groups, you'll get the added benefit of having something in common right away. Kira and Ellen read and discussed several works of fiction that dealt with matters of the spirit (see our "Spirituality in the Novel" list in chapter 8) at the adult learning center of a local church and found it to be spiritually and intellectually rewarding. These kinds of organizations are also great places to start if you want to get involved with children's or young adult book groups.

The Cons

If the group is sponsored by the organization, you may find that it's limited in scope or that you don't have the freedom to organize it the way you'd like. A few book groups we've worked with started this way and then moved away from the organization once they got things going. Another thing to keep in mind is that the reading you do may challenge some of your shared beliefs—if handled with sensitivity, this potential problem could actually become the most gratifying aspect of your group.

The Internet

We probably don't have to tell you on-line book groups are quite popular these days. Your challenge will be to find one that fits your needs and that meets regularly. Some on-line book groups are immediately engaging; others are more like virtual ghost towns. See appendix 3 for a complete list of reliable sources for on-line book groups of all kinds.

If you decide to join or to create an on-line book group, consider these pros and cons:

The Pros

The benefit of synchronous (real-time) chat-room book groups is that you can hold a conversation with people all over the world—while you sit in your living room, sipping tea in your jammies. The benefit of asynchronous bulletin board book groups is that they can store the comments of hundreds of book group members for months. When you finally find that passage you were looking for, or when you have a witty comeback for that annoying book group member in Skokie, you can add it—weeks later!

The Cons

We assume if you're considering this option, you're comfortable with technology and don't mind the fact that you can't see or hear the other members of your group. We don't want to offend anyone, but we must be honest: we don't think on-line groups will ever replace living room groups. Facial expressions; body language; live, flesh-and-blood contact—these are all central to the book group experience. That much said, there are times when such physical proximity isn't possible (as with Rose's group, which she formed with her sisters, who live scattered across the country), and on-line book groups offer a great alternative.

PUTTING THE "BOOK" IN BOOK GROUP: CHOOSING WHAT TO READ

Okay, by now you've made up your mind about two of the three most important elements of your book group experience: what you hope to get out of it, and who you'd like to share it with. Now, before we can move on to the nitty-gritty details, we need to tackle what you're going to read.

Books, you say? Well, yes, that's a start. Agreeing on the kinds of books you'll read and discuss is just as important as reaching a shared understanding of why your group is together. Will you read fiction, nonfiction, or both? What kind of fiction interests you most—literary novels, short stories, historical fiction, science fiction, mysteries, bestsellers, avant-garde experiments? If you choose to read nonfiction, what will you include—memoir, history, essays, biography, nature writing? If you're having trouble identifying whole genres that you like (or dislike), just jot down a list of your favorite books. If you're not sure which genre they fall into, check out our genre analyses in chapter 3. Now, look at the list you've created and decide which of these books left you so desperate for conversation, you called up your best friend in the middle of dinner to see if she'd read it. This is the kind of book you want to read in your book group.

What You Don't Want to Read

Here's a technique Ellen used to plan her wedding, one we've passed on to many book groups. When the DJ asked Ellen and her fiancé to pick out music, they put a unique spin on things. Instead of telling the DJ what they *did* want to hear, they gave him a list of songs he was *absolutely not allowed to play*. The "Macarena" and "Mony, Mony" were on their list—you get the idea. Ellen and her beau were so amused while putting together their long list of "absolutely-no-way" songs, we thought we'd borrow their technique and pass it along to you. Write down genres, authors, books, anything literary you don't want to touch with a ten-foot pole. We think you'll discover it's great fun playing the role of the cranky reader, and, believe it or not, you'll refine your reading choices along the way.

Agreeing on a Process

Do not underestimate the power of a sloppy book-choice process to threaten, undermine, and eventually destroy your book group. You may think we're exaggerating. We're not. Most book groups agree that choosing books is a chore, one that ranges from mildly frustrating to downright impossible. Lucky for you, we've gathered the wise advice of savvy book group members who suggest many different ways of handling this important process. Check out the helpful hints in appendix 1 for more ideas on how to streamline this endeavor. It can be an annual or semiannual meeting, a regular event, or something of your own devising. But don't forget that group consensus is necessary however you go about choosing books with your group.

Readers Recommend

"Annually, we have a potluck to discuss reading suggestions. Some members come with one book, none, or many choices. There is some discussion. If many of us have already read the book, it is knocked out. If some of us hate the author, it is knocked out. Hopefully, at least one person has read it or it is a group decision for selecting it." *—Susan, Greenwood Village, Colorado*

Susan emphasizes consensus, which is necessary no matter how you select books with your group. Organizing a special yearly or semiyearly meeting like Susan's potluck is a great idea for two reasons: (1) it will give you the time you need to make well-informed choices, and (2) it will make the chore of choosing books feel more like a special event, a celebration.

"We have high standards for our book selections . . . they have to be capable of generating interesting discussions. Because we have such a long history together, we have a good sense of which books will generate a two-hour discussion. While all of us read a lot, we make a clear distinction between a 'fun read' for our personal reading and a 'book group' selection." *—Dalene, Kansas City, Missouri*

Dalene is obviously experienced in the nuances of book choice and all its repercussions. As she points out, there are good books and then there are good book group books. These are not always the same thing. For an in-depth discussion of what makes a good book group book, check out the introductory section of chapter 8. It's true that feelings can be damaged in this process. Choosing a book you really love and having your group give it a lukewarm or even a negative reception just plain hurts. What's even worse is when you suggest a book without knowing much about it, and then it bombs. As Dalene points out, "That person has to be willing to endure the wrath of the group." Her group has taken the burden of choice off one person by requiring that two people recommend each title, which is a great idea. The last idea that Dalene offers is to shake things up a bit with short stories (or some other genre you don't usually read). We cover these "energizing" tactics in chapter 6.

> "Each month, one member of the group brings three choices and then the group votes on which one to read. Sometimes the person bringing the choices will have a theme, such as time, gay literature, etc., but sometimes the theme will be as simple as 'books I had sitting around at home that I want to read but haven't yet.' "
>
> —*Kathy, Pflugerville, Texas*

Usually, we try to steer groups away from dealing with the book-choice process at every meeting because it's so time-consuming. However, Kathy has a good way of making this work: have just one person present a few titles and then vote. Following a theme for several months is a great idea. If you're a planner, you'll probably prefer a model like Susan's, where the whole year is designed in advance. This has its benefits, but it doesn't allow for that oh-my-gosh-I-just-read-this-book-and-we-have-to-discuss-it-right-now kind of spontaneity. We suggest going for a happy middle ground—plan for three to six months in advance.

> "We either go to a book club consultant, or everyone brings several recommendations to our July meeting. Over a long lunch, we review the books, discuss, and then vote. Then we assign each book to a month and each month to a hostess."
>
> —*Susan, Evergreen, Colorado*

Susan's group also plans for one year in advance, and she makes this a special occasion. The book season usually peaks in the fall, so we recommend you hold your annual or semiannual meeting sometime in the fall or around the holidays to make sure you have access to all the newest, hottest titles. If yours is a living-room book group, you'll need to assign each meeting to a different member's home—we advise a rotation of this responsibility to lighten the load. What does Susan mean by "book club consultant," you may be wondering? You're reading the words of two right now! Good Books Lately provides reading recommendations in person, over the phone, and via E-mail. We've gathered our current favorites on our "Greedy Reader Menu" in chapter 8. Many bookstores are happy to offer a reading-recommendation service to book groups as well. If you do use an outside consultant, consider meeting in a restaurant, café, or bookstore to make the meeting festive.

"Well, lately we've sort of said, 'Who was supposed to choose the book?' Then someone else says, 'I think Terry was supposed to choose the book.' And someone else says, 'Terry's not here.' So then somebody says, 'Anyone got a book?' 'Um, uh, well, how about . . . ' There's a certain amount of discussion and then when someone remembers a book they want to read, we end up with that one. It's very informal."
—*Terry, Spokane, Washington*

Just when you thought this whole dang procedure sounded like a huge pain, Terry's humorous anecdote illustrates how a certain disorganized— or free-spirited and spontaneous, depending on how you see it— approach can work for some groups. As you can see, there are many, many ways to handle choosing books, not all of them formal. The fly-by-the-seat-of-your-pants approach Terry describes might prove frustrating over time, but the key is to find something that works for your unique group. This may require that you try out a few different techniques before you find the one that works best.

Finding Books That Work

Okay, you've read about several ways to navigate the tricky book-choice process with your group. But let's back up a step. Whether you choose books with your group once a year or at every meeting, whether you nominate and vote on candidates or select titles unceremoniously, you need to find the books first. Sure, you could just grab any book off the shelf, willy-nilly, and bring it to your group. But you wouldn't do that, would you? You want the books you suggest to be smart and provocative and haunting and funny and inspiring, right? You want every book you recommend to your group to be a winner. You want the earth to move under your book group's feet—and we want that for you.

In our years working with book groups and wading through the seemingly infinite number of books out there, we've fine-tuned our "good book group book" radar. We've got some tips for you, real steps you can take to find the best books for your group (see chapter 8). But chances are, at some point, you or someone else in your group will make a suggestion with all the best intentions, and splat! No one will like the book, and the discussion will be terrible. It's not the end of the world. At least your group will sharpen its sense of what it *doesn't* like. And you'll have a funny story to tell (in a year or two, after the sting wears off). We've discovered one of the best ways for us to get to know a book group at our first consultation is to ask the group to describe a book or two that absolutely bombed. There's usually lots of laughter and lots of "Oh, dear, I remember how much we all *hated* that book!" and it all comes out in the wash. However, there are things you can do to keep this kind of disaster at bay.

Define What *You* Mean by "Good Book Group Book"

We know exactly what we mean when we say, "That's a really good book group book" (see chapter 8). But that's only because we've been doing this awhile, and we've had time to discover what works and what doesn't. We hope the information we provide is helpful, but in the end, your group will need to discover this for yourselves. Once you've got a few book discussions under your belt, spend thirty minutes or so with your group designing some kind of shared definition of "good book group book." We have two basic criteria, which we expand on in chapter 8:

- A good book group book is enjoyable to read by yourself AND rewarding to discuss with your group.
- A good book group book asks more questions than it answers.

Browse the Shelves at Your Favorite Bookstore or Library

When people ask us how we find our books, we have a comical story to tell. Ellen was browsing the fiction shelves in her neighborhood bookshop, when out of the blue, for no apparent reason, a copy of Jim Crace's *Quarantine* shot off the tall shelf above her and hit her on the head. "My, oh my," Ellen said to herself, rubbing the bump that was swelling below her fingers, "what do we have here?" Reading the cover and discovering the book was a fictional account of Christ's forty days in the wilderness, Ellen guessed it must have been divine intervention, She sat down with Crace's novel and began reading. Two hours later, she got up from her chair, bought the book, rushed home and finished it in one sitting, and called Kira with the good news: "You won't believe the fantastic book I found today!"

The moral of the story, we suppose, is that you just never know how you'll find a great book (or how that great book will find you). Make use of the bookstores in your neighborhood, ask questions, request recommendations—use your bookstore *actively*. Likewise, visit your library once in a while. We believe librarians are among the kindest, smartest people in the world, and it's their job to help you. Give them a break from shelving those dusty old books and make use of their expertise. Libraries display new books, too, and once you develop an eye (yes, you can judge a book this way—check out our special feature in chapter 8, "How to Tell a Book by Its Cover"), you'll be able to whip right through a bookstore or library display in no time. The trick is to check out the cover, look at the blurbs on the back (see if any authors you like recommend the book, for instance), check out the review excerpts, and read the first five pages or so. If you have time, sit down, relax, and read some more. A good book should draw you in right away and make you forget about that appointment you have across town in just a few minutes.

Read Reviews (But Not Too Many or Too Often)

We have mixed feelings about reviews. On the one hand, they can be terribly useful; on the other hand, they can be just plain terrible. We don't mean that reviewers' opinions are wrong, or that their arguments are poorly constructed; no, what we're referring to is the way a reviewer's words can seep into your mind as you read, altering your perspective. Ellen reads only the first paragraph or two of a review—if she's convinced by what she reads, she'll leave the rest up to the book. Another technique is to find a reviewer whose opinion you usually agree with and then keep an eye out for her reviews. This can work in the other direction as well. For instance, Ellen knows from experience to avoid movies recommended by a certain ubiquitous movie reviewer—if he loves the movie, she's sure to hate it, and vice versa.

We do recommend the free Book Sense 76 newsletter, which is distributed every other month to independent bookstores across the country. In it booksellers select their favorite books of the moment and include a brief descriptive blurb—just enough to give you a sense of the book's flavor but not enough to ruin the ending (which some cruel reviewers are fond of doing from time to time). We hope you'll visit the Good Books Lately site at www.goodbookslately.com for up-to-date reading recommendations. We work with book groups every day, so we know what works and what doesn't; and because we're not affiliated with any one publisher, our independent opinions remain our own. If you can't find what you need on our Web site, e-mail us or give us a call—we're here to help!

Best-Seller Lists and Literary Awards and . . . Kelly Ripa?

We're just not sure how helpful best-seller lists are to the average reader. Sometimes really exceptional books, like *Girl with a Pearl Earring* or *The Lovely Bones,* makes it onto the best-seller list, but for the most part, you'll see the same five or so authors listed, month after month: Tom Clancy, Nora Roberts, John Grisham, Stephen King, Danielle Steele. Since you probably already know these authors and know whether or not you like their books, the best-seller list is not exactly the best way to expand your reading repertoire.

Of all the literary prizes, we tend to like the winners of the National Book Award, the National Book Critics Circle Award, the Booker Prize, and the PEN/Faulkner Award the most. You can go online to get lists of these prizewinners, but we recommend you do a little extra homework to discover if the book is right for your group. The best thing you can do is to sit down with the book and give it a try. The next best thing is to research the author and take a look at a few reviews, preferably from reviewers whose work you know and trust. Don't assume that because the book won a prize, it's an instant winner.

Since Oprah Winfrey disbanded her book group in spring 2002 (luckily for us readers, she has since continued Oprah's Book Club as a classics group), readers have asked us what we think of the TV book clubs that have come to fill the gap Oprah left. If you want some good old-fashioned beach trash, then "Reading with Ripa" (on *LIVE with Regis and Kelly*) is for you. If you're curious about which up-and-coming writers have captured the attention of big-time authors, check out the "Today's Book Club" on the *Today Show*. And if you're more interested in what book group members, like yourself, think is "hot," tune in to *Good Morning America*'s "Read This!" book club.

Last, but Definitely Not Least: Friends, Family, and People You Trust

We've collected many, many resources in appendix 3 to help you find the information you need to empower your book group and to find first-rate books. But when it comes to choosing books, nothing beats what booksellers call "hand selling." Literally, it means when someone recommends a book and places it in your hand. When this is done by a bookseller or by a librarian whose opinion you respect, or by a friend or family member whose taste you share, nothing—no best-seller list, no TV book club, not even Oprah—can compare. After all, that's what makes Oprah's Book Club so special—Oprah doesn't choose her book club books based on best-seller lists or prizes or the recommendations of publishers. Nope, she just does what we do. She gets by with a little help from her friends.

"SAME BAT TIME, SAME BAT CHANNEL": WHERE AND WHEN TO HOLD YOUR BOOK GROUP MEETINGS

Whew, you've gotten this far, which means the really tough stuff is done. These next few details are important, but they're the kind of thing you can decide with your group in no time. Before we take a peek at the details, let's take a moment to refresh ourselves.

Pass the Finger Food and Crack Open Another Bottle

For some groups—like the Mostly, We Eat book club in New Jersey— food is the highlight of the evening. We've devoted a section of chapter 6 to creative ways you can integrate your eating and reading experience, so we'll be brief: book group just isn't book group without fine food and good drink. Liven up your experience by connecting what you eat with what you read—a little Latin American cuisine when you're reading Isabel Allende, for instance. Ruth, of Denver, Colorado, tells us her book group has rather elaborate meals: the hostess prepares a full meal, and she always has two assistants, one in charge of bringing a side dish (which, like the meal, is related to the book), and one in charge of creating small party favors for each reader (again, linked to the story in some way). Don't underestimate the power of scrumptious chow: some tasty merlot and an inspired dish can save the night when discussion drags.

Meeting of the Minds

Before you can enjoy your literary libations, you need to decide where you'd like to meet. This is common sense, based on the kind of group you've joined or created. You can meet in book group members' homes; in bookstores and libraries; in corporate conference rooms; in (quiet) restaurants and cafés; in community centers, churches, and synagogues; and even in the great outdoors. Be creative! When things get dull, try varying your meeting place—you might be surprised by how transformative a simple change of venue can be.

Meetings, Meetings, Meetings

This last step is quick and easy. We'll give you the most common answers to these scheduling questions. Disregard our advice at will if your group has special needs or wants to try something different—it's completely up to you.

How often?
Once a month.

How many?
Eight to twelve times a year, depending on whether or not your group breaks for the summer months and/or holidays in December.

How long?
About two to three hours per meeting.

The 126-Year-Old Reading Club

By the time we encountered the Reading Club of West Medford, we thought we'd met some *really old* book groups. And we mean the groups, not the members, of course! We've had the pleasure of working with groups that have been meeting for twenty-five, thirty, even forty years. But nothing prepared us for this group, which in 2002–03 celebrated its 126th season. Yes, that's right: this multigenerational group of readers has been meeting continuously since 1877. The club's original written objective was quite serious: "To encourage whatever should tend to the development of good literary taste, to mental improvement, and to better the social life of its members." The club is well-organized, membership is highly sought after (there's a waiting list, and candidates must be formally nominated by an existing member), and each month club minutes are added to a well-tended file that records the club's fascinating history. Rather than reading a designated book each month and then discussing it as a group, the club provides a chance for members to present and exchange various—and we do mean *various*—intellectual topics of the day. Many times, the season's topics are organized around a common theme. The club benefits from male and female members and from the wide range of ages of its members, according to the 2002–03 secretary, Edward: "Over the years, we've had members in their nineties and members in their late twenties. It's the mix of people that makes it interesting." A few members are the descendants of original members of the club, while others are relatively new to the area, tracing their Boston roots back a mere hundred years.

Some things change, and some things stay the same, or so they say. It's no different with the Reading Club of West Medford. The topics of discussion have changed—in fact, one could trace a social history of the United States just by reading the meeting minutes of this group. Here's a selection of topics engaged over the years: "Old and New Utopias" and

"Italian Painters" (1889–90); "Civic Order," "Immigration," and "Dance Music" (1914–15); "Folk Schools of Northern Europe" and "The Fairyland of Modern Science" (1923–24); "America's Allies" (1942–43); "Tragic Heroines of Shakespeare," "Economic and Social Problems of the South Pacific," and "Rocket to the Moon" (1958–59). The thing that hasn't changed for the Reading Club of West Medford? Dessert. For all these years, the format of the club has remained constant: meetings occur once a month from October through May, a guest lecturer or a group member makes a presentation on a designated topic, followed by a congenial gathering around the dining-room table for tea and dessert, with the meeting adjourned, by tradition, at 10:00 p.m. Each season boasts a formal calendar, which is mailed to each member and includes information on the host and topic of each meeting, a list of current membership, and the elected officials of the group. The public and private histories contained in the club minutes of the Reading Club of West Medford are an inspiration to book groups everywhere—motivating us not only to keep it going every month, but to record what we read and what we discuss for readers in generations to come.

AVOID THOSE FIRST-DAY JITTERS: MAKING YOUR INAUGURAL MEETING A CELEBRATION

The Fun Stuff: Send Out Invitations, Give Party Favors, Name Your Group

Sure, you could just invite people over to your house, pick a book, and jump right into the discussion. But where's the fun in that? Mark the very special occasion of your inaugural meeting by sending out some kind of invitation. Create a small, book-related party favor. If you're meeting one another for the first time, spend this meeting getting to know about each other's lives as readers. Heather of Jacksonville, Florida, gave each member of her new book group a reading journal to record ideas and questions. First of all—and this is important—name your group! Have fun, be clever, capture the personality of your group in a name you'll be proud to share.

We've gathered an impressive collection of book group names in our files—we'll share a few of our favorites with you, just to get your juices flowing. Lots of book groups choose literary-sounding names, like The Bookworms, Between the Covers, Loose Pages, Women of Letters, The Thoughtful Eclectics, The Book Nook, Tea Time Readers Book Club, and Lone Tree Readers. Others are so inspired by one book, they name their group after it—for instance, The Pickles (named after *The Persian Pickle Club*). Many groups use a play-on-words to describe their character: Reading with Grace, Keen as Mustard, Inquiring Minds Want to Know, Literary Lunch Bunch, The Energizer Bunnies, and GAB (an acronym for Girls' Alibi to Blab).

If you're not feeling especially clever (or if your group is indebted to one particular member), you might want to choose something simple, like Bill's Book Club, Gene's Book Group, Anna's Reading Group, or Bev's Book Group—you get the idea. Another straightforward option is to designate your group with the affiliation shared by your members, like Weld County Liberal Democrats, Temple Beth Rishon Book Club, Kansas City Midtowners, St. Mark's Morning Book Group, Bicester Book Group, Keys School Parents and Teachers Book Club, and Lawrence Library Book Club. You can get more descriptive with titles like Law & Disorder Book Group, The Prettiest Town and the Dixie Chicks, or The Schizophrenic Book Club. You can even try to capture your group's mission in your name: Living on Purpose Discussion Group, Girls' Night Out, The Sisterhood, Enrichment of Life Book Group, and Fun with High School English Teachers Book Club.

Or, if you'd rather, you can make some kind of evaluative statement about your group in your name, like We'll Read Anything; A Pretty Good Book Group; Books Rock 2003; We're Smart, You're Not; and THE Book Club. Ah, we've saved the best for last. Here are some book group names we'll never forget: Right Now Misery Loves Company; "For Culture We Must Suffer"; Young Ladies and Old Broads; Read 'em and Reap; Urban Readers and Social Butterflies; Women Who Read Too Much and the Dogs Who Love Them; The Smokey Mt. Bookers, not Hookers; and perhaps our all-time favorite, Twelve Mouthy Chicks and Lamar.

The Fundamentals: Talk About Your Hopes, Goals, and Mission

Remember those words you wrote down describing what first inspired you to get involved with a book group? We hope you still have that scrap of paper because it sure will come in handy during your first meeting. New groups of all kinds have used this "getting to know you" exercise with great success. Before your first meeting, have the members write down what they'd like to get out of this book group. Have each person distill these thoughts into a few words. Share what you've written with the group, and then use these words to help you name your group. You may want to have members of your group write down a list of "top five most hated books or authors of all time" to help clarify what kinds of books you will (and won't) read together.

Most important, spend however much time you need to come to a shared understanding of why you're starting a book group. You may discover that some people have fundamentally different goals for the group, but it's best to find out now rather than run into this problem nine months down the road. Once you've defined your shared mission, record it in some way. Even the most casual book group will enjoy looking back on this written record of your first meeting. And you never know, it might come in handy later if you ever feel like you've lost your way.

The Details: Brought to You by OCD Girl

It's embarrassing but true, and now the secret's out of the bag. Kira's nickname among those who know her well is "OCD Girl," as in "obsessive-compulsive-disorder girl." Let's just say that nothing makes her happier than lamination. Even the most freewheeling book group will have a member who has Kira's tendencies, someone who is more than happy to take over the details and play the role of secretary. Don't worry, the secretary doesn't have to take minutes (although some do); rather, she's in charge of gathering everyone's contact information and keeping track of the reading schedule. If you don't have an OCD Girl in your midst, this position can be rotated, just like the hostess role.

6

A Shot in the Arm: Energizing Your Book Group with Lively, Crafty, Creative Ideas

Is your book group stuck in a rut? Is your dead-end discussion driving you crazy? Are you ready for a good old-fashioned shot in the arm? In this chapter we've collected the sage advice of savvy book group members who know what it's like to run out of steam and who've figured out where to get some more. Here you'll find some of the most unique, creative, and inspirational ideas for rejuvenating your book group. Even if your group has reached a state of book group nirvana, we hope you'll consider trying something different once in a while. As Kira's grandmother likes to say, "Sometimes you've got to grab life by the corners and shake it out, like a rug." We think your book group will enjoy shaking things up a bit—you may want to consider the ideas below for inspiration.

MEET THE AUTHOR (OR AT LEAST
LISTEN TO HER ON TAPE)

> Liking a writer and then meeting the writer is like liking goose
> liver and then meeting the goose.
> —ARTHUR KOESTLER

Many book groups have had great fun getting cozy with the author. There are different ways to do this: at a book signing at your neighborhood bookstore, by inviting a local author to visit your group, through an author lecture on video, by listening to the author read his or her work on tape, or through one of the many publisher-sponsored book group/author chats arranged via phone and/or the Internet. Check with your bookstore or library to discover local writers interested in meeting with book groups—most authors will be happy to visit for free just for the pleasure of discussing their book with a lively audience. You can also check the readings at bookstores and libraries near you— most post schedules for a month or two in advance, so your group can plan your reading accordingly and hear the author speak before your book group discussion. Visit publisher Web sites (like HarperCollins's Author Chat site) to find out which authors are willing to do book group outreach long-distance. There's just nothing like having the author in front of you (in person, on a discussion board, or through a speakerphone), so you can ask that burning question the book left unanswered.

Book Group Members Tell Tales

"We had a phone interview with Adriana Trigiani to discuss her book *Milk Glass Moon,* which is the third book in a series of books about a small town in Virginia. We met in my daughter's home because she has a speakerphone. Everyone brought food, and we had a party!! Ms. Trigiani was fantastic!! We loved talking to her, and it was so much fun. We hope to have phone interviews with other authors in the future."
— *Anna, Oak Ridge, Tennessee*

"When we read *Savage Beauty,* one member brought a tape of Edna St. Vincent Mil-
lay reading her poetry."
                                                    —*Annie, Plano, Texas*

"Our favorite book discussion would definitely have to be the time that the author
Jodi Picoult joined us one night in our chat room! It was just unbelievable to get to
'talk' with her. I think that's a HUGE advantage of having an on-line book club . . . it
is MUCH easier to get authors to visit with us!"   —*Carrie, St. Louis, Missouri*

"Inge Sargent, who wrote about being a Burmese princess, visited our group. It was
fascinating—she brought props, like an enormous snakeskin that was one of the
few things she got out of Burma (now Myanmar). She was so compelling and
warm and wonderful. Her book wasn't terrific, but she's the first to say that she's
not a writer and just felt the need to tell her story."

                        —*Nancy, Lafayette, Colorado; Not the Blue Heron Book Group*

One Book Group's Taste of Fame

A few years ago we became aware of a couple of women who were working as facilitators for book clubs with Good Books Lately [all right, we admit, it's yours truly!]. Our group thought that it would be a growth experience to have someone come to us with new ideas on how to discuss books. The book club consultants sent us abundant resource materials [ReadSmartGuides®] in order to prepare for our discussion of Zadie Smith's White Teeth. They included character studies, a chapter-by-chapter plot outline, comparisons to other literature, as well as questions designed to promote discussion. It was a wealth of material. A few weeks before our scheduled meeting, Ellen from Good Books Lately called. She asked if it would be okay with us if a film crew came and taped our session for a spot on CBS's Early Show. Oh my gosh, how exciting! I called the members of the book group to see if everyone was willing to appear on national TV. Much to my surprise, everyone agreed.

The evening of the book club came quickly. Everyone was abuzz with nervous excitement. Soon we were involved in a discussion about books, book clubs, and White Teeth. We became oblivious to the cameras moving around the room, sometimes practically right in our faces. A few weeks later, our spot aired. Even after an hour of filming, our brush with fame lasted only a few minutes. Still, it was a huge thrill. Of course we taped the show to show friends and relatives."

—Susan
Between the Covers Book Club
Evergreen, Colorado

A quick note about The Early Show segment: We, too, gathered around our TV sets the morning the show aired. Much to our surprise, the usual host, Bryant Gumbel, was nowhere to be seen. As it turns out, Richard Hatch—of Survivor fame—was a special guest host. Perhaps needless to say, the entire show was organized around the "survivor" theme, which didn't exactly make for a smooth transition to our little book group story. "Will Susan survive her book group?" just didn't seem like a dramatic enough (or even relevant!) question. So the story ran, and of course, Susan's book group was articulate and smart and funny and charming, proudly representing the rest of us book groupies.

We were delighted to have been interviewed by none other than Lisa Birnbach, author of *The Official Preppy Handbook,* which was, as you'll recall, *the* book of 1980. The only catch came when the story concluded in the studio with the show's cohost Jane Clayson, who said something like (forgive us if our memory is a bit hazy), "Well, thanks so much for that story, Lisa. It seems that book groups aren't really about books, are they? They're mostly about women getting together and chatting." Oh dear. But still, we were delighted to have been part of a great story—perhaps a few of you out there saw us on CBS in May of 2001.

One other thing we should mention about Susan's book group: they were among the first to be selected by HarperCollins for its inaugural "Invite the Author" program. Susan heard about the contest through our e-newsletter *LATELIES,* and figured, "What the heck, I might as well enter." She then forgot about entering and didn't tell anyone in her group that she had done so. "A few weeks later," she recalls, "I received an E-mail from HarperCollins saying that my group was one of two winning book clubs nationally, and would receive a call from Ann Patchett." The speakerphone conversation with Patchett was a huge success and made for "a truly memorable evening."

We encourage you and your book group to get involved—many publishers have special programs designed just for book groups. A visit from one of your favorite authors could be just a click away. For more information on the "Invite the Author" program and other publisher programs for book groups, check out the "Book Group Help—Other Resources" page at www.goodbookslately.com.

WATCH THE MOVIE, SEE THE PLAY, LISTEN TO THE OPERA

You know what they say: read a book before Hollywood ruins it. We've all had the experience of going to see a movie based on one of our most adored books, only to leave the theater feeling perplexed and sometimes downright angry. "What were they thinking?" we ask indignantly. And sometimes it's true—Hollywood can trash a fine work of fiction. But more often than not, the filmmaker just makes some necessary adjustments to move the story from the page to the screen. We would provide a complete list for you, but so many movies are adaptations of novels, it's difficult to think of a film these days that's based on an original screenplay. Take advantage of the current climate: read the book and then watch the movie with your book group. Of course, you can do it the other way around, but we recommend you read the book first. It's great fun to compare and contrast the different methods of storytelling and to trace the way the written *word* is translated into visual *image*. We recommend these great book/movie pairings: *The Hours*, *To Kill a Mockingbird*, *Cold Mountain*, *Seabiscuit*, *Rebecca*, *Persuasion*, and *Adaptation* (the movie) and the book that inspired it, Susan Orlean's *The Orchid Thief*. And don't forget about your local performing arts centers—you'd be surprised how many literary favorites have been reworked for the stage. Seeing the story reenacted live before your eyes can be a magical experience.

Book Group Members Suggest

"We read *A Handmaid's Tale* and we are going to see it performed by the Minnesota Opera in May. None of us has been to an opera before."

—*Laura, Saint Paul, Minnesota*

"We gather two weeks after reading a book to view a movie: for example, when we read *Father of Frankenstein* by Christopher Bram, we followed it with the film adaptation, *Gods and Monsters*."

—*Paul, Colorado Springs, Colorado*

"Once every year, we 'read a book, then see the movie' (*A Tree Grows in Brooklyn, Howard's End, Emma*)."
—*Ellen, Eden Prairie, Minnesota; Newcomers Club (of the Southwest Suburbs) Book Group*

CHANGE THE SCENERY AND DO A WORLD OF GOOD

Sometimes nothing works better than a field trip to shake things up for your group. Investigate scenic literary spots in your area: authors' homes, author museums, off-the-beaten-path places where stories have been set, art exhibits with a literary connection. Your friendly librarian can help you find out which authors are from your area and which books are set near you. You may not be able to do something as extravagant as the book group we met with in Santa Fe, New Mexico, who had traveled there from Denver to discuss Willa Cather's *Death Comes for the Archbishop* (we held our discussion in the cathedral on the plaza), but you'll be surprised at what a little change of scenery will do. Even moving your meeting once or twice a year from your living rooms to a quiet restaurant, café, or bar can do the trick and give your group that much-needed boost.

Book Group Members Get Out

"We went to 'Martini and a Movie' at Atlanta's IMAX theater. We had dinner and martinis and watched the movie version of *Into Thin Air.* It was fascinating to see the actual footage of what we had read about, and we had a great time socializing outside of the normal book club setting. We plan a 'field trip' of some sort every year now."
—*Angels, Canton, Georgia*

"Another thing we are going to try this year is to have an overnight meeting at a member's cabin on a lake in Richmond, Minnesota. That should be a great bonding experience."
—*Laura, Saint Paul, Minnesota*

"Last fall, three of us went to Bouchercon, the annual mystery writers' convention. Bouchercon is three and a half days of panel discussions, signings, and readings. We split up so we could attend different discussions and readings, spent tons of time in the booksellers' room, and spent each evening recapping the things we'd seen and heard that day. We had so much fun that the whole group has decided to attend this fall's convention." —*Jennifer, Temple, Texas; We're Smart, You're Not Book Club*

"The most poignant book group [meeting] that we will never forget was discussing Doris Kearnes Goodwin's *No Ordinary Time* at a naval officer's home on base on 9-10-01. We were all in agreement that 'the youth of today would not rise to the occasion of war as they did during the World War II era because they are too soft and much too used to the creature comforts that our society has to offer. They would not choose to go to war unless it was on our own soil.' Needless to say, we were all in shock the next morning when the twin towers were struck and collectively felt as if we should have spoken in hushed tones the previous day."

—*Barbara, Norfolk, Virginia*

SATISFY HUNGRY MINDS WITH FOOD AND DRINK

Most book groups eat and drink as they're merrily discussing books, so why not connect the food you're eating with the book you're reading? It's easy to do with Latin American, African, Chinese, Italian, and French books, but don't limit yourself. Sometimes the smallest detail in the book will inspire you to create something different for your group. And by the way, we know that many book groups have the same person host the meeting and lead the discussion, and that can work well. It can also be exhausting, especially if you want to try something special. We suggest you break it up a bit and assign the discussion and food responsibilities to separate members each month. That way, when it's your turn to play host, you can really have some fun.

Book Group Members Share Recipes

"In the past year, we have been trying to choose a cuisine for dinner that relates to the book we are discussing. With *The Year of Jubilo,* we enjoyed pork barbecue with all the fixin's. For *The Lion, the Witch and the Wardrobe,* which we read around Christmastime, we tried Turkish Delight. Obviously, this works better with some books than with others. For example, when we read *Catcher in the Rye,* we realized that the only appropriate fare would be a carton of cigarettes and a fifth of whisky. For such occasions, the rules are temporarily suspended."

—*Ruth, Richmond, Virginia; Law and Disorder Book Club*

"When we read *Fast Food Nation,* I suggested having the discussion at McDonald's and to bring in our own sandwiches, but the group opted to have it in a bakery instead." —*Laura, Saint Paul, Minnesota*

"One fun meeting was when we did *Sweet Potato Queens' Book of Love* and served several of the dishes from this book, including the 'Fat Mama's Knock You Naked Margaritas.' "

—*Brenda, Cheraw, South Carolina; Prettiest Town and the Dixie Chicks Book Club*

"We have the discussions at individual houses and the host/hostess usually tries to incorporate something from the book. We read *Jitterbug Perfume* and our hostess made a dish with beets and used beets in her centerpiece."

—*Angela, Canton, Georgia; Twelve Mouthy Chicks and Lamar Book Group*

"For Patricia Highsmith's *Strangers on a Train,* black-and-white food, including black caviar on white toast, was served to set the mood."

—*Kathy, Austin, Texas; "For Culture We Must Suffer" Book Group*

"We recently read *The Red Tent* by Anita Diamant. We dined on lamb stew, hummus, flatbread, couscous, and olives. There was plenty of beer and wine to wash it down (inspired by the book, of course). We refrained from sampling the honey-dipped grasshoppers that were mentioned in the book. Looking back, I suppose we should have run around barefoot and in linen robes, but slacks and sweaters seemed more appropriate . . ."

—*Pam, Centennial, Colorado; GAB (Girls' Alibi to Blab) Book Club*

BRING THE STORY TO LIFE
WITH PROPS

When we read a book, we create a visual image in our mind. If the author is really good, that image is so strong, we feel like we can step right into another world. The beauty of reading, of course, is that each of us creates a slightly different and always unique image of the places and people in the story. However, sometimes images or objects in the book are so distinct, so connected with the story, they're inescapable—everyone recognizes them. When you run across one of these, make use of it! Find a way to bring the story to life with some kind of prop: use all the senses. Even the smallest gesture can reinvigorate your group and inspire a lively discussion. Bringing in props is a great way to lighten up a difficult or heavy book as well, as you'll see with some of the examples below.

Book Group Members Get Creative

"We just finished reading *The Hiding Place* by Corrie Ten Boom, and since my grandfather fought in WWII and liberated a few concentration camps, I brought a nine-prong Nazi leather whip that he brought home from Buchenwald to the meeting and retold some of his stories. It was powerful." —*Laura, Saint Paul, Minnesota*

"When we read *The Persian Pickle Club* by Sandra Dallas, one of the ladies brought in an antique quilt to show us. Several others brought quilts that had been made by their grandmothers." —*Anna, Oak Ridge, Tennessee*

"For *The Red Tent* the reviewer wore a robe and other attire (appropriate to the biblical setting of the book), which she borrowed from our church. She also made out 'work assignments' for each of the women at the group—several tasks that each would have had to perform had they been one of the multiple wives of Jacob. These included weaving, cooking, collecting herbs for medicines, etc., and ALL had as their last assignment 'servicing Jacob.'"

—*Susan, Omaha, Nebraska; Presbyterian Church of the Master's Women's Book Group*

"I am presenting *Bel Canto* this week and will be playing Renee Fleming arias in the background. In an interview, Ann Pachett referred to Fleming as the real-life diva who inspired her."
—*Mimi, Englewood, Colorado*

"We use 'totem objects.' For instance, when we read *Corelli's Mandolin,* we had a real mandolin as the centerpiece of our table. When we discussed *The Greatest Generation,* we shared memorabilia from WWII. Especially for historical fiction, bringing these objects into the discussion really adds something special."
—*Ruth, Denver, Colorado*

"When we read Lewis Carroll's *Alice in Wonderland,* the host had her niece dress up like Alice and greet us at the door, after which we had a fancy tea party."
—*Kathy, Austin, Texas; "For Culture We Must Suffer" Book Group*

CELEBRATE THE HOLIDAYS WITH YOUR GROUP

Many book groups hold special holiday parties around Christmas, Hanukkah, and the New Year. You can make the most of the holidays in many ways: read a holiday-inspired book; take a break from reading altogether and make this time a purely social event; lighten the pace a little by reading a children's or young adult novel, entertain each other with a literary gift exchange, or use this time to plan next year's reading schedule. Don't forget about the other holidays, too. Discuss a Maeve Binchy novel around St. Patrick's Day and fill up on bangers and mash. Get yourself in the mood by reading to each other passages from your favorite love stories for Valentine's Day. Celebrate your independence around the Fourth of July and read some great American historical fiction. Be creative!

Book Group Members Recommend

"Our holiday meeting is always special. We get 'gussied up' and go out to a special Christmas dinner. Everyone purchases and wraps a book, we set them in the center of the table, and, one by one, members make a pick. The member who brought the book has to tell us a little about it and why she wanted to share it with someone."

—Felicia, Charlotte, North Carolina; Friends of Lorraine, a Reading Group

---

"We don't have time to decorate our houses for each and every holiday, but because we have book club each month, we get to celebrate with each other. We plan our year's reading around the holidays. The hostess gets to pick which holiday she wants, so she can dress up her house with all the knickknacks she usually leaves stored in the basement. It makes every meeting festive."

—Fran, Jacksonville, Florida

GO ALL OUT: SET A STAGE FOR YOUR DISCUSSION

Some of us are a bit more ambitious than others. If you have that fiercely driven person in your book group, plant a seed in her head with this next idea and get her to go all out. Once a year it's satisfying to have your book group meeting be completely over the top: coordinate food and drink, decorate the house, wear costumes, give out party favors, play games, involve the family. Set a stage for your discussion. Even if the book is just lukewarm and your discussion falters, you'll have so much else to enjoy you'll never notice! We suggest that unless you have a truly gifted Martha Stewart type in your midst, you divide up the responsibilities for this kind of extravagant meeting.

Book Group Members Get Busy

"The book was *Modoc: The Story of the Greatest Elephant Who Ever Lived.* The book took place in Germany, India, and the United States, and Modoc was a circus elephant. I did Under the Big Top circus invitations, rolled them up and tied them with ribbon, attaching a peanut and an elephant cutout with each member's name written on the ear. We had German and circus-type food. The tables were done in red, blue, and yellow, with pictures of elephants and ceramic elephants with helium balloons tied to them. Before dinner, accompanied by traditional circus music, my son juggled flaming torches. The group agrees that this was the loudest meeting they have ever had." —Sarah, Littleton, Colorado; Loose Pages Book Club

"One member was particularly excited to have us read Truman Capote's "Hand-carved Coffins," her favorite short story, which, she was sure, was based on a true story. At some point in the discussion we found that we had an irreconcilable difference, and the group divided into two camps—those who thought Capote's yarn was based on a true story and those who insisted it wasn't (and couldn't possibly be). The member who had recommended the story was certain it was true and left the meeting determined to prove her point. A writer herself, she set out on what turned into a major investigation. She made over fifty calls to a wide range of people who might have information, including the Kansas detective Capote had befriended when he was writing In Cold Blood; the Nebraska (where the story was set) FBI; the Kansas FBI agent who had cooperated with Capote on In Cold Blood; and George Plimpton, one of Capote's friends and an author him-self. She researched the microfilm collection of Capote's notes and interviews at the New York Public Library. At a subsequent meeting, she presented us with a written report of her findings, with details of her contacts and things learned along the way." —Dalene, Kansas City, Missouri, Rockhill Book Club

MOVE FROM READER TO WRITER

Are you one of those people who is inspired to grab that dusty old jour-nal and write a few pages after reading a really powerful book? Even if you're not a diary-keeping kind of person, it can rejuvenate your group in fascinating ways to bring writing into the discussion experience. You don't have to be a writer to enjoy writing together collaboratively, or, if you're comfortable, sharing your own personal musings with the mem-bers of your group. You can make time during your meeting for free-writing on a topic related to the story and then share what you've written. You could provide a few discussion questions before the meeting, have everyone respond to them, and then read the responses anonymously to get the discussion going. We know of one book group that, after reading *The Hours,* began by reading a passage where the main character tells her daughter about a profound moment in her life: a truly happy moment, a moment she thought was the beginning of happiness. The discussion leader asked each member to take ten minutes or so to jot down her thoughts about a moment like that in her life. Writing with your group doesn't have to feel like homework or like a pop quiz.

Book Group Members Become Authors

"One member wrote a small play and got some other book clubbers to volunteer for the parts."

—*Annie, Plano, Texas*

"For my own pick, Susan Minot's *Evening,* I did something personally risky—reading a long passionate piece from my own journal that had been provoked by the heroine's end-of-life memory of an early unforgettable love affair."

—*Jan, Cherry Hills Village, Colorado*

GET INVOLVED: REACH OUT TO YOUR COMMUNITY

Don't feel bad—we think reading a book every month and talking about it with friends is itself a kind of community service. But if you're energized enough to take this to the next level, you can get involved in your community in a variety of ways. Not only will you be doing some good out there in the world, you'll have shared an experience with your book group members that will solidify and deepen your connection with each other.

Book Group Members Advocate

"When the Itty Bitty Reading Group read *Nickel and Dimed,* we brainstormed ways that we could help the homeless in Minnesota. We are going to help build a house with Habitat for Humanity sometime this summer." —*Laura, Saint Paul, Minnesota*

"We bring books to donate to a local Christmas program."

—*Langhorne, Covington, Virginia*

"We got involved with the local chapter of Big Brothers/Big Sisters. Now we all meet together once a month, all the Big and Little Brothers and Sisters, and talk about a kid or young adult book we've all read in our individual pairs."

—*Jaime, Chicago, Illinois*

BRING IN A PROFESSIONAL FACILITATOR

Now of course, for obvious reasons, we think professional facilitators are a superb idea, and we meet with some book groups each and every month. But others use our services just once a year for a particularly demanding book or to help reinvigorate the group on a special occasion. Hiring someone trained in leading book group discussions shouldn't make you dependent on that person; it should give you the resources and models you need to make your discussion satisfying every time, even when the facilitator isn't there. Check your local library or bookstore, or go to www.goodbookslately.com to find a facilitator in your area. Sometimes it's nice to just sit back and relax and let someone else do the work. That person doesn't have to be a book group expert, either. As Ellen from Eden Prairie, Minnesota, points out below, it's rewarding to have someone who has some kind of expertise related to the book speak to your group. For example, if you're reading *Girl with a Pearl Earring* or *Girl in Hyacinth Blue,* consider asking a docent from your art museum or a curator from a local gallery to speak to your group about Vermeer. If you're reading *Bel Canto,* you could call the political science department

Book Group Leaders Advise

And now a few words from the Voices of Experience. If you are interested in becoming a book group leader, either professionally or casually, you may want to check in with these two venerable visionaries who've been active in this arena for over thirty years.

Bob of Boulder, Colorado, is a Methodist minister, currently serving as chaplain of the Jefferson County Detention Center. In the thirty-two years of his ministry, he has founded a successful book group at each of his four churches. Bob was originally inspired by his mother, who had been an enthusiastic member of her church book group (one that discussed primarily nonreligious books). "When I became ordained, I knew I wanted to start a group like that," Bob says. Borrowing a name from an article in a Methodist magazine, Bob called his groups The Order of Literate Laity. He still participates in the one he started at Mountain View Methodist Church.

The Order of Literate Laity decides as a group what to read. Bob brings in his ideas just like everyone else. His trusted sources of inspiration include reviews from the *New York Times Book Review,* the *Atlantic Monthly,* the *Washington Post,* the *Christian Science Monitor,* the *Bloomsbury Review,* and the local *Rocky Mountain News.* He also depends on the "wonderful recommendations" of his local bookstore (Tattered Cover). The pastor says his group likes to choose books that are controversial, intense, that address hot social issues, even that push certain political buttons. Some of Bob's personal favorites include: *Guns, Germs, and Steel, A Prayer for Owen Meany, The Poisonwood Bible, The Name of the Rose, A Civil Action,* and *Snow Falling on Cedars.* Each month Bob presents a fifteen-minute summary of the book: major highlights of each chapter, important moments, events, and characters (publisher reading guides have been extremely helpful!). He then opens the discussion to the room at large. Bob says he doesn't worry about choosing or leading books that might be too "sensational" for a church group. "I have found that many of the 'little old ladies' are much less embarrassed or taken aback by racy sex than I am. Of course, I have a dual role as their pastor, which makes it even weirder!" As a leader, Bob is guided by the philosophy of book groups building a sense of community and belonging. In our increasingly fractured and stressed society, he says, it's wonderful to see these intergenerational groups of twenty year olds meeting with 'seventysomethings.'

Janet of Chicago, Illinois, started her literary career as a Ph.D. candidate at Northwestern University but found the department less than supportive when she became pregnant. "Things were different back then. One professor pointed out to me, 'If your husband should get a job offer in a different city, we'd be left high and dry. But if we found a job for you, you couldn't move because of your husband.'" Upon request, Janet started book groups for her local Jewish Community Center and for the parents of the children who attended her daughter's nursery school. She wanted to provide something like the quality of the classroom for her groups—intellectually rigorous, challenging, focused. Thirty-six years later Janet is currently leading fourteen groups. Two or three of these have been with Janet for her entire tenure (including the Bernard Horowich JCC!). Her newest group is one of young women in their thirties—mothers of young children who were, at the time of our interview, having great luck with Dante's *Inferno*.

In order to prepare to lead a discussion, Janet rereads the book each and every time. A self-described "mad nipper and clipper," Janet keeps a file on each book she has done (or thinks she might do) with a group—reviews, author profiles, connected themes. Janet loves a good Google search—favorite sources are the *New York Times, The New York Review of Books, The New Yorker,* and *The London Times Literary Supplement.* "If a book belongs to a particular genre (*Madame Bovary*), we look at writing on French literature, its traditions and influences. As a 'big picture' type of person, I like to put a book in some sort of context, to put it back in the world—social, political, philosophical. All arts are central, not peripheral, to society, intrinsic to each other." Janet is interested in

the preponderance of big family epic books in the past couple of years—
*Middlesex, Amazing Adventures of Kavalier & Clay, The Corrections,
Fortress of Solitude*—books that seem "almost nineteenth century in
spirit" yet also focus on comic book characters. "What's this saying about
our culture?" Janet wonders. "Do we need escapists and heroes more
than ever?" She enjoys mixing the old and new in reading choices.
"Everyone's scared of *Ulysees* initially: 'I won't be able to do this!' But the
act of reading and discussing this novel creates a lasting confidence in
reading slowly and closely."

Janet is astounded by incredible media attention to book groups right
now. "It used to be that people didn't know what I did. Now they get it
right away." Yet she feels that there is still some prejudice undermining
the validity of women's intellectual contributions. The Oprah/Jonathon
Franzen conflict, she thinks, is indicative of a commonly held assump-
tion that "women's intellectual activity is not up to par somehow—very
unfortunate and very unfair." Let no such aspersions be cast upon the
family. That nursery school daughter is now a tenured professor of
American Literature at Northwestern, while her mother, for the past four
decades, has fused the experience of classroom and living room into a
completely unique educational opportunity.

at a local college or university and see if a professor there is willing to
share information about Tupac Amaru, the Marxist revolutionary who
inspired Patchett's novel. If you're reading Sebold's *Lovely Bones,* invite
a representative from a spiritual center to speak to your group about
various notions of the afterlife. It's amazing how many people out there
are willing and eager to share their knowledge with a captive audience.
Plus, just having an outside person join you for a meeting can keep you
on your toes in a good way, refresh things a bit, and remind you why
you all liked each other so much in the first place.

Book Group Members Advise

[Please excuse the following gratuitous, self-agrandizing testimonial. We include it to show how powerfully energizing a visit from a professional facilitator can be.]
"Hard to narrow this down, but I give high marks to the two facilitated discussions we have had with *Good Books Lately,* not only because of a great guide and discussion leader, but because book club members came primed and pumped to show their colors and discuss the book in detail. The first event, for *The Group,* was rollicking fun and full of laughter; the second event, a bit darker but rich with discussion of place and character, covered *The Power of the Dog.* (The wine helped loosen our tongues, too, something we usually don't have!) In both cases I think we might have missed these books from earlier eras without the suggestion of Good Books Lately, and they were ripe for deep discussion. I also think GBL showed us a way for the inclusion of all members in the discussion, beginning with going around the circle of members and asking each to pick their most memorable or powerful scene, so that we have fuller, more all-encompassing discussions."

—Jan, Cherry Hills Village, Colorado

"Once during the year we ask a person outside the group to speak (a prison social worker after we read *Newjack: Guarding Sing Sing,* a high school instructor after we read *Another Planet,* a horseracing expert after we read *Seabiscuit*)."

—Ellen, Eden Prairie, Minnesota; Newcomers Club
(of the Southwest Suburbs) Book Group

INVITE THE FAMILY!

We know some of you out there are thinking, "Invite the family? Have you lost your mind? I joined my book group to *escape* my family once a month! It's my only refuge!" That may be true, but consider this: you love your book group experience, and it's an important part of your life. Why not find a way to share it—just once a year!—with those you love? If you have children (especially kids between the ages of nine and thirteen), try reading a young adult book with your group and invite the little ones to join you. They'll feel all grown-up hanging out with the group, and you'll set a great example, showing them that reading is something you do for fun, not just for school. You can build a bridge between the generations moving in the other direction as well. We've worked with many book groups who bring their parents together (or go visit them in assisted-living centers, etc.) for a book group discussion. It's amazing how older folks are inspired to tell their own stories and reminisce after reading a good book set in a time when they were growing up. This can be a real learning experience—for both child and parent. Or consider inviting the spouses for a special meeting. This can get tricky, though, as you can imagine. Marital dynamics come right to the surface when talking about books, especially books with sensitive topics. If you try this, do your best to choose a book that will appeal to everyone.

Book Group Members Relate

"We have a holiday party every year where the spouses/partners/whatever bring a book. We've had some really good meetings come from those books."

—*Nancy, Lafayette, Colorado*

"We had a great Harry Potter costume party with our spouses/partners invited. We read the first book and dressed as characters from the book. We ate Muggle stew, played Harry Potter games, and had a scavenger hunt in a house decorated with suspended brooms and owls."

—*Sally, Kansas City, Montana; The Girls, or The Bookworms*

CREATE BOOKEND PAIRINGS

This is one of our very favorite things to do with book groups. Pair up two books that are related in some way—sometimes the less obvious the connection the more intense the discussion, so put on your thinking caps for this one. If you're an industrious group, you can read and discuss both books in one month; however, we find most groups do best when the books are discussed in back-to-back meetings. Here are some of our favorites (we'll let you tease out the connection, but most of them are "revisionist" versions of the original story): *The Hours* and *Mrs. Dalloway*, *Jane Eyre* and *The Wide Sargasso Sea*, *Beowulf* and *Grendel*, *The Tempest* and *Philadelphia Fire*, the Arthurian legends and *The Mists of Avalon*, *Moby-Dick* and *Ahab's Wife*. You can also pair two books by the same author, two books in a series, two books in the same genre, two books with the same setting, two books with similar themes—you get the idea. The nice thing about trying this out is that it expands your conversation and connects it from one meeting to the next, so you're able to look back at what you said last month and bring it into the discussion. If you try this and you like it, you might want to consider doing thematic blocks of reading each year—say, six months of Latin American fiction, or four months of modernist fiction, or three months of novels set during WWI.

Book Group Members Advise

"[We had] a double-book night that featured a contrast of Louis L'Amour's *Last of the Breed* with Slavomir Rawicz's *Long Walk* and included a letter from the author of *The Long Walk*."

—*Betty, Grand Saline, Texas; Friends of the Library Book Discussion Group*

GET THE JUICES FLOWING WITH
CREATIVE DISCUSSION

We're always on the lookout for creative ideas to get the discussion going, and these book groups have some great ones. Sometimes it just takes a little ingenuity to pick things up when the pace starts to slow!

Book Groups Propose

"Each of us writes a question about the book on a piece of paper. Then I cut up the questions, fold them up, throw them in a hat, and we take turns leading the question we draw."

—*Elaine, Denver, Colorado*

"If the discussion is flagging, we have an Activity Bag to resort to—containing slips of paper with ideas and discussion topics on them—someone pulls out a slip, and off we go again!"

—*Mary, Bicester, Oxfordshire, United Kingdom.*

"One of our members could not make the meeting when we were discussing *Back Roads* by Tawni O'Dell. So she sent an E-mail to the hostess with her comments. One of the other members read her E-mail to the group, point by point. After each point was made, we either agreed or disagreed with each of the statements. We had one of the longest book discussions ever!"

—*Sue, Coatesville, Pennsylvania*

"The book group's host of the month always prepares notes on the author's life and works, and every host has given us a surprise at one time or another. For *The Count of Monte Cristo* by Alexandre Dumas, the host plotted out the timelines of the book and corresponding social and political events."

—*Kathy, Austin, Texas; "For Culture We Must Suffer" Book Group*

"We choose an author and each read something different by that author. We then discuss common themes, differences between the books, etc. We have done Robert Frost's poems and Ernest Hemingway's works."

—*Eileen, Canadian Lakes, Michigan; Monday Morning Book Club*

DO SOMETHING SILLY AND EASY,
JUST FOR FUN

Ever feel like your book group is more work than it's worth? Is your group getting too serious? Have you read too many heavy-hitting titles in a row? Then listen to these book group members—they've got some absurd ideas to put the lightness back in your book group step. Don't be afraid to get silly with your group! This is supposed to be fun, right?

Book Group Members Give Hints

"We start each book discussion with a toast: 'To good friends, good books, good yard saling—yada, yada, yada.' Small, embossed, silver chalices 'stolen' for a mere pittance at a yard sale are used for this toast."

—*Janet, Fleetwood, Pennsylvania; Stodgy Tomes*

"Everyone brings their favorite children's book and reads it aloud. Everyone brings their favorite movie clip to share. Make up book titles that would best suit each book club member. Each member brings a favorite book to give to a member who is moving away." —*Julie, Jackson Hole, Wyoming*

"One book we read had a very pompous author that used all of these words that we had never heard of and the leader did a vocab quiz where you had to match the word to the definition. It was hilarious." —*Shari, Westin, Massachusetts*

7

"A Thousand Different Types": An Assortment of Diverse, Distinctive Book Groups

Americans of all ages, all stations of life, and all types of disposition are forever forming associations. There are not only commercial and industrial associations in which all take part, but others of a thousand different types—religious, moral, serious, futile, very general and very limited, immensely large and very minute.

—ALEXIS DE TOCQUEVILLE, *DEMOCRACY IN AMERICA, 1831*

In conducting our book group survey, we heard from book groups of all shapes and sizes, with all kinds of membership, and reading tastes, and discussion habits. Each respondent was asked to give us a word that describes the personality of his or her group, and here are just a few:

eclectic	social	lost
cozy	intense	chaotic
diverse	bold	smart
yuppie	weary	fun
comfortable	inquisitive	vibrant
low-key	elderly	thoughtful
serious	insatiable	loyal

nonintellectual	challenging	zany
lively	life-affirming	accepting
supportive	intellectual	thought-provoking
middle-aged	noisy	committed
relaxed	critical	harmonious
wacky	gregarious	well-read
mouthy	vocal	exuberant
passionate	vivacious	open
informal	friendly	neighborly
opinionated	dynamic	adventurous
erratic	engaged	energetic

As we point out in chapter 1, the explosion of interest in book groups in the late 1990s resulted in the creation of increasingly diverse book groups. We've selected some fascinating facts from a varied bunch and include them here (in no particular order). As you'll see, each group is organized differently: around reading interests, associations, professions, regions, political or social convictions. By no means do these groups represent *all* book groups out there—just enough to get you thinking about the possibilities. We've identified some general group "types," and we've included one piece of information that captures the character of each group: a description of the book group's mission, a juicy blurb for a favorite book group book, or a tale of a book that bombed. The stereotypical image of book group members doesn't necessarily hold anymore: as you'll see, they're not all necessarily white, middle-class, educated, suburban stay-at-home moms (and even when groups share similar demographics, their reading interests and discussion experience make them unique). We hope you'll enjoy reading these delicious tidbits and discovering just how varied book groups can be!

SERIOUS-MINDED, LITERARY BOOK GROUP

"For Culture We Must Suffer"

Kathy
Austin, Texas

BOOK GROUP MISSION

Any book club claiming it reads great literature cannot dodge the fiction of Henry James, and just one month after our formation, we put ourselves to the task. Our choice was *Portrait of a Lady*. Raring and avid, we sallied forth on our trek, keen to explore a novel at the very pinnacle of greatness. At our meeting, after a month of Herculean exertions, what a relief to confess it was an exhausting climb. From the heights, we acknowledged the view: the rarefied literary achievement and artistry, magnificent plotting, the eye-opening psychological examination of consciousness, the grand sweep of his sentences, and his pinpoint clarity of observation. Naïve and ungrateful, perhaps, but not one of us enjoyed the trip. That's right: we did not enjoy reading this book. Let's not mince words. It was worse than that. We suffered the entire way through. Was it time to concede we were lost, that our group might be beyond redemption, might never love or revel in the great tomes of Mr. James or in the masterpieces of other greats? Time to backtrack to the ground level of Danielle Steele? Hold on. At the end of the meeting, a club member unfolded a small clipping from the *New York Times Magazine* of the previous Sunday. All doubt was clarified as she quoted from a letter to the editor from a man [who suffered through a long reading of Henry James at his local bookstore, during which the annoyed reader told the slowly disappearing audience, "For culture, you must suffer!"]. Of course! That was it! Even if redemption was impossible, we were staying put: just apply the soothing balm of validation, keep climbing, and, in the name of culture, suffer. For Culture We Must Suffer. The name was swiftly adopted by a unanimous vote.

WE JUST WANT AN INFORMAL,
FUN CHAT BOOK GROUP

Books and Bites

Sue
Coatesville, Pennsylvania

BOOK GROUP BOMB

The Shipping News by Annie Proulx has become a running joke with our group. None of us had read this book prior to it being voted as a pick. One of the members had suggested it, and it sounded rather interesting. It also tends to pop up on other book clubs' lists of favorite reads. Well, how did we go wrong? It was not well received. Now, there were several members who thought it was okay, but most of the members hated it and some never even finished it. We have had some good laughs over it, and it was a memorable pick.

WE'RE ALL NEIGHBORS
BOOK GROUP

Mariana Cove Neighborhood Book Discussion Group

Phyllis
Loveland, Colorado

BOOK GROUP FAVORITE

The Diary of Mattie Spenser by Sandra Dallas, a fictionalized account of a young woman marrying a man she barely knows and leaving with him immediately after the wedding to establish a home on the western prairie, presents a realistic picture of pioneer life from a woman's perspective. All is not as it seems. Mattie must make difficult decisions. Readers differ on their reactions to these choices.

GREAT BOOKS FOUNDATION
BOOK GROUP

Rockhill Book Club

Dalene
Kansas City, Missouri

BOOK GROUP MISSION

We grew out of an adult Great Books group hosted as a class at a community college twenty-five years ago. After only one semester, we became an autonomous group, meeting in members' homes. We work hard to find literature that operates on multiple levels, contains "controversy" or room for interpretation, provides different points of view, and invites literary analysis. We try to select readings that challenge us to think and grow intellectually (perhaps things we might not read on our own) and that engage us in challenging and enjoyable discussions. We find that these little masterpieces generate terrific discussions and lend themselves quite well to careful literary analysis.

BEEN TOGETHER MANY, MANY YEARS
BOOK GROUP

The Girls, or The Bookworms

Sally
Kansas City, Missouri

BOOK GROUP MISSION

Read, drink, and be merry. We came together thirty-three years ago, after college. We were all in the same high school class (forty-two girls graduated, and any of the forty-two who live in Kansas City are welcomed into the group; presently there are ten of us). We see ourselves as "compatible through conflict"—loyal and constant in spite of very differing life views and opinions.

WE'RE ALL NEW TO THE AREA
BOOK GROUP

Newcomers Club

Ellen
Eden Prairie, Minnesota

BOOK GROUP MISSION

The group was formed by members of Newcomers Club of the Southwest Suburbs (of Minnesota's Twin Cities) to provide a means of socialization for new residents of our community. As well as socialization, we receive intellectual stimulation from being members of the group, and our horizons have been broadened through interaction with women from throughout the country.

20-SOMETHING BOOK GROUP

Shirley's Angels

Shirley
Flagstaff, Arizona

BOOK GROUP BOMB

Our worst-ever book discussion happened when we tried to read something we thought would be "good" for us. Most of us graduated from college a few years ago, and we started the group when we realized we missed reading and weren't going to read much unless we were forced to. That sounds terrible, I know, but we're all so busy, we just wouldn't make the time if we didn't have our book group. Anyway, maybe we were feeling nostalgic or something, but we decided to read *Moby-Dick* because none of us had read it in school. Only two of us finished it. The discussion lasted about ten minutes. But that wasn't the worst part. We decided to try another tactic and this time choose a book by an author we all knew and liked. So the next time we met, we discussed Barbara Kingsolver's *The Bean Trees*. Actually, I'm using the word "discussed" loosely. There really wasn't any discussion because we all just kept saying how much we loved it. We decided from then on to avoid these kinds of books—both kinds.

WE'RE ALL MOTHERS OF TODDLERS
BOOK GROUP

Prettiest Town and the Dixie Chicks
Book Club

Brenda
Cheraw, South Carolina

BOOK GROUP MISSION

The group started seven or eight years ago, when a group of pool moms discovered they had a common interest in books and read the same types of books. As the children floundered about in the water, we got excited hearing about the books our neighbors had read and began swapping books. Alas, summer ended; though sad, we still wanted to talk about our books. So we began meeting once a month at a home and made plans to read the same books so we all knew what was going on. It's been great fun! Our group's membership has changed over the years, but our laid-back formula has been great, especially for those who find themselves overwhelmed at times. We read a variety of genres and try to keep a healthy balance between what we consider a "beach" read and some more intellectual works.

MOTHER-DAUGHTER BOOK GROUP

Moms and Gals Book Club

Julie and Sara
Amsterdam, New York

BOOK GROUP MISSION

My ten-year-old daughter, Sara, and her best friend, Allison, love to read; and after I read about mother-daughter book groups in the newspaper, I thought I might try to start one. Turns out Allison's mom was interested, too, so we got a copy of Shireen Dodson's book *The Mother-Daughter Book Club* and put a sign up in the library asking other mothers and daughters to join us. Now we have eight pairs of "moms and gals" in our group, and we meet once a month to discuss a new book. We let the girls choose the books. At first I think the moms all thought we'd have to force the girls to talk or at least make sure we weren't taking over the discussion. We had nothing to worry about! They go on and on without us, and usually we're the ones who leave the meeting seeing the book in a whole new way. The toughest part is trying not to talk with Sara about the book before we meet with our group. We sneak in a little discussion with each other now and then (don't tell our group—it's against the rules!). This is one of the best things I've ever done with my daughter. I've met all these other moms with daughters Sara's age, Sara's made new friends with girls from different schools, and we're able to talk about things in a whole new way. I just hope this carries over into her teenage years!

FATHER-SON BOOK GROUP

The Curse of the Bambino Book Club

Jack and Braxton
Brookline, Massachusetts

BOOK GROUP MISSION

I'm a single dad, and I wanted to spend more time with my son, Braxton (he just started junior high). He's a rough-and-tumble kind of kid, obsessed with the Red Sox like every other male in my family. I thought I'd better try to get him interested in something other than baseball. He'd never been much of a reader, but a friend of mine suggested that I give him a copy of *For Love of the Game*. He loved it and wanted more books on baseball. He started reading Kinsella's books; and when he talked to his English teacher about it, she told him about her husband's book club. Long story short, it's a father-son club with boys about Braxton's age, and he dragged me along. We read mostly sports novels. Right now, I'm reading *The Brothers K*, and I think we'll try it with our group. It's a hard one, but I think we can do it.

The Personalities in Your Book Group: Understanding and Making the Most of Each Individual Reader

Our opinions and observations about any book frequently reveal something very essential about our character, as does the way we make (or avoid making) these observations. As we come to appreciate the multitude of different ways people experience the world, we can learn something more about our own unique approach to existence. You don't join a book club, obviously, so you can enhance your intolerance of everyone who isn't exactly like you or so you can remain happily ignorant of other people's troubling perspectives. Check out the nine personality profiles below and see if you can find one that reminds you of anyone in your group. Perhaps this may help you appreciate the particular contributions of another member—even someone that you find chronically irritating—or inspire you to think about your own participation in a new way. These very basic profiles are inspired by a personality-typing system called the Enneagram. Check out Dr. Helen Palmer's or Don Richard Riso's works on the subject if you'd like to explore the types in more depth.

THE IDEALISTIC PERFECTIONIST

Idealists know their own minds. For them, there is a clear division between right and wrong, an ultimate reality of Truth and Justice. Idealists are happiest on the side of a good cause, especially when they are joined by others who are also seeking a higher path. Most perfectionists have a certain "control freak" quality and can become frustrated or depressed when life doesn't match up to their lofty expectations. A book group member of this type will maintain a certain fresh capacity for outrage each time he or she is confronted by irresponsibility or laziness. Such members are invaluable to any group in terms of the high standards they will inspire, perhaps in terms of creating or sustaining a highly effective organization, suggesting tactics to promote insightful discussion, or selecting the most promising books. Idealists are natural crusaders, and most will take their campaign into a book group discussion; they don't suffer fools gladly, either within the pages of the book or within the commentary of the group. It's important to remember that an outspoken Idealist is not trying to pick a fight with you just for the sake of argument but because he or she feels it's important to get to "the truth." **Famous Idealists:** Mahatma Gandhi, Margaret Thatcher, Al Gore, Martha Stewart, Joan of Arc, Mr. Spock of *Star Trek*, Nathan Price of *Poisonwood Bible*, Mr. Darcy of *Pride and Prejudice*.

THE SELFLESS GIVER

Is there a person in your book group who might stand a chance to win the award for Nicest Person in the World? Such Givers are consistently kind and responsive, always asking, "What can I do for you?" They feel most secure and valued when they can serve others in some way, but it's hard to give most of them a compliment. Praise a Giver and get some version of the response, "It was nothing, and anyone could have done it much better than I could." The Giver of your book group will stand out for sweetness of temper and willingness to serve the needs of the group. Perhaps because the internal world of these Givers is so generous and accommodating, some can take forever to get to a point, while others seem to leap from thought to thought in a perfect flurry of non sequiturs. If your book group is graced by the presence of a rambling speaker, interrupt gently and ask for clarity. Or, if this voluble member has fired off several brilliant starting points of discussion in a row, you might say, "Wow, so many great questions—which one should we talk about first?" **Famous Givers:** Mother Teresa, Eleanor Roosevelt, Richard Simmons,

Princess Diana, Melanie Hamilton of *Gone With the Wind*, King Arthur of *The Once and Future King,* Marmee of *Little Women.*

THE STAR PERFORMER

Scratch the surface of a highly motivated and attractively charming person, and you'll likely find a turbo-powered Performer smiling beneath. Many of the most prestigious and powerful people of the Western society are Performers—our fast-paced, status-oriented culture provides a stimulating climate in which such energetic people can thrive. Performers strive to distinguish themselves in whatever manner and medium their particular social environment deems most valuable. In an effort to help the book group become the best on the block, an organized Performer might be the member to find some great new outside book group resource or to arrange for a distinguished speaker to visit. Sometimes a preternaturally social Performer may have a certain amount of trouble sticking to the topic of the book rather than sharing a personal story or may be caught whispering with his or her neighbor while another speaker has the floor. Rely on your leader or "gatekeeper" to bring the conversation back on the book track. **Famous Performers:** Bill Clinton, Tom Cruise, Whitney Houston, Jennifer Lopez, Annette Benning's character in the film *American Beauty,* Rachel Price of *Poisonwood Bible,* Mrs. Rachel Lynde of *Anne of Green Gables.*

THE ROMANTIC INDIVIDUALIST

Individualists exhibit a passionate investment in self-expression and self-actualization, and most will strongly resist conformity or confinement. The Individualist doesn't want to go with the crowd but with his or her own personal flow. This maverick's intense imagination fosters a highly personal inner world. Such people are compelled by beauty and creativity, often choosing careers in the arts. They will most likely make their strongest mark when it comes to unique book choices and discussion, will be drawn to passionate stories, strange characters, wild situations, and surreal coincidences. Because the Individualist has the natural gift for zeroing in on what is special in even the most ordinary of circumstances, this member will bring some very different and unexpected insights to your discussion. Wise book group members will take the time to follow up on an idea or perspective that they don't understand, even if it initially seems mysteriously off-base. **Famous Individualists:** Michael Jackson, Judy Garland, Virginia Woolf, Bob Dylan, Andy Warhol, Cathy and Heathcliff of *Wuthering Heights,* Blanche Dubois of *Streetcar Named Desire.*

THE INTELLECTUAL OBSERVER

It's hard to tell an Observer anything that he or she doesn't already know. Observers have an absolutely rapacious appetite for knowledge of all kinds. These "brainiacs" are the scientists, theorists, philosophers, and innovators of the human race. Observers tend to keep just on the edge of your group, watching, listening, evaluating. They shine brightest in one-on-one conversation, focusing intently and sharing some scarily accurate hypotheses. Such eggheads tend to be fairly private—open with their opinions, if someone asks, but reserved about their feelings and convictions. Most Observers have two discussion modes: on and off. When they do have a contribution to make, Observers will be eager to convey this information in the most comprehensive manner possible. In their efforts to present the listener with the "whole picture," they are sometimes prone to slip into "dissertation" mode, to settle back into coherent but lengthy diatribes on the subject of their expertise. Most Observers won't mind if you ask for the "short version." **Famous Observers:** Albert Einstein, Stanley Kubrick, Sigmund Freud, Emily Dickenson, Stephen Hawking, Arthur Conan Doyle's Sherlock Holmes, Meryl Streep,

Mary Shelly's Frankenstein (the doctor, not the monster), Velma of the cartoon *Scooby Doo*, and Data from *Star Trek: The Next Generation*

THE DEVIL'S ADVOCATE

The Devil's Advocate is the person who questions everything, who tests people and things and situations, looking for hidden landmines. Devil's Advocates are looking for something to believe in, but their default mode is one of doubt and skepticism. They are by nature extremely loyal and loving people, but it takes time and consistency to earn their trust. Advocates are constantly anticipating the worst-case scenario, which tends to make them run very hot and cold. As the most paradoxical of personalities, they are "easy to like but hard to get to know." Notoriously quirky, charming, usually blessed with a wonderfully dry sense of humor, Advocates are generally very self-aware, even of their own most oxymoronic leanings. The Advocate in your book group will be invaluable in providing an alternative viewpoint to a majority consensus of opinion, questioning any judgments of character or situation that seem too easy or facile. Occasionally, the Advocate will disagree simply to challenge the group assessment, even if he or she secretly concurs. **Famous Advocates:** Malcolm X, Marilyn Monroe, Richard Nixon, Marilyn Manson, Hawkeye of *M.A.S.H.*, Jane Fonda, Rev. Jim Jones, Shakespeare's Othello and Hamlet.

THE PLAYFUL HEDONIST

No one does fun quite like a Hedonist. These pleasure seekers enjoy themselves like no other personality type, often packing in a staggering amount of activities and events into a single day. While Hedonists may resemble outgoing Performers in their seemingly endless enthusiasm for energetic group activity, their core motivation is a different one. Performers like to stay in the thick of things so they can please themselves by pleasing others; Hedonists strive to surround themselves with interesting people and entertaining activity for the sheer thrill of motion and choice. They will engage in book group organization and discussion with gusto but will prefer to keep things "light" rather than heavy or deep. Intelligent Hedonists will eagerly take part in complicated intellectual arguments, but they won't want to dwell on intensely negative topics nor stick with emotionally weighty group discussions. This can be a frustrating characteristic for members who feel the Hedonist is circumventing a thorough postmortem but an energizing element for a group that might get bogged down too often in existential angst or despair. **Famous Hedonists:** John Belushi, John F. Kennedy, Bette Midler, Goldie Hawn, Moll Flanders, Miss Piggy, Peter Pan.

THE CHARISMATIC BOSS

The Boss is always the "biggest" person in any room. These people are the natural leaders of any group—extremely outgoing, articulate, witty, often very funny. They "take command" of people and situations; it's usually impossible to ignore their presence. Bosses like things to run smoothly, but they aren't afraid of confrontation. These powerful leaders enjoy a good challenge from a worthy opponent; they feel invigorated by the chance to match wits or to test their strength. The Boss in your book group may not be the official leader of the group, but you will definitely be aware of his or her guiding hand and forceful opinions. Despite the unmistakable confidence and charisma of most Bosses, they often aren't aware of just how overwhelming they can be—some of their bravura masks a hidden insecurity that they aren't as invincible as their self-presentation would suggest. **Famous Bosses:** Martin Luther King Jr., Frank Sinatra, Janet Reno, Barbara Walters, Roseanne, Saddam Hussein, and Darth Vader.

THE EASYGOING MEDIATOR

Do you remember the book *I'm OK—You're OK*? This is the dominant worldview of the laid-back Mediator. The Mediator's natural mode is one of all-inclusive accessibility; these are people who can always (or almost always) see both sides of the question. In this they resemble the Devil's Advocate, but Mediators seek to smooth things over rather than stir things up. Because Mediators can see most issues or choices from a wide variety of perspectives, they tend to look on most as equally valid— "She's got a good point, but his point is good, too." The Mediators in your book group will generally provide a calming and comforting presence as they will usually attempt to keep discussion fair and balanced, intense but not chaotic. On the other hand, the too-agreeable Mediator can be frustrating in the tendency to remain on the fence, exhibiting an unwillingness to make a stand for one idea over another. **Famous Mediators:** Abraham Lincoln, Ronald Reagan, Janet Jackson, Edith Bunker of *All in the Family,* Gen Watanabe of *Bel Canto*, Marge Simpson of *The Simpsons*.

BOOKSTORE BOOK GROUP

WordsWorth Book Club

Janet
Cambridge, Massachusetts

BOOK GROUP FAVORITE

One of our best discussions happened when we decided to read something completely different. We're all avid readers—we met at Wordsworth Book Store in Harvard Square—and we'd been reading all the popular book group books: *The Poisonwood Bible* and *Bel Canto* and *The Lovely Bones*. Good reads, all of them, but we wanted to try a new genre. "How about science fiction?" one member suggested. Turns out a lot of us had heard about *The Sparrow*, so we decided to read it for our next meeting. Oh my god. Half of us (and I mean half, six against six) LOVED the book and half of us HATED it. We'd never had that happen before, and it was surprisingly great! We argued back and forth for hours. I must admit, if the book had been more serious, I don't think we would have felt so free to air our strong opinions. But the heated debate was fun.

LIBRARY BOOK GROUP

Friends of the Library Book Discussion Group

Betty
Grand Saline, Texas

BOOK GROUP BOMB

James Joyce's *Dubliners* stopped all of our members in their tracks, and only one faithful member could even finish the book. Discussion consisted of incredulous amazement at the book's standing in the literary world.

CHURCH/SYNAGOGUE BOOK GROUP

The Friends of Lorraine, a Reading Group

Felicia
Charlotte, North Carolina

BOOK GROUP MISSION

Our group was started as part of an Emmaus offering for St. Matthew Church to reach out to new members and develop a camaraderie. We now even have members who do not belong to our church, so we have accomplished our embracement of others. We have a list of those waiting to join. Our name, the Friends of Lorraine, came about after we lost one of our charter members to cancer. Lorraine was an avid reader, and we wanted to honor her. We have donated books in her name to an assisted-living facility.

ON-LINE BOOK GROUP

ANZ LitLovers

Lisa
Melbourne, Victoria, Australia

BOOK GROUP MISSION

The group was formed to discuss Australian literary fiction because other E-groups were dominated by international literature, and the inclusion of Aussie books was rare. My comoderator and I set it up as a closed group because we didn't want to have to keep explaining local issues or vocabulary/slang to non-Australians. Along the way, we wanted to reach out to other keen readers across this vast continent of ours, and now we have members from every state except Tasmania (and we're working on it!).

INSPIRED BY OPRAH'S BOOK CLUB

The Smoky Mountain Bookers, Not Hookers

Anna
Knoxville, Tennessee

BOOK GROUP MISSION

Our book group started as an Oprah book discussion group, reading and discussing the books Oprah picked for her book club. We started meeting at a bookstore in Knoxville, Tennessee. When the leader of the group moved, she asked me to become the discussion leader, and I was delighted to say yes! When the bookstore closed, we moved to the activity center of a local church. When Oprah was no longer having her book group, we continued and are now choosing the books we discuss. This group is absolutely wonderful. Everyone takes part in the discussion and feels free to offer her opinion. We have a good time!

LESBIAN/FEMINIST BOOK GROUP

The Nine Muses

Eva
Dana Point, California

BOOK GROUP MISSION

Our book club, The Nine Muses, is made up of nine women (we've decided to keep that number, so we won't take another member unless one of us moves away). We live in the same small community, and several of us knew each other from the local art scene. Years ago I was part of a different book club, one that I didn't fit into. This group had read Dorothy Allison and decided that her work was "too dark" and "too feminist." She's one of my favorite authors, so that was a clue I was in the wrong group. I left. Now this may not seem like a good way to start a group, but I was so bitter, I decided I would start my own group and would invite only women who loved Dorothy Allison's books as much as I do. Turns out it was a good litmus test—better than I could have hoped if I had planned it. The nine of us are all feminist-lesbian-artists, and we bring this point of view to everything we read.

GAY MEN'S BOOK GROUP

Colorado Springs Gay Male Fiction Book Club

Paul
Colorado Springs, Colorado

BOOK GROUP FAVORITE
The World of Normal Boys by K. M. Soehnlein is a great coming-of-age story. Good boy goes bad . . . and that's good. About growing up, being a teenager in the late seventies, being tossed around by friends, parents, and other people without knowing where to stand or what to do. Drugs, sex, rebellion, longing, and rage.

COUPLES BOOK GROUP

The Saving Grace Book Club

Elayne and John
Denver, Colorado

BOOK GROUP FAVORITE
Our group is made up of middle-aged married couples. Can you guess why we call it the Saving Grace Book Club? Some of us have joked that this little club has saved our marriages on more than one occasion. We met at a seminar at the Tattered Cover Book Store. Kira put us all together because we mentioned that we wanted to be in a co-ed

group with our spouses. Here we are, about eight years later, still going strong. Our favorite book group book is *The Republic of Love* by Carol Shields. It's about two middle-aged people who fall in love, and the story is told from alternating points of view, first the woman's, then the man's, and so on. We had a fabulous discussion of this book. Some of the men thought the author's male character was a caricature, and others thought he was right on. We wish there were more books like that, told from both points of view. It's a perfect kind of book for our group since we tend to see things in a "male/female" way, and we're constantly on the lookout for books that will appeal to all of us.

The Book Group Hall of Shame

Book group people are smart people, no doubt about it. But just like the rest of us, they occasionally make a mistake. Sometimes this mistake can turn into a legendary story for the whole group to cherish for years. . . .

"We had a member under house arrest for white-collar crime, and we had to vote as to whether or not to change our meetings to her house and keep her as a member. I am proud to say she is still with us."   —*Barbara, Norfolk, Virginia*

"One night I returned home from an especially excruciating day at work. I threw on my pajamas, a mud face masque, and settled down with a bottle of red wine. I hadn't had time to take out the trash or the recycling or empty the dishwasher for weeks, and my house was a sty. I was on my fourth glass of wine when the doorbell rang. Five members of my book group were waiting outside. Apparently, not only had I forgotten that it was book group night, but that it was my night to host the group. At least there was enough wine and ramen noodles and frozen pizza for everybody!"   —*Anonymous*

"I belong to a public library group, and one month the reviewer for the meeting had a family emergency and asked me to substitute two hours before the meeting. I frantically prepared for the discussion, only to have NO ONE SHOW UP."   —*Susie, Omaha, Nebraska*

"We were reading *Einstein's Dreams* for our summer read, and I got a call from another member who was attempting to read the book while vacationing with her family. She was complaining that this was the hardest book she had ever read and didn't understand why it had been chosen for our book group. I thought this was a little strange, since she is one of our most intelligent and perceptive members. Imagine all of our surprise when she showed up at the next meeting having read all of Einstein's *Theory of Relativity.*"   —*Anne, Evergreen, Colorado*

"One of our members left the group to live in Japan for two years. When she returned, she mentioned something about her experiences abroad. Another long-term member looked very surprised and asked, 'Oh, were you gone?' Dead silence in the group. Luckily, the returning member has a good sense of humor."

—Mary Jane, Fairfax, Virginia

"We have a holiday party where the men present books. People got so drunk that by the time the men were presenting, a lot of people just talked and didn't listen. I relinquished my position as 'queen of the book group' shortly thereafter."

—Nancy, Lafayette, Colorado

"We were reading T.C. Boyle's *Tortilla Curtain*, and I thought it might be fun to re-create the strict 'have' versus 'have-not' divisions of the book in our meeting. I served half the members an elegant organic spread and the other half cold refried beans out of the can. The organic diners got good silver and the refried bean eaters got a single spork (a spoon-fork hybrid) to share among them. It didn't go over quite as well as I had hoped."

—Ann, Naperville, Illinois

"My friend Rebecca invited me to join her book group for a meeting that was being held at another member's apartment. I read the book (Wally Lamb's *She's Come Undone*) and showed up to join the group for appetizers before the discussion. I introduced myself as Rebecca's friend, and a member told me she was probably running late. I had a great time, but Rebecca never showed. I didn't hear from her until the next day when she called to ask why I hadn't come to her book group. Get this: I got the address right but the apartment number wrong. Two totally unrelated book groups were meeting in that complex on the same evening at the same time to discuss the same book. I joined the one that I crashed because we all got along so well."

—Jolene, Madison, Wisconsin

"We had the privilege of having Nien Cheng, author of *Life and Death in Shanghai*, come to our book club. We were all expecting some little old lady. Well, in she comes, in a gorgeous full-length mink coat and a designer suit. She looked like a million dollars, and we all looked like the little old ladies."

—*Mary Jane, Fairfax, Virginia*

"When I was a leader, I accidentally read and prepared the wrong book: *The Girl with the Pearl Earring* instead of *The Girl in the Picture.*"

—*Rosalind, Zionsville, Indiana*

"Our member Sandy was spending a few months in Florida. Another member suggested we all take a week and drive down to visit her for our meeting on *Ahab's Wife*. Everyone was packed and ready to go when the infamous "Beast of the East" storm put an abrupt halt to our trip down south. To top it off, the author of the book was in Florida at the time: Sandy was able to meet her and get autographed copies of her book for all of us. After we got dug out, the five of us met at a chilly local eating place (instead of a warm beachside café) for our discussion. This was one meeting of the Stodgy Tomes that we will never forget!"

—*Janet DeAngelo, Fleetwood, Pennsylvania*

"A member of our group had just gone through a nasty divorce—cheating husband and all that—when we formed the book club. Coincidentally, our very first book choice dealt with the theme of a cheating husband (*Sullivan's Island*). Three selections later we read another book with this theme (*The Pilot's Wife*). Our rather new divorcée got a bit disgruntled with us, and with the author, for giving the 'wronged woman' true love and happiness by page 300. 'True love does not come quickly after an ugly divorce!' she said. 'And can we please avoid this theme for a while?' We have." —*Stephanie, Hays, Kansas; Read 'em and Reap Book Club*

"Our boisterous group met at a fondue restaurant one time, and the waiters asked us all about our group and the book we had read. We all hated the book so much that we handed every copy to the waiters on the way out the door!"

—*Jennifer, Redwood City, California; We're Booked Up! Book Group*

COED BOOK GROUP

Swingin' Singles

Camille
Perry, Florida

BOOK GROUP MISSION

I didn't want to be in a book group of just women, so a neighbor told me about the book group she's in with her husband. I can't imagine anything worse than trying to talk about books in a room full of couples. So I asked some people at work if they'd like to start a book group with me. Our group has seven men and six women, most of them from our company. We're not real formal, and we don't like to have to cook and all that, so we meet at various bars and restaurants around town. Most of us are single, and once in a while we bring a new person to the group. At first we called ourselves Swingin' Singles, but now that two members of the group are getting married, we might have to change our name. If people keep hooking up, I might have to find myself a new group.

CROSSING GENERATIONS
BOOK GROUP

Books Anonymous

Margaret
Charleston, South Carolina

BOOK GROUP BOMB

Many people don't understand our name until we explain that we're in BA, Books Anonymous, a twelve-step program for people addicted to books. I think our group is special because our oldest member just turned eighty-nine and our youngest member is seventeen (I'm right in the middle). Our worst book group experience was when we discussed a book by Penelope Lively called *Moon Tiger*. Now I've enjoyed some of her other novels, but this one I did not like. And it caused a problem in our group because it raises a delicate topic: incest. The narrator is a woman with a brain disorder who looks back on her life and recalls a sexual relationship with her brother. I must tell you that the older ladies in our group were not prepared for that, and some of them didn't finish the book once they got to that part. The younger women wanted to talk about it, but it was too upsetting. That was the only time I remember our group not being able to bridge the gap between our generations.

RETIRED WOMEN BOOK GROUP

We're Retired, Not Tired

JoAnn
Englewood, Colorado

BOOK GROUP FAVORITE

I hadn't thought about Mary McCarthy's *The Group* in years. Then a member of my book group said she saw it in Good Books Lately's newsletter, and we decided to read it. Many of us had read it before, but it had been years and years. It was very different the second time around. I think we were all surprised by how naïve the girls in the book seem. And we were also discouraged that things have changed so little since then, for women I mean. All but two of us are retired high school English teachers, so we talked about the style of the book and the setting and the way McCarthy sort of tears apart her characters. It was the closest thing to a "classic" we've done in our group (we've all taught classics for too long to want to read them again), and it was a real success.

BUSINESS BOOK GROUP

Just Book It, a Book Club

Monty
Dallas, Texas

BOOK GROUP MISSION

One of the goals of a private dining and business club of ClubCorp is to develop "clubs-within-a-club" as a tool for members and guests to connect with one another. In 1995 one of the members strongly urged the club to support the formation of a book club. We did, and the group has grown, and true friendships have been established, reestablished, and nurtured. The one main goal was to select not only a variety of books but to intentionally seek out books that normally would not be seen on our nightstands. I can honestly say that I am quite certain that we may be the only book club in the world to have Dr. Phil as a guest author!

LAWYERS AND PARALEGALS
BOOK GROUP

Law and Disorder

Ruth
Richmond, Virginia

BOOK GROUP FAVORITE

Revolutionary Road by Richard Yates is a modern classic about an "average" couple of the *Donna Reed Show* era, who try to rise above the banality of their suburban surroundings. Not quite as cynical as *The Ice Storm*, this book had the men and women in our group pitted against each other as we tried to defend the attitudes and actions of the male and female protagonists. There is at least a small piece of this book for each person to relate to, whether it is emotional, situational, or intellectual.

WRITERS BOOK GROUP

Writers, Inc.

Alan
Los Angeles, California

BOOK GROUP MISSION

We're a group of freelance screenwriters who started a book club because, frankly, people in this city don't read. Especially in the film industry. Strange but true. We read the usual book group stuff. I think our only challenge is not to be too critical when we discuss it. It's hard sometimes to be a writer and read for pleasure. I think we look at things differently, from a writerly perspective, and we're constantly analyzing how the author puts things together instead of just letting ourselves get pulled into the story. At least that's how I read. In the last few years, our group has read book after book that's been adapted into film. The only problem is, being in our profession, we tend to see the movies first, and that colors the way we read the book.

SELF-HELP BOOK GROUP

Living on Purpose Discussion Group

Nancy
Philadelphia, Pennsylvania

BOOK GROUP MISSION

[We recently celebrated] the fourth anniversary of our Living on Purpose discussion group at Barnes & Noble. Four years of reading books that assist in our living a rich, fulfilling life! To celebrate, we

[went] back to the book that started it all: *Coaching for a Rich, Fulfilling Life* and talk[ed] about how our lives have changed over the last four years as we've share[d] successes, possibilities, laughter, and the joy of being a community.

MIDWESTERN BOOK GROUP

Lone Tree Readers

Jackie
Central City, Nebraska

BOOK GROUP MISSION
Our group has several retired teachers and other retirees. We enjoy some of the classics and authors from our state of Nebraska, such as Willa Cather, Mari Sandoz, Bess Streeter Aldrich. Most of us have visited the locations that these books describe and feel a personal attachment to the authors. We are midwesterners who stretch ourselves to try to understand other parts of the country while holding fast to the values of our moral, conservative upbringings.

AFRICAN-AMERICAN BOOK GROUP

The Hue-Man Experience Book Club

Geneva
Denver, Colorado

BOOK GROUP FAVORITE
We've read everything by Toni Morrison—her novels, her essays, even some of her children's books. Many years ago our group was started by Denver's African-American bookstore, the Hue-Man Experience. Our group has changed over time, but we keep reading Toni Morrison because she defines what it means to be a strong black woman in America.

We do read books by other African-American authors, and we're glad to discover a new voice in our community. Right now we're reading short stories by a young up-and-coming writer named Z. Z. Packer.

MYSTERY BOOK GROUP

Get a Clue Book Club

Annie
Fort Worth, Texas

BOOK GROUP MISSION

In our club we don't discuss the books like other book clubs I've visited. We don't sit down and talk about characters and theme and all that stuff. We're mystery fans. We all read constantly, and most of us read at least two or three books a week. Our club gives us a chance to show each other new authors and to remind ourselves about new books coming out. Sometimes one of our members will give a "book report" on writers who aren't as well known. Then, if any of us pick up books by these authors, we can discuss them and compare them to other authors. That's what we do most of the time, compare authors and enjoy each other's company. It's nice to be with people who love the same kinds of books as much as you do.

SCIENCE FICTION BOOK GROUP

SF Book Club

Matt
Shelby, Montana

BOOK GROUP BOMB

One thing people don't understand is the difference between science fiction and fantasy. I tell people to remember it this way: if there are spaceships and robots in it, it's sci-fi; if there are dragons and wizards, it's fantasy. Some people think this distinction doesn't matter. But when you're a purist like me, it does. Our book club is a SCIENCE FICTION book club. Apparently, one of our new members didn't realize this when he recommended *Eragon* by Christopher Paolini. Now, I can handle Tolkien, but not some eighteen-year-old kid who thinks he's Tolkien. We tore that book to shreds.

ROMANCE BOOK GROUP

In Love with Books

Kay
Pueblo, Colorado

BOOK GROUP MISSION

When I tell people I'm in a romance book group, they look at me like I'm crazy; like all we read are Harlequin novels with Fabio on the cover. We do read those, but we don't usually discuss them in our group. We try to up the ante and find new romance novels. It's hard to find them sometimes, especially when you read as many of them as we do. We all have our favorite authors, and we read them a lot. One recent favorite was *Like Water for Chocolate*. We even made some of the recipes! We just like to escape into a story about love and romance.

8

The Greedy Reader Menu: Read Any Good Books Lately?

> The vital thing is that you have your own favorites—books that are real and genuine, each one brimful of the inspiration of a great soul. Keep these books on a shelf convenient for use, and read them again and again and again until you have saturated your mind with their wisdom and beauty.
>
> —GEORGE HAMILTON FITCH, *COMFORT FOUND IN GOOD OLD BOOKS*

THE WHO WANTS TO BE A MILLIONAIRE QUESTION: WHAT MAKES A GOOD BOOK GROUP BOOK?

What if you could find a way to determine, precisely and without any margin of error, what exactly makes a certain book gain best-selling momentum in the book group world? What if you could predict exactly which books will be a smash hit with book groups? Well, first off, that's kind of creepy—are you channeling Oprah? But if you could do this, then you could, in fact, go ahead and quit your day job.

Of course, there are many people in the publishing world whose jobs are based on the ability to discover and promote wonderful books. There are also lots of "book group experts" like us (although, hopefully, not exactly like us) whose job it is to identify and promote great book club reading. We wish that *we* were the ones who could tell, 100 percent of the time, which books will ignite the torch of the worldwide book group community—we'd be sure to keep our day jobs. But even if we did possess this uncanny power, that wouldn't necessarily make us the best-qualified leaders to recommend good books for book group readers. As we all learned long ago, "popular" and "good" can go hand in hand, but they are not synonyms. It's one thing to predict which books will be popular with book group readers, but it can sometimes be quite another thing to choose the books that will inspire the imagination, arouse the curiosity, challenge the intellect, and start a feisty book group debate.

Let's be clear on this point. The majority of books that have won the hearts and minds of book group readers are verifiably excellent, as book group readers are a very discerning lot. However, we all know of at least one example of a book that was reputed—by someone who allegedly knew her hindquarters from a hole in the ground—to be a fabulous book club read, a smashing discussion vehicle, but which, when our group eagerly pounced on it, turned out to be a major disappointment for one reason or another. There are certain select books (that shall remain mostly nameless) to which countless numbers of our readers and survey respondents have pointed, again and again, as prime examples of the baffling mystery of "popular" taste. Now that we've addressed that little issue, let's move on to the true million-dollar question: *What makes a book a great book group book?*

Book Group Readers Weigh In

"I've found that a lot of the best book group books—the ones that seem to inspire the most lively discussion—are those that feature a culture or a character or situation that is somewhat foreign to us as readers. I don't necessarily mean 'foreign' as in a foreign country, but foreign as in 'not like our everyday lives.' I like to read to see the world from another perspective, so I like to read about people who are different from me in some way, about problems and choices that I will probably never face. I think these kinds of books make for good conversation because there is so much to debate and try to understand." —*Chris, Ann Arbor, Michigan*

"On a fundamental level, I think that most of us like to read and discuss books that we can relate to. I know that I do, anyway. A few of our choices have been so far out in left field that I don't begin to know how to analyze or discuss them. That said, I guess I like books that also inspire us to talk about our own lives . . . to mix a discussion of what's going on in the book with what's going on in nonfictional reality." —*Marguerite, Rockford, Illinois*

"We look for books with controversy . . . stories that invite multiple interpretations, operate on several levels, are open to literary analysis, that deal with some human conflict, some moral or broad issue." —*Dalene, Kansas City, Missouri*

"A novel is like an inkblot, a Rorschach test: the way you respond will reveal something about you." —*Shari, Boston, Massachusetts*

"Anything that features group sex, S&M, bondage, role-playing, etc." —*"Rachel," Ft. Wayne, Indiana*

Anyone who tells you that all book groups are the same doesn't know "Rachel"!

Our Demands for a Fantastic Book Group Book

Compelling Read, Stimulating Discussion

First and foremost, a fantastic book group book must demonstrate its excellence in *both* of the arenas that make up the book group experience. You start out in the private sector, reading by yourself, and then you move on to the public forum, talking about what you've read. In the perfect book group world, each of these two activities should enhance and invigorate the other. An extraordinary book group book is both a fascinating, compelling read *and* a provocative source for energetic, animated discussion. We have all run across a book or two in our time that performed admirably in one aspect but miserably in the other—the book everyone loved but no one had a thing to say about, or the book no one enjoyed reading but everyone had a great time tearing to shreds. It's not that such books have no value whatsoever. But they do not belong in the A-list category. Because there are so many deliriously wonderful books in the world, you can and should demand the best of both worlds when it comes to book group choices.

Now that you're comfortable having it all, what is it, exactly, that makes a particular book the exceptional star in both private and public arenas? Obviously, this is a subjective matter. But since this is our book, we're going to seize the opportunity to lay down the law. Not so much the law, exactly, but the rules of thumb, the guidelines that we consistently use to figure out whether a certain book is, in our estimation, truly great or just kind of good.

Fascinating in Story, Intriguing in Subject

A truly interesting book should be about something interesting. It should feature interesting characters who are individuals, not types. It should bring a strongly individualized world to life—while you're reading this book, you become submerged in the realities of its characters, of its setting, of the particular points of conflict that are specific to this book, and, in a way, to this book only. A great book group book may remind you of another book on a similar topic, but it must occupy a distinctive space all its own. Not every book, even those generally acknowledged as wonderful, compelling, important, can be a great read for every single reader. But the superlative book group book should encourage a fiendish form of addiction in the readers who give it a chance—this book should suck you in, should make you hungry for more. Call us old-fashioned, if you will, but we are putty in the hands of a truly absorbing story.

Distinctive in Style

The books that belong in the very top tiers of the Book Group Greats category are ones that feature a distinctive, commanding, and appealing writing style. Yes, certain stylistic tendencies are more obvious than others, easier to pick up on. It is definitely worthwhile to focus on the intricacies of a certain noteworthy style, but it's okay if you can't describe exactly why a particular writer's word choices do it for you. The main point is that this gifted individual combines words and phrases in such a way as to excite your senses and agitate your imagination, and that's what really matters. Don't waste your time on a stylistically flabby writer or story.

Complex and Challenging

Complexity is a good, good thing. In life, of course, it can be a bad, frustrating, or upsetting thing—sometimes we long for nothing more than to "simplify" our lives to some degree, or we reminisce about a time when everything seemed straightforward. However, life has a funny way of squirming around our efforts to keep everything in order. The good news is that when it comes to reading about other people's lives, the more complicated and convoluted things get, the better it is for you! In real life you may prefer to skip surprises, but a great book group book should surprise you in some manner, inspiring different members to find very different ways of making sense of its contents.

However, if a book is so complicated, so riddled with trickiness and cleverness, so wrapped in foggy layers of multiple meanings that you begin to feel either too bored or too intimidated to read it, then it is not a fun book group book. At least *some* part of the reading experience should be fun—remember: fascinating and intriguing.

Ambiguous and Open to Interpretation

A gold-standard book group book does not offer you all the answers. Instead, it encourages you to keep asking more questions—questions about the characters, questions about meanings, questions about larger social or philosophic issues that extend to the world outside of the book. The best book groups are ambiguous enough to encourage a variety of different interpretations but not so ambiguous that they frustrate every attempt to make sense or meaning of what they describe. A great book group book will give you plenty of room to roam in your search for meaning and will provide plenty of fodder to keep your discussion fast and furious.

Great from Start to Finish

Nothing spoils a good book like a rotten ending. By rotten we don't necessarily mean depressing, tragic, disappointing, or frustrating—many great novels do finish on a less than ideal note for their main characters, for instance, and that's all part of the story. A rotten ending is one that does not go with, that does not match, that does not live up to the excellence of the rest of the story. You know the feeling. You're whizzing along through an excellent read when suddenly, toward the end, everything turns sour. Somehow this ending, in your opinion, just doesn't do justice to the book. A truly amazing book group doesn't trip you up like this—instead, the last page is as good as the first, and perhaps even makes you sad only for the sad fact that you've come to the end of the book and you can never, never read it again for the very first time.

Exactly as Long as It Should Be

A phenomenal book is not so phenomenal if it tries to be phenomenal for too long. It's so frustrating to follow a fascinating story for the first three hundred pages only to watch it wheeze and cough through a seemingly endless next two hundred pages. A great group book is neither too long for what it has to say, nor so short that you get teased but not satisfied. Many book group readers we know stick to the "around three hundred pages" rule, which is perfectly reasonable. Of course, there are plenty of stories that are much longer and that still hold our attention at every line, as well as others that are STILL too long at two hundred pages.

Discussion Questions by Subject Category

If you've looked over some of chapter 3, you'll know that we have already divided up the most popular book group books by category. But guess what? We're going to do it all over again! How do you like them apples?

In our discussion of customized reading and discussion considerations in chapter 3, we divide books by genre—the mostly traditional literary categories that together comprise the vast majority of book group reading: classic literary fiction, contemporary literary fiction, short stories, popular fiction, memoir, essays, nonfiction, and, of course, the genre category you won't find in most college textbooks, "the book I hated and sort of hated you for choosing." But on our Web site, and in our lists of recommended reading ("The Greedy Reader Menu"), we also divide books by subject matter, by locations, themes, or topics that a large number of books share. In this chapter we'll be telling you about some of the very best books (in each of our subject categories) that we have encountered in the past ten years of leading book groups and book discussions. You will also find some additional reading and discussion questions along the way.

Certain books on the list could easily belong to more than one category. A "'Coming of Age" novel might also be a "Domestic" story that travels mostly in the realm of "Spirituality in Fiction." For example, Alice Sebold's *Lovely Bones* could be placed under any of those categories. In such multifaceted cases, we try to identify the most dominant and distinctive elements of the book and to place it under the heading that seems most appropriate.

Because our diligent editor came down hard and insisted we find a way to make this gargantuan chapter a bit shorter, we made the painful decision to eliminate full descriptions for some of the books on this list. In most cases we chose to cut the blurbs for the books we think you may already know something about. However, you can find the unabridged descriptions for each of these books on our Web site, www.goodbookslately.com: just type in the title or the author's name in the Search box at the top of our homepage. We've also written reading guides for several of the books on this menu; again, you can preview or purchase these online at our site. These books are marked by "Read *Smart*Guide® available at www.goodbookslately.com" following the description. One last word about our tiresome Web site and we're done: since recommended reading lists can become dated even in the time it takes to publish this book, we would also direct you to the site for weekly updates on hot new books. Forge ahead for some ideas to appeal to everyone in your group or on your gift list.

PEOPLES AND CULTURES: INTERNATIONAL GRAB BAG OF THE WORLD'S GREATEST TALENTS

The books we chose to place in this category are written by authors of a different national or cultural background or are set in countries or places that are somewhat different from our own. This category reflects, of course, a specifically North American perspective on our part, that is, if you live in or hail from a "foreign" (to Americans) country, then you'll want to pick a different category to discuss the books we listed here.

Some Discussion Considerations for Books in This Category

- Describe the setting of this story: time, place, and specific social atmosphere and/or cultural traditions of the people. Do you see this setting as vital or intrinsic to the story—that is, can you picture a similar version of this story taking place somewhere else?
- In your opinion, what are the major points of conflict in this story—the issues and events and dilemmas that push the story along? Are these points of conflict specific to this particular cultural climate in some way?
- If you have included this story in this category, can we assume this culture or country or region is in some way very foreign to your own or just somewhat unfamiliar? If so, what, if any, expectations

or ideas do you tend to associate with the people of this country or culture? How were any of your assumptions or unconscious images confirmed, redirected, or refuted by the book?

Becoming Madame Mao
Anchee Min. Mariner Books: 2001 (paperback). 352 pages.

How does a simple concubine's daughter grow up to be one of the most feared and hated women of the twentieth century? In Anchee Min's imagined life story of the woman who became Chairman Mao Tse Tung's wife, we watch a very determined girl fight her way up to a very powerful, very precarious position. Min's novel traces the events and circumstances that turn a young girl into a fiercely ambitious actress, and then place that actress in the path of a man who offers her the role of a lifetime. On the edge of death, Madame Mao demands that her daughter, a historian, document her contributions to the revolution, chronicle her sacrifices to the cause, in order that she may claim her rightful place in history. Although she has a different perspective on her mother's career of service, Nah agrees to record Madame Mao's account. The result is an irresistibly commanding tale of greed, vanity, and good intentions gone wrong.

July's People
Nadine Gordimer. Viking Press: 1982 (paperback). 190 pages.

South Africa's most famous white writer, Pulitzer Prize winner Nadine Gordimer is at the top of her craft in this short but incredibly important, amazingly comprehensive novel. As the "political situation" in South Africa grows increasingly tense, Maureen and Bam Smales (a white liberal couple) make a desperate run for their lives. The only person who can save them is their black servant, July, who brings the Smales and their children to his village. As the balance of power shifts, former masters and former servant must rethink the structure of their relationship, and Maureen Smales must confront her most basic assumptions about the way that blacks and whites should interact. Fans of Barbara Kingsolver's *Poisonwood Bible* will recognize lots of connections and inspirations here.

The Looking Glass
Michèle Roberts. Picador USA: 2002 (paperback). 288 pages.

Are you ready to meet France's best-kept secret weapon? Michèle Roberts's novels read like literary powerhouses, like the European classics of yesterday—she's got that much sheer punch, deft ambition, and tight control. No insult intended to such earlier French masters as Stendhal, Balzac, and Flaubert, but we'll be happy to read *anything* Roberts is willing to offer up to us. In this novel, set in Normandy at the turn of the last century, Roberts gives us an absolutely drop-dead-amazing portrait of a singularly charming man through the eyes of the four women who love him to the point of destruction. In essence, you get four great love stories for the price of one and every line rippling wonderfully with the force of Roberts's incomparable writing. You are about to discover a new favorite author today.

Moth Smoke
Mohsin Hamid. Picador USA: 2001 (paperback). 256 pages.

If you don't like to read stories about young people getting in all sorts of trouble—the sex, drugs, and violence kind—skip this one altogether. If you don't like to read stories that feature less-than-lovable characters, move ahead to more sympathetic pastures. If you do like stories that celebrate the East as an exotic, sensual, dreamy realm of magic, you're still out of luck. Hamid's vivid portrait of life in contemporary Pakistan owes little to the standard mystical myth of Eastern culture. His hero, Daru, gets fired from his job at a bank, sulks over his failure to keep up with the Land Cruiser and cell-phone set, mistreats his servant, falls in love with his best friend's wife, and gets hooked on heroin. Oh, and we first meet Daru in court, on trial for the murder of a young boy. Now before you say thanks but no thanks, please be aware that this is a truly captivating, genuinely unprecedented beast of a first novel. We loved it.

White Teeth
Zadie Smith. Knopf: 2001 (paperback). 464 pages.

Smith's novel (penned at the tender age of twenty-four) was one of most eagerly awaited debuts in the year 2000. It's about the peculiar and sometimes ferociously funny relationship between two very different families living in North London in the 1990s. First we meet the Jones: ordinary Archie, who makes life-changing decisions by flipping a trusty coin; Clara, his beautiful, toothless Jamaican wife; and Irie, their witty teenage daughter, whose buck teeth, wild hair, and wide hips can't quite camouflage the beauty she'll soon become. Then we meet the Iqbals: Samad, a Muslim Bengali who has never really made London his home; Alsana, his fiery wife (from an arranged marriage), who likes to settle arguments with her husband by wrestling him to the ground; and their twin teenage sons Millat (a pot-smoking wannabe Muslim terrorist) and Magid (a wise teenager who manages to be both otherworldly and nerdy at the same time). While the intricate story is plotted cleverly at a page-turning pace, the unusual characters are what make this hefty novel an extraordinary first.

❧ **ReadSmartGuide®** *available at* www.goodbookslately.com

A Gesture Life
Chang Rae Lee. Riverhead Books: 2000 (paperback). 356 pages.

A respected pharmacist must confront the memories of war and a Korean comfort woman who shaped his inclination to dispense drugs rather than love.

The Poisonwood Bible
Barbara Kingsolver. HarperPerennial Library: 1999 (paperback). 556 pages.

An American family of Baptist missionaries discover new definitions of fellowship in the Congo. Required reading for all book
groups, says Oprah and says us.

⚛ **Read*Smart*Guide®** *available at* www.goodbookslately.com

Disgrace
J. M. Coetzee. Penguin USA: 2000 (paperback). 220 pages.
Winner of the 1999 Booker Prize: a South African college professor confronts the powers of persuasion and brute force. Harsh but
amazing post-Apartheid stuff.

⚛ **Read*Smart*Guide®** *available at* www.goodbookslately.com

Krik? Krak!
**Edwidge Danticat. Vintage Contemporaries: 1996
(paperback—reprint). 224 pages.**
Terrific short stories that give distinct faces and voices to the sur-
vivors in and from Haiti. A 1995 National Book Award Finalist.

The Kite Runner
Khaled Hosseini. Riverhead: 2003 (hardcover). 324 pages.
A powerful story of a childhood friendship gone wrong, by the
first native Afghani to write a major novel in English. Topically
important, deliciously readable.

LOST IN AMERICA: TODAY'S AUTHORS
EXPLORE LIFE IN THE LAND OF
THE FREE

Books in this category feature, of course, stories that are set on American soil. The choices, issues, and conflicts that the characters face
will in part be shaped by some specifically American culture and/or

concerns. The "lost" part comes in because the main characters of these books will be wandering through some kind of temporary abyss, looking for all the wrong things in all the wrong places.

Some Discussion Considerations for Books in This Category

- How is this story in some way a specifically "American" one? That is, can you picture things breaking down in a similar way someplace that is not America?
- Consider one or some of your favorite main or minor characters in this book. Do you see components or characteristics of this character's personality, expectations, and dilemmas that are distinctively shaped by those of the United States?
- You've heard for years about the Great American Novel. What exactly does that phrase mean to you? Does this novel aspire to any such glory, do you think? Where does it fit in the tradition of American literature?

The Subtle Art of Recommending Books

IF THE BOOK FITS, READ IT

**Fitting people with books is about as difficult as fitting
them with shoes.**
—SYLVIA BEACH, SHAKESPEARE AND COMPANY
BOOKSHOP

In her many years working as a bookseller, Kira was often called upon
to recommend books. A bookseller talented in the subtle art of recommending books listens carefully, waits patiently, and asks astute questions. Kira learned this lesson the hard way. One afternoon as she was
minding her own business and shelving books in the Fiction section, she
heard someone behind her say quietly, "I really liked *The Bridges of
Madison County*. Could you recommend a book like it?"

Kira paused for a moment before stepping down off her ladder. It wasn't
the question that stumped her—after all, this happened in 1992, when
everyone was reading Waller's saccharine novel of love—no, it wasn't the
question, it was the person asking it. A man, a middle-aged man in overalls
and work boots, was asking for something similar to *The Bridges of Madison County*. Puzzled, but proceeding to do what she'd been doing repeatedly every day for weeks, Kira took the customer over to a table display
filled with a dozen or so books selected to satisfy the appetites of Waller's
insatiable readers. After several minutes, the man came back, looking perplexed. "I didn't quite see what I was looking for. Could you recommend
some others?" Kira wracked her brain for other sappy love stories and
showed him them all, each time expecting that bright "yes, that's it!" expression to pass over his face. None of the love stories appealed to him.
This went on for about twenty minutes, until Kira asked that all-important
question she should have asked in the first place: "So what was it about

The Bridges of Madison County that you liked?" The man's face lit up. "Covered bridges," he said. "I love those covered bridges."

WHY "IF YOU LIKED THIS, YOU'LL LIKE THIS" DOESN'T ALWAYS WORK

Okay, we've got a pet peeve here we just have to get out in the open. It involves an annoying trend in the book and movie world, one pioneered by Blockbuster Video. Have you ever tried to use the sometimes seemingly arbitrary movie recommendations on the back of Blockbuster Video cases? You know, the ones that begin, "If you like this movie, try these!" Most of the time, there's a clear connection between the movies mentioned, usually having to do with the film's plot or star.

"If you liked *Clueless*," the anonymous blurb will suggest with confidence, "try *Sweet Home Alabama*, *10 Things I Hate about You*, and *She's All That*." Now, before you rush over to your local video store, let's just stop and think about this for a moment. What do these four movies have in common? They're all teenybopper flicks, right? Well, if that's why you liked *Clueless*, then you're in business. But what if you despise all the lame John Hughes rip-offs of the nineties? What if what you liked about *Clueless* had nothing to do with fluffy tales of teenage life in America and everything to do with Jane Austen (*Clueless*, as you may know, is a revision of Austen's *Emma*)? Or what if you didn't care much for the film but loved Alicia Silverstone? What if you want to see other movies directed by Amy Heckerling? You see what we're getting at—without a context or an explanation of any kind, these kinds of recommendations are potentially meaningless. Even worse, sometimes they can lead you astray. A good recommendation tells you not only the title of other related works, but *how* and *why* they're related. That way, you can make an informed decision whether or not to follow the suggestion. In our "Greedy Reader Menu," we try our very best to make these potentially pleasing (and relevant!) connections clear.

The Average Human
Ellen Toby-Potter. MacAdam/Cage: 2003 (hardcover). 270 pages.

The Average Human, maybe, but so far above and beyond the Average Novel! The nebulous heroes of Toby-Potter's novel are the members of the Mayborn family. Every pleasant small town in America is home to at least one family like the Mayborns, social outcasts who suck the class right out of the neighborhood: front yard claimed by discarded household items, sons perpetually in jail, daughters perpetually pregnant. When fourteen-year-old June Mayborn accidentally kills the aging leader of a former local cult, the funeral attracts a new crop of visitors and a new focus on just what it means to be a Mayborn. Are the Mayborns so far removed from the average human that all hope is lost? Wonderfully strange and unique, *The Average Human* will freak you out, not in a creepy, gross way, but in a remarkably original way. The writing is brilliant, reminiscent of Barry Hannah in the creativity and perfection of images and metaphor. This book would be the perfect choice for any book group stuck in any kind of rut—you won't have read the like of this before!

Drown
Junot Diaz. Riverhead Books: 1997 (paperback). 208 pages.

We'd always remember this book in any top-ten-of-all-time list we made. Diaz's American immigrant characters are from the Dominican Republic, a country that shares its war-torn island with Haiti. As the setting shifts from jungle to concrete jungle (in this case, urban New Jersey), you may become increasingly aware that Diaz has it all—the faultless ear for dialogue, the sharp eye of the impartial observer, the natural sense of the perfect balance between lyricism and restraint. But his stories are so engaging, so exciting and interesting to read, that it's equally probable you'll read too fast to worry about his technique. Diaz captures the essence of so many cultural edges, especially those formed by race, immigration, and urban/suburban sprawl, but never allows either his narrators or his characters to drown in self-pity. This literary debut is a collection of short stories, but since the stories are about the same people it reads like a novel of sorts, much like Louise Erdrich's first book, *Love Medicine*.

Feast of Love
Charles Baxter. Vintage Contemporaries: 2001 (paperback). 308 pages.

"Every relationship has at least one really good day," according to Bradley Smith. Bradley is an unlikely connoisseur of love, a man often described by friends and lovers as "an exceptionally handsome toad," a man who seems, well, rather ordinary. But one of this novel's greatest pleasures is the way it slowly immerses us in Bradley's life until his desires and heartbreaks are both familiar and extraordinary. Through Bradley, we meet a pair of young lovers whose appetite for each other is insatiable: Oscar, a pierced and tattooed post-rehab heroin addict, and his wise and profane girlfriend, Chloe. We meet Harry, an old philosophy professor, and his wife, Esther; and we witness the repeated devastation of their domestic harmony by their suicidal son, Aaron. Like Charlie Baxter, the Ann Arbor creative writing professor who begins the novel with a stroll into the cool quiet of a summer's early morning, each of these narrators shares a surprising tale of love. We've grown wary of novels that feature the author as a character—usually they're self-consciously clever. But in *The Feast of Love*, Baxter has crafted a finely tuned, warm, and deeply humane novel.

Middlesex
Jeffrey Eugenides. Picador: 2003 (paperback). 529 pages.

The Greatest American Hermaphrodite Epic of the twenty-first century! Calliope Stephanides will soon become your favorite intersex character in all of literature.

Seabiscuit: An American Legend
Laura Hillenbrand. Ballantine: 2002 (paperback). 339 pages.
 The fat little horse that could! When he wasn't taking a nap.

House of Sand and Fog
Andre Dubus III. Vintage Books: 2000 (paperback). 365 pages.
 Whose side are you on in this battle to the death over a California
 house of dreams? Andre Dubus III keeps you struggling on the
 fence to the last heart-racing page.

American Pastoral
**Philip Roth. Vintage Books: 1998 (paperback—reissue). 423
pages.**
 This 1997 Pulitzer Prize winner tells the life story of a man who
 personifies the American Dream until his daughter decides to
 blow it up. Philip Roth at his greatest.

THE AMERICAN WEST:
FICTION THAT KNOCKS THE DUST
FROM ALL THE MYTHS

Books included in this category will—shocking, we know—be set in
the American West, either the West of the present or the past. We
have a lot of favorites in this category, which, we'll admit, is partly because we live here. But it's also because the literature of the American
West is currently going through a powerful boom—writers like Annie
Proulx, Kent Haruf, and Thomas Savage are making this area one of
our current national literary hotspots.

Some Discussion Considerations for Books in This Category

- When you hear the words "American West," who or what does that make you think about? What about when you hear the words "Western Fiction"? What sort of expectations do you have for a story that is set in the West?

- How would you describe your picture of the "Old West"? What are some of the common images and traditional ideas that are associated with this place and time? How do the people or the issues or the themes of this story fit in with or reject some of our ingrained assumptions about the Old West?

- What sort of picture does this book present of the American West of today? How does this book represent the evils versus the joys that are particular to Western living? Whose West are you reading about—that of cowboys, or Indians, or ranchers, or the women who love them?

Close Range: Wyoming Stories
Annie Proulx. Scribner: 2000 (paperback). 285 pages.

Pulitzer Prize–winning author Annie Proulx offers up a haunting and powerful collection of short stories that connect the isolated people of a vast and hostile landscape: the state of Wyoming. These interconnected tales of farmers, ranchers, cowboys, rodeo riders, storekeepers, freeloaders, tractors, and the men and women who attempt to love them are riddled with a sense that blunt violence is the logical option in a place of too much space and too little security, but they also open up surprising moments of pure elation. The last story in the collection must be read to be believed—you'll never look at the Marlboro Man in the same way again.

⁓ **Read*Smart*Guide®** *available at* www.goodbookslately.com

The Life of an Ordinary Woman
Anne Ellis. Mariner Books: 1999 (paperback). 301 pages.

Most of us don't tend to include women in our mental pictures of the Old West (unless we've spent a lot of time with *Little House on the Prairie*). If we do include a woman in our Old West vision, she tends to be dressed in cheap satin and feathers, the flashy hooker with a heart of gold. Well, as you'd probably guess, most of the real women who settled in the West resembled this stereotypical floozy about as much as most actual Native Americans of the period resembled the Lone Ranger's Tonto. But you may be astounded to discover just how many of these women wrote about their frontier experiences. Trust us, Anne Ellis isn't exactly your ordinary woman. She doesn't try to pretend that life in Colorado's turn-of-the-century mining towns was a wonderful adventure; but nonetheless, after the first few pages, you know you are in for a wild and funny ride.

⚞ **ReadSmartGuide®** *available at* www.goodbookslately.com

Plainsong
Kent Haruf. Vintage Contemporaries: 2000 (paperback). 320 pages.

Spare. Magical. Perfect. And right in our backyard. Haruf's novel, set in Holt, Colorado, will take its place among the great small-town stories, the great Western stories, the great American stories, of the century. Its narrative voice is unlike anything else you've encountered, so simple that it takes your breath away. It's easy to describe what happens in this book: seven ordinary people encounter some of life's most common problems, coming together in the end to form an unusual but logical sort of family. But to describe how Haruf makes this happen is a much trickier matter, and efforts to do so guarantee an intense book group discussion. A finalist for the 1999 National Book Award.

⚞ **ReadSmartGuide®** *available at* www.goodbookslately.com

Angle of Repose
Wallace Stegner. Penguin USA: 1992 (paperback). 569 pages.
The double-jointed masterpiece that no book group can afford to skip: two astounding stories (of historical past and troublesome present) for the price of one.

✻ **ReadSmartGuide®** *available at* www.goodbookslately.com

The Tortilla Curtain
T. C. Boyle. Penguin USA: 1996 (paperback). 355 pages.
Politically correct California liberals versus illegal Mexican immigrants—winner takes all.

✻ **ReadSmartGuide®** *available at* www.goodbookslately.com

SMALL WORLD: REVEALING TALES FROM INTIMATE, ISOLATED COMMUNITIES

The books we have chosen to place in this category all share one very specific structural and thematic element—all these stories take place within some very small or isolated or intimate setting. These books demand a distinct category because it is the very nature of their enclosed, specialized setting that shapes the story and the characters' dilemmas.

Some Discussion Considerations for Books in This Category

- How would you describe or define the specialized "world" of the people in this book?
- Does this insular world have any particular rules or customs or values that are very different from those you might find in a larger or metropolitan setting?

- How does this isolated setting or distinctive world shape the lives of the people who live in it? How many of these people are here by choice or by default? Who represents the ideals and traditions of this world, and who is fighting or reacting against these norms?

Homestead
Rosina Lippi. Mariner Books: 1999 (paperback). 210 pages.

A Good Books Lately favorite. The initial draw of this novel, composed of several linked short stories, is its tiny, isolated, rural setting, an insular Alpine village in a remote corner of Austria. Lippi's practical but passionate female narrators quickly involve us in the intimate domestic details of village life: its values, quarrels, and the intricate family relationships and jealousies. But what is perhaps most intriguing about this eighty-year fictional history is the way that, as the twentieth century moves on, the established traditions and fixed expectations of the Rosenau villagers become increasingly subject to the demands and intrusions of the modern outside world. We have yet to meet the reader who doesn't like this book, and most readers tell us they've shared this hidden gem with friends and family.

≈ **ReadSmartGuide®** *available at* www.goodbookslately.com

Any Small Thing Can Save You
Christina Adam. Little, Brown and Company: 2002 (paperback). 223 pages.

We don't encounter too many bestiaries these days, but once upon a time, long ago, such stories were as common as grown-ups without teeth. The bestiary, a moral and allegorical tale that focused on the behaviors of uncommon and often imaginary animals, was all the rage in the medieval world. We're counting on you to ensure that this stunning collection of tales by Christina Adam will bring this ancient genre back in vogue. The animals in Adam's book are generally those of the more ordinary sort: asps, bats, cats, doves, etc. But for the characters in Adam's stories, their often unexpected encounters with these animals provide flashes of insight into the most complicated aspects of their own needs and desires. Together, the twenty-six vignettes that make up this book (and the animals, A through Z) create a totally unique reading experience. This seems like just the right sort of book to unstick a group stuck in a rut of the same old, same old.

The Beach
Alex Garland. Riverhead Books: 1998 (paperback). 436 pages.
Forget the film. This riveting story of been-there, done-that, thrill-seeking young backpackers in search of the ultimate un-spoiled destination simply can't fly severed from Alex Garland's taut, precise prose. Although this book has been repeatedly compared to *Lord of the Flies,* repeatedly called the *Heart of Darkness* or *On the Road* for the postmodern generations X and Y, Garland's novel manages to avoid cliché and sidestep simplification, while saying something new about forces that are very old: the human desire for utopia and the teenage desire to escape authority and tradition and to embrace something more real than real life. This novel offers an intriguing commentary on the new breed of politically correct colonialism, asks lots of interesting moral questions, and is an amazingly irresistible read about what happens when an international cast of young people try to re-create paradise lost on the most isolated, forbidden, and secret of beaches.

Bel Canto
Ann Patchett. Perennial: 2002 (paperback). 336 pages.
Somewhere in South America, a birthday party is going terribly wrong. This incredibly moving tale of colluding guerillas and hostages is poised to become a book group favorite for the ages. Winner of the 2002 PEN/Faulkner prize.

❧ **ReadSmartGuide®** *available at* www.goodbookslately.com

Geek Love
Katherine Dunn. Vintage Books: 2002 (paperback—reissue). 368 pages.

A pair of starry-eyed carnies decide to breed their own bona fide show stoppers by indulging in arsenic, amphetamines, and radioisotopes. Not for the squeamish, but heartily endorsed for adventurous "Norms."

A FAMILY AFFAIR: FICTION THAT TACKLES THE OLDEST INSTITUTION

These are stories in which the main centering (or dividing) point is a family unit of some kind. Traditionally, stories that focus mainly on the dramas of a single family or several distinct families are known as **domestic** narratives: the domestic novel or the domestic memoir.

Some Discussion Considerations for Books in This Category

- Can you come up with some adjectives or phrases that describe the unique social world or sphere of this family? Is it fair or possible to describe an entire family, composed of many different members, with certain words and phrases that nonetheless apply to each member in some way and the family as a whole?
- Look at each of the members of this family and describe his or her relationship to each of the other members—you might want to draw some kind of rough chart with this one, it's fun! Who is the most powerful or influential member of this family? Who is trying to gain more power in the family circle and how? Who is its biggest rebel—that is, rebelling against the values of the family, not necessarily of society at large?

- Look at the family's relationship to the larger social world that sur-rounds it, and each member of the family's attempts to fit in, run from, or react against this world. How does this particular family's unique makeup affect each of its members attempts to succeed in the greater world beyond the home?

Disobedience
Jane Hamilton. Anchor Books: 2001 (paperback). 288 pages.

Tired of mother-daughter books? How about a mother-son book? Jane Hamilton isn't exactly known for her light touch; however, her latest page-turning novel is filled with quirky characters that lighten the load of what could be a heavy story. Hamilton writes once more about what happens to people when things go terribly wrong (think of the poor woman in *A Map of the World*), but here the story is told by Henry Shaw, who discovers his mother Beth's affair while reading her E-mail. It's a twenty-first-century twist on a very old story, and Hamilton's teenage narrator makes it fresh. At first Henry's voice seems impossibly sophisticated; but quickly we realize that while Henry may know a lot, he hasn't experienced enough life to know as much as he thinks he knows. Henry's de-pressed mother is a musician, his idealistic father is a history teacher at a prestigious private high school in Chicago, and his younger sister, Elvira, perhaps the most complicated character in the novel, is a thirteen-year-old Civil War fanatic who dresses only in "authentic" soldier uniforms. This novel has an unusually powerful ending and a great cast of characters, each drawn with precision and care, each learning something about love and loss along the way. Henry looks back and tells his mother's story be-cause, as he puts it, it's "the only one I seem to have in me. . . . It is always about her."

A Heartbreaking Work of Staggering Genius
Dave Eggers. Vintage Books: 2001. 496 pages.

You've got to hand it to Dave Eggers for that eye-catching title. It is an appropriately self-demeaning, self-conscious name for a memoir that wallows in self-awareness in an irresistible, irreverent, joyfully exuberant manner. It's the true story (if, as the author questions, there can be any such thing) of the adventures of two modern-day orphans. When both of his parents die within weeks of each other, Dave is left to take care of his seven-year-old brother, Toph. As Eggers relates the story of the brothers' move to San Francisco and their efforts to regain some sort of stable family life, you can feel how uncomfortable he is with the stigma of grief, with the problem of sliding into the Oh Poor Me tearjerker. But his fear, paranoia, and frantic need for control leak out of every wonderfully written scene. Don't be alarmed by the book's unusual thirty-four-page preface, which allegedly explains everything, but press on. Or you could take the author's suggestion and just skip over the whole thing.

Make Believe
Joanna Scott. Back Bay Books: 2001 (paperback). 246 pages.
It must feel pretty darn good to be the kind of writer that other writers rave about. Turn to the back of Scott's fourth novel, *Make Believe,* and you'll find praise from some of today's most celebrated authors—Michael Cunningham, Rick Moody, David Foster Wallace. Wallace, in fact, calls Scott "the absolute cream of our generation." This is the story of Bo, a three-year-old orphan trying, like any three year old, to make sense of the world around him. It's a tough job, especially considering that his two sets of grandparents (one white, one black) are fighting to get custody of their parentless grandson. Scott's story is no legal thriller, nor is it a tear-jerking tale of innocence besieged. Rather, she accomplishes the astonishing feat of getting us inside the head of a very young child while giving us a riveting story for intelligent adults. This is one of the great ones—don't miss it.

⇝ **ReadSmartGuide®** *available at* www.goodbookslately.com

About a Boy
Nick Hornby. Riverhead Books: 2002 (paperback). 307 pages.
   A young geeky schoolboy and wealthy irresponsible bum form a
   strange but profitable alliance.

Will You Miss Me When I'm Gone?: The Carter Family and
Their Legacy in American Music.
Marc Zwonitzer with Charles Hirshberg. Simon & Schuster:
2002 (hardcover). 432 pages.
   A wonderful nonfiction account of the astounding Appalachian
   family who almost single-handedly established the sounds and
   styles and rhythms that grew into modern folk, country, and blue-
   grass music.

COMING OF AGE: INNOCENCE
COMES FACE TO FACE WITH THE
LARGER WORLD

Also known by the German name of bildungsroman, the coming-of-age
novel or story is one of the most popular breeds on the block. A coming-
of-age story features a young character (or characters) who is (or are)
traveling the rocky road from childish innocence to adult understanding.

Some Discussion Considerations for Books in
This Category

- Describe the main young or naïve character (or characters) at the
  beginning of the story. What sort of person is he or she? Can you
  describe any of his or her most basic assumptions about life at the
  start of this narrative?
- How much interaction does the coming-of-age character have
  with a larger world outside his or her family, town, home? How
  does this change from the beginning of the story to the end?

- Traditionally, a story that we call "coming of age" features a young or innocent or oblivious character who undergoes some transformative emotional or intellectual experience. What are the major points of change and revelation for this character? Do you think the knowledge or experience that he or she requires will be ultimately good or bad for the character in the long run?

Atonement
Ian McEwan. Anchor Books: 2003 (paperback). 368 pages.

If you haven't yet tangled with the unstoppable, mind-boggling, jaw-dropping force that is British author Ian McEwan, now is the perfect time to take him on. Just last year McEwan's novel *Amsterdam* was nominated for (and won) pretty much every major literary award going—but apparently it's no big deal for Mr. McEwan to pop out a truly great novel every fourteen months or so. This year's contribution is *Atonement,* one of the most beautiful and frustrating love stories you will ever read, ever. The action begins in 1935, when thirteen-year-old Briony—a precocious aspiring writer who knows much more than most kids of her age, but not enough to know that she's too inexperienced to interpret adult behavior just yet—misinterprets a flirtation between her older sister Cecelia and the gardener's son. Feeling proud of her entry into the adult world of intrigue and passion, Briony commits a terrible crime against her sister and her sister's lover, one that will shatter the former lives, hopes, and expectations of all three. The story continues through the ravages of World War II, as each of the three main characters fight to get back to the one place that he or she belongs.

⋙ **ReadSmartGuide**® *available at* www.goodbookslately.com

The Curious Incident of the Dog in the Night-Time
Mark Haddon. Doubleday: 2003 (hardcover). 226 pages.

No matter how many times you've encountered fifteen-year-old autistic genius narrators over the past few years in your reading, we think you'll find Christopher John Francis Boone a deliciously readable storyteller of a most distinctive cut. He knows all the prime numbers up to 7,057, enjoys solving quadratic equations with larger coefficients (to make them a bit harder) in his head, can explain some of the finer points of Occam's Razor in Latin, but refuses to have anything to do with the colors yellow or brown, and tends to scream maniacally but methodically when anyone touches him. The curious incident that inspires Christopher to begin writing his book is the discovery of his neighbor's dog dead in the yard, apparently murdered by a garden fork. Christopher determines to solve the mystery of Wellington's demise, an investigation that is doomed to shred the rigidly controlled order of his world into increasingly chaotic tatters. It's no easy matter for any teenager to confront the raw emotions of family secrets hidden in the closet, but how much harder is it for a teenager who has no immediate experience of most human emotion? It's a safe bet that Mark Haddon himself, a children's book author, screenwriter, and creative writing teacher, is not, in fact, an autistic mathematical genius, but his brilliance in giving us access to the mind of one such as Christopher represents an unprecedented leap into literary quantum physics.

⚘ **ReadSmartGuide®** *available at* www.goodbookslately.com

Four Corners
Diane Freund. Harvest Books: 2003 (paperback). 256 pages.
Sometimes you can just feel a great novel coming on from the very first sentence. Take this one, for example: "I was ten the summer that we drove my mother crazy." The time is the early 1950s. The setting is the small rural town of Four Corners. And the narrator, ten-year-old Rainey, is one of the sharpest young voices ever to tell the story of the murky journey from childhood trust to adult resignation. The middle child of five confused siblings, all under the age of thirteen, Rainey isn't sure why her mother is in a sanatorium. She can't ask her dad because he's al-

most always at the bar. She doesn't have to ask her aunt because Merle rarely lets a moment go by without reminding the children who is to blame. Merle has left her husband and son back in the Bronx, she tells the kids, "to come to this frigging sorry excuse for a Shangri-La because we had finally succeeded in driving her sister crazy." Merle, by the way, is one of the best fictional characters ever to slash and burn her way across a page. And what Merle can't teach Rainey about the harsh, greedy reality of human love, her teenage daughter Joan certainly can. As frequently funny as it is dark and terrifying (you almost hate yourself for laughing), *Four Corners* is that rare first novel—a flat-out, hands-down, must-read.

The Miracle Life of Edgar Mint
Brady Udall. Vintage: 2002 (paperback). 423 pages.

A perspicacious young orphan (whose first memory is of a United States postal jeep running over his head) sets out from the San Carlos Apache Indian Reservation on a brave journey of self-determination, earning your eternal devotion in the process.

Northern Lights
Howard Norman. Picador: 2001 (paperback). 236 pages.

Deep in the wilds of northernmost Manitoba, fourteen-year-old Noah meets Pelly Bay, the flying boy whose tragic trajectory inspires Noah's return to civilization. Stupendous!

Everything Is Illuminated
Jonathan Safran Foer. HarperPerennial: 2003 (paperbook). 288 pages.

Savor the delights of this irreverent, touching novel about an American Jew who has traveled to the Ukraine to trace family roots. Featuring the funniest narrator ever, known to his family as "Alexi-stop-spleening me!"

≈ **ReadSmartGuide®** *available at* www.goodbookslately.com

Diamond Dogs
Alan Watt. Little, Brown and Company: 2001 (paperback). 256 pages.

Neil Garvin's father would do anything to ensure his son's successful football career, including covering up the fact that Neil might be responsible for the death of a fellow high school student—making for an almost unbearably tense psychological thriller.

WOMEN ON WOMEN: DARING FEMALE AUTHORS DELIVER DYNAMIC FEMALE CHARACTERS

Not hard to figure out this category. Books under this heading will address issues and concerns that are, at least in part, specifically important to those of the female persuasion. And they will also be written by women.

Some Discussion Considerations for Books in This Category

- Would you agree that this book is in some way specifically geared toward female readers or addresses issues and concerns that are specific to the world of women? Why or why not?
- Consider the major female and male characters of this story. How does this story represent the experience, desires, and fears of women as opposed to men?
- Would you describe this author, or any of the major characters in the story, as a feminist? What does this word mean to you in this day and age?

How to Tell a Book by Its Cover

You can't, or so the old saying goes. But just the same, we keep trying. Like any average reader who possesses the gift of sight, we are suckers for a great visual presentation, for a book-jacket design of such startling or provocative appeal we are compelled to pick it up. Publishers know this, of course. Cover art has become a highly specialized if not exact science (compare the practical, sedate covers of thirty years ago with those of the books that are competing for your dollar today). While front covers may attract the eye, it's the "endorsement blurbs" from the back covers that most influence our decision to take a book to the cash register. With some practice, you can start to pinpoint words of praise from certain people and publications as reasonably fair indicators that you might like this book.

We all know, for instance, that an excerpt from a rave review from the *New York Times* is always a positive sign. Resounding excerpts from both the *New York Times* and *People* might be an even better sign—this book is probably both distinctive *and* enjoyable. We have our own favorite, lesser-known sources here at Good Books Lately. We are motivated, for example, by a positive plug from the *Charlotte Observer,* an uncannily and consistently prescient source of reading recommendations. Ellen is always susceptible to an enthusiastic endorsement from *Entertainment Weekly*—you may not be aware just how witty and sophisticated this magazine is—while Kira is a huge fan of Salon.com. We are also likely to check out any book that made a "notable" or "best" list of books for the year, especially from any of the major metropolitan newspapers. By contrast, a positive quote from *Publishers Weekly, Kirkus Review,* or *Library Journal* tends to come from a plot summary, so doesn't mean so much to us unless it's a "starred" review. Your favorite reviewers and media don't have to be ours; the key thing is to keep track of whom you trust, whose taste is similar to yours.

Another factor to consider is literary-prize winners, and it helps to know something about what each stands for. The Nobel, for instance, is a lifetime award—so while you know you're reading an author of international importance, you don't know much about a specific book. The Pulitzer is a yearly award, rewarding American works of journalism, letters, and music that address "the largest themes in life, the raw passion and tragedy of the human condition." The National Book Award is presented annually in America, while the Booker is awarded to a writer from Great Britain or its former Commonwealth, including Canada, Pakistan, and South Africa. Lesser known but equally valuable awards are the PEN/Faulkner (best fiction by American writer) and the PEN/Hemingway (best fiction by a first-time published author). Both are presented by an international association of writers who confer this honor on their peers. One award you won't ever see mentioned as an enticement to buy is the Bulwer-Lytton, the prize for the book containing the worst first sentence in the spirit of "It was a dark and stormy night," the opener *Peanuts'* Snoopy made famous. For a complete run down on awards, check out www.literature-awards.com or the link on our site at www.goodbookslately.com.

One final thing to consider is the publisher of the book. Most of us aren't accustomed to looking for this, but we might want to be. Again, if you start to pay attention, you'll notice you do have a taste for the products of certain publishers (as you might for certain designers or directors or vineyards). Books from Vintage, Picador, and MacAdam/Cage will always warrant immediate attention in this office, but you may discover your own favorite "brand" over time.

Amy and Isabelle
Elizabeth Strout. Vintage Books: 2000 (paperback). 304 pages.

In her finely crafted debut, Strout writes about the unspoken and sometimes volatile emotions that make the mother-daughter the most complex of relationships. Her portrait of Isabelle, the single mother of sixteen-year-old Amy, is uncompromising, and we may at first judge Isabelle harshly for her seeming detachment from the world around her; but as the story unfolds and as our understanding of her increases, we begin to respect her quiet strength. The story takes place during a very hot summer in the small mill town of Shirley Falls as Amy explores her growing sense of independence while Isabelle must deal with the truth of her past. Strout makes every word count, and the story is told with genuine warmth and provocative honesty. The revelatory plot makes *Amy and Isabelle* a great page-turner; the taut beauty of Strout's prose makes you want to savor every scene.

❧ **ReadSmartGuide®** *available at* www.goodbookslately.com

Flight of the Maidens
Jane Gardam. Plume: 2002 (paperback). 278 pages.

Wow. Absolutely and unquestionably awesome! This modest little tale of three young women coming of age in post—World War II Britain is a stunner, a wonder, and a must-read for your list. At turns bitingly funny and bitterly moving, this is nothing less than a perfectly constructed "easy" read that nonetheless captures emotions and issues of real and lasting importance. We got so attached to the three main characters—aspiring intellectual Hetty Fallowes, wandering refugee Liselotte Klein, and class-jumper Una Vane—that we could have happily followed their adventures for another three hundred or so pages. But Gardam is one of those increasingly rare writers who knows how to bring her story to a heart-racing and warmly truthful conclusion. Don't miss this one!

Highwire Moon
Susan Straight. Anchor: 2002 (paperback). 320 pages.

The *New York Times Book Review* called this 2001 National Book Award Finalist "an eye-opener of a novel, a road map to the real California." *Highwire Moon* is an immigrant story that yanks a population of overlooked characters out from under the rock that camouflages their presence for most of us; it's also a mother-daughter novel that turns that genre on its ear. An unfortunate accident earns illegal migrant worker Serafina a trip back to her home country of Mexico, and an even more unfortunate oversight sends her back without her three-year-old daughter. Twelve years later, Serafina sets off on a dangerous journey across the border to find Elvia. Elvia, for her part, now fifteen and pregnant, determines to find the mother who so inexplicably abandoned her. As Serafina and Elvia track across an increasingly hazardous landscape of people desperate enough to try anything twice, we are treated to a portrait of individual determination and family love that burns a passage from the page to our core. Straight steadily resists any temptation to play this story for cheap sensation or easy tears, and the result is gutsy, gritty, and ultimately uplifting.

Emotionally Weird
Kate Atkinson. Picador USA: 2001 (paperback). 355 pages.

Emotionally weird but enormously entertaining. In 1970s Scotland, twenty-one-year-old Effie Stuart-Murphy and her mother, Nora (who is allegedly still a virgin), share their darkest family secrets to hilariously edifying effect.

SPIRITUALITY IN THE NOVEL: COURAGEOUS CHARACTERS ON A QUEST FOR MEANING

This is a category we coined to cradle the amazing number of modern books and stories that feature some kind of spiritual, religious, or philosophic quest. One thing's for sure: the search for God, Truth, and the Soul is definitely *not* dead.

Some Discussion Considerations for Books in This Category

- Consider the perimeters of the spiritual belief system that is important to the majority of the characters in this story. That is, how would you describe the spiritual "norm" of this book or story? Which of the characters are satisfied or comforted by this tradition, and which seek or find some alternative spiritual reality?
- To what degree does the supernatural, or life after death, or the miraculous play a part in this story? Is any conflict generated between those who believe or have experienced some supernatural reality and those who do or have not? How important is God or the gods to any of these main characters?
- Describe the unique spiritual battle or search for each or any of the main characters. What does he or she hope to find through a spiritual connection? What is he or she most afraid of in this regard?
- Can you identify the major cause that instigated this character's spiritual quest? Does this original source seem human- or God-oriented?

Mariette in Ecstasy
Ron Hansen. HarperPerennial Library: 1992 (paperback). 192 pages.

Surely one of the most intriguing, unusual, deceptively simple, and flat-out creepiest novels ever written, Ron Hansen's astonishing story must be read to be believed. This compact little book delivers an absolute knockout in less than two hundred pages—you'll want to read slowly to make it last at the same time that you're tearing through the pages to find out what happens. We don't want to say too much about the subject matter, lest we spoil the surprise, but we'll tell you what we can. This is the story of Mariette Baptiste, a brand-new postulant to the convent of Our Lady of Sorrows. None of the nuns know quite what to think of this brand-new novice, especially once she begins to manifest the unmistakable signs of a soul in ecstasy. But is Mariette's alleged connection to Christ the real deal or the boldest of shams? Perhaps "creepy" isn't the right word, but it's something very close to that—you may well feel the hair on the back of your neck rise as you follow the attempts to decipher a stupefying mystery.

ᘔ **ReadSmartGuide®** *available at* www.goodbookslately.com

Quarantine
Jim Crace. Picador USA: 1999 (paperback). 243 pages.

How many writers out there are bold enough to attempt to envision the forty days of Christ's fabled fast in the wilderness? In this daring, hypnotizing, utterly one-of-a-kind novel, Crace's Jesus Christ sequesters himself in a desolate cave, preparing to empty his body in order to meet God. You might think that the choice to live in a cave in an arid desert would guarantee a guy some privacy, but Christ is not entirely alone. His neighbors, a group of exiles and malcontents who seek salvation in the dusty cluster of caves in the hills, grow increasingly curious about the gangly stranger from Galilee. As you might imagine, some lives are changed in some very significant ways, but not in the ways that either you or the characters will expect. Enough said. Read this book instantly if not sooner.

ᘔ **ReadSmartGuide®** *available at* www.goodbookslately.com

Bee Season
Myla Goldberg. Knopf: 2001 (paperback). 288 pages.

The miraculous story of Eliza, a C+ student who becomes a spelling-bee mystic, unlocking a fascinating portrayal of four family members struggling to satisfy their deepest needs while remaining oblivious to those of their nearest and dearest.

🌿 **ReadSmartGuide®** *available at* www.goodbookslately.com

The Lovely Bones
Alice Sebold. Little, Brown and Company: 2002 (hardcover). 328 pages.

A murdered teenage girl tells the story of her family's grief as she looks down from heaven. Sixty-eight weeks on the *New York Times* best-seller list and counting!

The Friendly Persuasion
Jessamyn West. Harcourt: 1991 (paperback). 214 pages.

Who knew that life in a Civil War–era Quaker community could get so hot? A *San Francisco Chronicle* Western 100 Best Book of the Twentieth Century.

LATIN AMERICAN FICTION: ABSORBING SAGAS OF FAMILIES AND POLITICAL TURMOIL

This might seem like a culturally prejudiced or exclusionary category. Sure, we feature lots of American novels because we're from America. But why don't we include a category on literature from France, or from Australia, or from Asia? Just give us some time, and we will; we promise. The only reason we can pinpoint this particular national or regional category is because of the absolutely incredible amount of literature that has poured out of the countries of South and Central

America and the incredible popularity of these stories worldwide, especially in North America.

Some Discussion Considerations for Books in This Category

- What does the term "Latin American fiction" mean to you? What assumptions or associations do you bring to a work of "Latin American" literature? Where, exactly, is Latin America—which countries or regions are included or excluded?
- Some "non–Latin American" readers have been especially intrigued by what they see as certain motifs, themes, characters, or cultural traits that seem to appear in many works of Latin American fiction. Some examples we've heard are: passionate and domineering men, even more passionate and rebellious women, intense spiritual/religious undertones or quests, major political upheaval, and the vital, central importance of family. Do you see any of those allegedly "common" ideas or characteristics emerging in this book? How does the author or narrator play with any of these "traditional" elements?
- Latin American fiction is also famous for the way some of its major authors—such as Gabriel Garcia Marquez, Isabel Allende, and Mario Vargas Llosa—practice the art of "magical realism." These authors include descriptions of supernatural or surreal events presented in a very matter-of-fact way. Take a minute to look at our definition of "magical realism" in appendix 2, and then think about whether you've come across any moments or elements of this current in your present book.

The House of the Spirits
Isabel Allende. Bantam Books: 1986 (paperback). 433 pages.

A spectacular work of magical realism this is one of the most moving, most compelling novels in the Latin American tradition. Allende has delighted readers worldwide with her novels, but this, her first, is still our very favorite. It tells the story of the astonishing

Trueba family, connecting their unique, fantastic history with a century of change in Chile. Although the terms "epic" and "saga" are too frequently bestowed on the undeserving, this is a romantic, magical, and important story that truly deserves these labels. When Esteban Trueba's breathtakingly gorgeous green-haired fiancée dies suddenly, he takes her clairvoyant sister, Clara, as his wife. As one corrupt political regime replaces another, each member of the Trueba clan fights for his or her own distinctive place in history. As the niece of Chile's assassinated president Salvador Allende, the author is well versed in the chaos and violence that has rocked the country for so many years—but that doesn't explain how she became such a damn good storyteller.

❧ **ReadSmartGuide®** *available at* www.goodbookslately.com

Sirena Selena
Mayra Santos-Febres (translated by Stephen A. Lytle). Picador: 2000 (paperback). 214 pages.

"You know the desires unleashed by urban nights. You are the memory of distant orgasms reduced to recording sessions." Puerto Rican writer Mayra Santos-Febres's novel *Sirena Silena* is a stunning little creation that would make the perfect choice for any reader who yearns for something fresh and provocative. It's the story of an unbelievably sexy chanteuse, the breathtaking, barely legal singer whose voice has the power to render an audience prostrate with longing. Only thing is, this overpoweringly exotic girl used to be just another dirty little homeless boy roaming the streets of San Juan in search of a trick or a fix. But fortune, in the shape of drag-queen diva Martha Divine, smiles on fifteen-year-old Leocadio, transforming a scared young man into a dangerous young woman. *Sirena Selena* offers a surprisingly substantial mix of both giddy and serious pleasures. You get to meet a cast of gutsy transvestite performers who share the kind of black-comedy insight you can only gain by shaving your back and stuffing it into a cocktail dress. But this is also a deeply serious novel, which offers a startling look at the boundaries of gender that separate man from woman and the boundaries of love that separate each of us from our heart's desire.

In the Time of the Butterflies
Julia Alvarez. Penguin USA: 1995 (paperback). 321 pages.

Julia Alvarez's family emigrated from the Dominican Republic in 1960, seeking refuge in the United States from the Dominican tyrant Trujillo. Alvarez first came to American literary attention with the publication of her novel *How the Garcia Girls Lost Their Accents,* a story about four sisters making the difficult adjustments required of immigrants. But Alvarez never forgot four real-life sisters who never got the chance to escape or to begin a new life. *In the Time of the Butterflies* tells the story of the four Mirabel sisters, privileged young women who trade in their easy lives for ones of terrible hardship and danger in order to resist Trujillo's bloody dictatorship. Alvarez imagines the winding paths that led the sisters from luxury to rebellion, from static security to the defining moment of their lives, a moment that made international press. Alvarez's fluid, often irreverent writing captures the Mirabels' defiant spirit of freedom, a spirit that still inspires a nation to exclaim, *"¡Vivan Las Mariposas!"* This novel is on Ellen's personal all-time favorite list. "Keeps me up till four in the morning, every time."

❧ **ReadSmartGuide®** *available at* www.goodbookslately.com

The House on the Lagoon
Rosario Ferré. Plume: 1996 (paperback). 407 pages.

Matriarch and patriarch of a powerful Puerto Rican family offer competing accounts of the family's personal history and its connection to the island's politics.

THE SOUTHERN NOVEL:
CONTEMPORARY AUTHORS STEP OUT
FROM FAULKNER'S SHADOW

We told you the literature of the American West is going through a boom time of quality and quantity, but the literature of the American South (an older part of the country) has already risen once and has recently started to rise majestically once again. These contemporary southern authors do more than appropriate justice to the great legacy left by authors such as William Faulkner, Eudora Welty, and Walker Percy.

Some Discussion Considerations for Books in This Category

- Consider and discuss your past experience with "literature of the American South." Do you remember reading or are you familiar with any particular celebrated works of southern origin? When you think of the phrase "southern fiction," what immediate associations or pictures snap to mind? Where is "The South" exactly, in your mind—which states or regions are included or excluded?

- Can you pinpoint any characters, situations, or themes that seem specifically "southern" in some way to you—that is, that would not or could not emerge in the same way if they had come from or happened somewhere else in the country? How would a non-southerner's reading of this book's major ideas and meanings be different from what somebody from another part of the country would pick up on?

- Many writers and critics, southerners and otherwise (those damn Yankees!) have argued that much of the cultural life of the South was shaped by its brutal defeat in the Civil War. These pundits sometimes claim that the South has been "left behind" or isolated from the rest of the country in some way. Do you see any evidence to support or refute this in this book?

The Long Home
William Gay. MacMurray & Beck: 2000 (paperback). 257 pages.

The big bad southern novel rears its gritty head once again, and it's about time. Much as we have enjoyed the recent flood of comfy, wacky, zesty novels from and about the American South, it's a pleasure to discover an author who deserves to walk in the footprints of the historic greats. Set in rural Tennessee in the 1940s, Gay's novel is populated by a cast of archetypal characters—the bold young man, the beautiful young girl, the wise old man, and the omniscient villain with a heart as black as night. But these characters are more than stock types; in each we recognize the stubborn elements of individual humanity that insist on pushing through to the surface. In the villain, especially, Gay has managed to create the kind of ominous presence that lurks on the edge of nightmare, waiting to take advantage of a person's most private weaknesses. Even the physical landscape conspires to enhance the novel's sense of a hidden evil lurking within the dark and leafy forest. Brrrrrrrr . . .

So Far Back
Pam Durban. Picador USA: 2001 (paperback). 259 pages.

Durban's provocative novel gives us an amazing perspective on how family members from the past can influence our everyday lives today. Through the 1837 diary of Eliza Hilliard, we learn about the Hilliards—a venerable Charleston clan whose family tree stretches back 250 years. Past and present and black and white clash and dance back and forth as Louisa (the last of the family and the discoverer of Eliza's journal) struggles to understand how her own family could have justified slavery and how its slaves could have survived. In the way this haunting story examines America's deepest collective wound, it bears some resemblance to Toni Morrison's *Beloved* (and, like *Beloved,* it's beautiful and wrenching at the same time). While there's lots to think about and lots to talk about, Durban tells the story without hitting us over the head with a political agenda, so what shines through are the all-too-human moments in some of the biggest and darkest events that shaped our nation.

Yonder Stands Your Orphan
Barry Hannah. Grove Press: 2001 (paperback). 336 pages.

"He was undergoing stress, a rapid melancholy that overcame him once he had vomited on another person. This thing wanting out of him so quickly, like a hot weasel in a tube." How's that for an image, folks? And yet that whimsical little sentence is but one of thousands of brilliant bits of wordplay from Barry Hannah's unexpectedly charming novel, *Yonder Stands Your Orphan.* If you care about truly great writing, you are about to be reduced to a twitching, slobbering, and insatiable slave to this Major Talent, who turns Faulkner's rural Mississippi on its proverbial and ragged ear. In this alternately sweet and hilariously nasty cautionary tale, Hannah creates a cast of characters who are doomed to lurk in the corners of your consciousness for the duration, as each takes his or her particular brand of revenge on the small town of Eagle Lake. These include frustrated pimp Man Mortimer, who mourns the fading of his youthful Fabian looks by launching a cheerful campaign of terror; Isaac and Jacob Allison, two prepubescent brothers who discover a mysterious pair of skeletons in the trunk of a car they've borrowed; and the fabulously detestable, perpetually nauseous Sidney Farté, who watches aging town beauty Melanie Wooten with lazy, hooded eyes. "He could barely stand her presence. Oh, he wanted to sodomize her and puke on her back, but he certainly didn't respect her." Genius, friends, genius.

TALES OF NEW YORK: FRESH VOICES
FROM ALL FIVE BOROUGHS

A fun little special-interest category for all those of you out there who might joyously declare "I (heart) NY!" or, conversely, for those of you who would do nothing of the kind.

Kissing in Manhattan
David Schickler. Delta: 2002 (paperback). 288 pages.

We remember reading a short story called "The Smoker" in the *New Yorker* and thinking to ourselves, "What kind of sick, brilliant mind came up with this?!" The answer is David Schickler, the talented young writer whose short-story collection, *Kissing in Manhattan,* is perfect for anyone who loves short stories, the city, and sex. The stories are expertly told, strangely erotic, filled with surprising images, clever dialogue, and plot twists that move in directions you might never have imagined. Schickler's collection is a sort of *Sex and the City* from a guy's point of view—funny, smart, and stylish, with characters like no one you've met before in relationships you never knew existed. We are introduced to many of these characters from the outside in, meeting them first through the eyes of another narrator and then, sometimes shockingly, in a later story, we see things through their eyes. The shifts in perspective are enough to make you dizzy (in a good way). What ties the separate stories together—and this is so well done, surely one of the book's most satisfying characteristics—is that most of the characters (whether they know it or not) live in the same building on the Upper West Side of Manhattan. The Preemption Building lurks behind each story as a sort of character itself, adding a foreboding sense of gothic atmosphere and bringing the characters together in surprising ways.

Plum & Jaggers
Susan Richards Shreve. Picador: 2000 (paperback). 228 pages.

Susan Richards Shreve starts her story with a literal and literary explosion of such force that it almost knocks you off the page. The four McWilliams children—Sam, the oldest, at seven, and younger siblings Charlotte, Oliver, and Julia—are waiting for lunch aboard the express train from Milan to Rome. Their parents, James and Lucy McWilliams, have just stepped into the café two cars down to get the meal, when a terrorist bomb goes off, killing everyone in the first two cars, James and Lucy included. In telling the story of the McWilliams orphans, especially the story of Sam, vigilant new head of a shattered family, Shreve begins with a bang and never stops for breath. This novel makes you dizzy with fear and fierce with hope all at the same time, taking you in one after another unexpected direction. Just like Sam, who turns the family tragedy into the family enterprise. In creating the dynamic dark comedy of *Plum & Jaggers,* a laugh-'cause-it-hurts double-brother/sister stage routine, Sam launches an entertainment vehicle that will rocket the McWilliams kids from Second City to *Saturday Night Live* and beyond. But as Sam and his siblings know all too well, you're never safe from surprise, and at the height of the McWilliams's professional success, a stranger comes a-knockin' on the door.

～ **Read*Smart*Guide®** *available at* www.goodbookslately.com

Twelve
Nick McDonell. Grove Press: 2003 (paperback). 256 pages.

Flip to the back flap of this precise, prematurely wise, and chilling novel to look at the author's jacket photo. Now read the bio underneath—one simple sentence—"Nick McDonell was born in 1984 in New York City." Yes, folks, that's right, this guy is nineteen—he was seventeen when this book was published—and he can already tell a story that is vastly more compelling than about 90 percent of what's out there on the shelves. We were tempted to dismiss this cautionary tale of spoiled-rotten teen life on the Upper East Side of present-day Manhattan, but the novel is too straightforward and fresh to resist. McDonell's hero is White Mike, a strangely clean, disturbingly moral drug dealer who has mostly dropped out of his very prestigious prep school to sell dope to kids from pretty much every prestigious prep school in town. As White Mike makes his rounds during the week between Christmas and New Year's Eve, we meet a variety of his disenchanted and disenfranchised clientele—somehow, McDonell wins our caring, and occasionally our compassion, for these zany kids who have so much and appreciate so little. You sort of want to yank away their cell phones and Discmans and offer them a snack and an afghan. As you might expect, kids with tons of money, plenty of free time, and a complete lack of parental care or supervision can whip up a hell of a New Year's party. But the week, the novel, and the evening culminate in a surprising crescendo of passion that's enough to smack the apathy out of the most jaded reader or character.

IRISH YARNS: THE GIFT OF GAB
AT WORK FROM BOTH SIDES OF
THE ATLANTIC

Kiss the Blarney stone, the legend promises, and inherit the gift of gab. These marvelous contemporary authors write of the Irish experience both at home and abroad, circumventing any dated notions regarding the rustic charms of blarney, leprechauns, shillelaghs, or thatched cottages.

At Swim Two Boys
Jamie O'Neill. Scribner: 2003 (paperback). 567 pages.
For those of you out there who are still feeling guilty about never having read James Joyce, here's a Irish novel that, while extremely

Joycean in style and spirit, is also aggressively readable. In addition, it's one of the most authentic, appealing, and evocative love stories yet to grace our new century, even as it recounts events of almost a century ago. Set in the year preceeding the Easter Uprising of 1916, *At Swim, Two Boys* chronicles the passionate, confrontational relationship between Jim Mack, an aspiring scholar and son of a delusionally ambitious shopkeeper, and Doyler Doyle, a notorious ruffian waste collector and son of Jim's dad's old army buddy. The boys make a secret pact to claim a new country for themselves; meanwhile, adults in positions of both responsible and corrupt authority make other plans for these two promising young boys—everyone, it seems, has already laid claim to a little piece of each of them. You might think you can guess the ending, but you won't. Let's just say it hits you right where it counts. The writing is truly exquisite and the story is bold as brass—this book's going to get a lot of very well-deserved attention for a very long time.

Felicia's Journey
William Trevor. Penguin: 1994 (paperback). 213 pages.
A masterful literary thriller that will keep you guessing and hoping till the final page. When we meet Trevor's young Irish heroine, Felicia, she is vomiting repeatedly in the public washroom of a ship bound for England, having gotten herself into the oldest kind of trouble. She had some help getting herself into this kind of trouble, of course, and now she is seeking her passionate hometown beau, Johnny, in his new adopted country, confident that together they will start a new family infinitely more supportive and loving than the one she has left behind. The only problem is that Felicia isn't exactly certain of Johnny's precise whereabouts. As Johnny proves harder and harder to find in the heavily industrial English Midlands, Felicia comes to depend more and more on the help of her new friend, the infinitely respectable Mr. Hilditch, a middle-aged catering manager. Little does Felicia know that Mr. Hilditch has enjoyed the friendship of many a pretty, unsuspecting girl before she stumbled across his path. Trevor's penetrating

psychological portrayal of his two principals rapidly heats to a boiling point in such an unexpected manner that you hardly know what or who to root for, making for the utmost reading satisfaction you are likely ever to find in two hundred pages.

My Dream of You
Nuala O'Faolain. Riverhead: 2001 (paperback). 528 pages.

Prepare yourself for one of the loveliest love stories we have ever encountered. Despite her own better judgment, London travel writer Kathleen de Burca makes the bold move to journey back to her homeland in Ireland several decades after her initial escape from family hell. She simply can't help it, as she's totally obsessed by a very old scandal—a sordid affair that took place over a century ago between an English landlord's wife and an Irish servant. Having spent her entire adult life as a slave to passion, Kathleen is finally ready to stare disastrous love in its greedy face, hoping to gain a tiny smidgen of personal insight into her own highly irregular relationships. What she discovers as she researches this old story is quite a surprise, both to her and to the utterly absorbed reader. Ready to lose your heart to a truly worthwhile book? This is the perfect candidate.

A Star Called Henry
Roddy Doyle. Penguin USA: 2000 (paperback). 384 pages.

Young desperado Henry Smart joins the newly formed IRA just in time for Easter Monday 1916. It's safe to say that you won't find a more charismatic hero who uses a wooden leg to kill for his country in your reading in this or any other year.

Charming Billy
Alice McDermott. Delta: 1999 (paperback). 243 pages.

This winner of the 1998 National Book Award opens in a dingy Bronx bar after the funeral of a longtime alcoholic. As his large circle of family and friends share their stories of Billy, we discover one man's meaning to a struggling but supportive community.

HISTORICAL FICTION: FASCINATING STORIES SET IN A DAY GONE BY

The titles in this category belong to a time and place that is not our own, are set sometime and someplace in the past. Just how far past? Good question. Could a novel set in the American 1960s, that is in some way specifically "about" the sixties, be considered a historical novel? Sure it could, if you want it to. But many people might argue that a "historical" setting is one that is at least fifty years old or older. Why fifty? Who knows? Guess that just feels about right.

Some Discussion Considerations for Books in This Category

- Describe the specific historical setting of this novel: time, place, and specific social atmosphere and/or cultural values. Does the author make this world come alive for you?
- How intrinsic or vital to the story is the setting? How are each of the main characters' personalities, aspirations, desires, fears, or conflicts shaped by the specific time and place in which he or she lives? Or can you imagine a similar version of this story taking place in a completely different time and place?
- Was the specific historical setting of this story part of the reason that you wanted or were excited to read it? Is this setting familiar to you, in some ways, from other stories that you might have read that are set in this place and time?

In Sunlight, in a Beautiful Garden
Kathleen Cambor. Perennial: 2002 (paperback). 272 pages.
We'd like to take this opportunity to introduce the perfect summer novel that's good for all year round. Cambor's moving historical novel is set against the backdrop of a not-so-perfect Memorial Day weekend 112 years ago, the weekend in 1889 when a shaky

dam perched precariously above Johnstown, Pennsylvania, finally broke down, killing more than two thousand people below. Cambor employs a large cast of characters, some purely fictional, others the fictional representatives of the real people who managed to turn a blind eye to a big problem. However, because she makes you care about each and every one of these people almost instantaneously, you won't have any trouble remembering who's who. This is one of those novels that's dangerous to begin unless you've got some free time, because otherwise you're going to get slightly annoyed at everyone and everything in your life that keeps you from reading it straight through to the end.

Spies
Michael Frayn. Picador USA: 2003 (paperback). 261 pages.

Michael Frayn, that notorious Triple Threat, pulls off yet another masterpiece, once again, making it look so effortless and easy that we feel like it must be about as difficult for him to knock out a mind-boggling literary thriller as it is for us to clean our bathroom sink. Frayn, author of prize-winning plays and screenplays, as well as numerous novels, including 1999's international hit *Headlong,* treats us to yet another chilling, challenging, perfect page-turning story. The spies in question are two young boys living in a London suburb during World War II. The games of their childhood screech to a halt when Keith, the alpha dog of the pair, utters the six fatal words that will change the lives of everyone in the neighborhood forever. As the boys move deeper into an intrigue that they cannot hope to understand, we begin to learn of a secret forbidden love affair that is destined to outwit and outlast the ravages of war and the bonds of family ties.

The Year of Jubilo: A Novel of the Civil War
Howard Bahr. Picador USA: 2001 (paperback). 384 pages.

We wonder if Howard Bahr, in his impetuous youth, told his friends that he was going to write a Great American Novel. If any bets were made, now's the time to pay up, boys. How to explain this very unusual Civil War story? Well, it starts with a vicious double murder, as described by a blind eyewitness, in the last year of the war, 1864. Next, Bahr jumps forward a year, and we join up with Gawain Harper, a forty-year-old Confederate veteran making his weary way home, with many a mixed feeling about what he's going to find when he gets there. He's particularly anxious about the matter of Morgan Rhea, the unusual woman whose fierce determination propelled Gawain, a peace-loving professor, into serving the Cause. On the way into town, Gawain meets Harry Stribling, a cheerful, interfering man of unexplained background, who calls himself a philosopher and whose mission appears to be to shake and stir Gawain's already mixed-up world. Back at home, they find a Yankee regiment allegedly keeping order, a brilliant, cold-hearted killer picking off the soldiers one by one, a tortured Rebel spy-turned-guilty-entrepreneur, a fresh-faced young boy who takes a walk and gets his throat slit, and a barbarian backwoodsman who lurks in the cover of the forest, watching it all. Great cast of characters, great Smalltown novel, great mystery, great story of what happens to defeat, violence, and hatred in light of a second, brighter chance.

Girl with a Pearl Earring
Tracy Chevalier. Plume: 2001 (paperback). 233 pages.
Chevalier imagines the story behind one of the world's most celebrated and mysterious paintings by Dutch artist Johannes Vermeer. A phenomenal story, terrific heroine, and a must read for book groups who don't want their union card taken away.

❧ **ReadSmart Guide®** *available at* www.goodbookslately.com

The Book of Ebenezer Le Page
G. B. Edwards. Moyer Bell Ltd: 1995 (paperback—reissue). 241 pages
The only book you'll need when you get marooned on that desert island: the glorious, heart-breaking epic of one Guernsey fellow's

trip through the twentieth century. Average Amazon.com rating: five stars. We give it six.

The Greenlanders
Jane Smiley. Fawcett Books: 1996 (paperback). 582 pages.
It's fourteenth-century Greenland, and life is harsh, so don't be surprised when major characters meet, die, or disappear without fanfare. If you stick with this unusual story, it will reverberate in you for a lifetime.

Cloudsplitter
Russell Banks. HarperCollins: 1999 (paperback). 758 pages.
What would it be like to be the son of the country's most notorious activist, terrorist, and martyr? Banks attempts to answer this question in his portrait of Owen Brown, the only son to survive John Brown's attack on Harper's Ferry.

The Polished Hoe
Austin Clarke. Amistad: 2003 (hardcover). 462 pages.
Mary Mathilda kills her husband and spends the night with the local chief of police, telling the story of her rise from field laborer to mistress of a sugar plantation on a small island in the West Indies—set in the postcolonial thirties and forties.

CONTEMPORARY CLASSICS:
TWENTIETH-CENTURY WORKS THAT
WILL STAND THE TEST OF TIME

The stories in this category are what TNN might call the "New Classics," or what you might call "Classics in the Making." These are books that are relatively new—that is, written in the past ten to thirty years, but which have already earned an established place in the limelight, and which seem destined to do so for the foreseeable future. (For reading considerations and discussion questions, please see chapter 3, page 70.)

The Group
Mary McCarthy. Harvest Books: 1991 (paperback). 487 pages.
Could this classic story of eight Vassar grads, class of '33, be the ultimate book group book? Well, it's certainly one of the most insightful, wickedly funny, embarrassingly accurate renditions of the group life of women that has ever been written. As our eight heroines leave the shelter of the university to explore new worlds their mothers didn't dream of, they never, of course, leave the shelter of class or privilege. These are the women of our mothers' or grandmothers' time; but as we read about their expectations, their ideals, their debates over the nature of womanhood in a brand-new era, it's truly unnerving to see how little, in some ways, things have changed. McCarthy's ability to make you care about these women, even while you're laughing at their naïveté and sense of entitlement, makes *The Group* an endlessly fascinating classic.

∽ **ReadSmartGuide®** *available at* www.goodbookslately.com

I Capture the Castle
Dodie Smith. St. Martin's Griffin: 1998 (paperback). 343 pages.
J. K. Rowling raves: "This book has one of the most charismatic narrators I've ever met." If the unparalleled popularity of Rowling's main character (some boy named Harry Potter) is any indication, it would appear that she knows a thing or two about charisma. As it happens, we couldn't agree more—you'll find it hard not to fall in love with seventeen-year-old Cassandra Mortmain and her delicious account of life in a a most unconventional British family. True, the Mortmains live in a castle, but they're wearing the rags of clothing purchased in an earlier decade and wondering about the exact whereabouts of their next meal. As

Cassandra decides to devote herself to writing, hoping to pick up a literary career like the one her father has so inexplicably left off, a new family moves into the neighborhood and provides ample material for her diary. Originally published in 1948, and brought back into print to the thunderous gratitude of worshipful readers the world round, *I Capture the Castle* is a reading experience utterly unlike any other we have encountered. It's one of those awesome family stories that might have earned your undying loyalty as a youngster, but it's clever enough to capture even the most sophisticated reader long past the coming of age.

The Power of the Dog
Thomas Savage. Back Bay: 2001 (paperback—reprint). 276 pages.

If we were forced at gunpoint to pick an absolute favorite book group book, this would be it. Thomas Savage is a Great American Writer. And when we say great, we mean great like William Faulkner, like Ernest Hemingway, like Toni Morrison, like Philip Roth. Good authors can write great books, but great authors write the books that change things forever, that disarm and redefine current literary expectations. Thank you so much for that lecture, you say, but how come I've never even heard of this guy? Well, we hadn't ever heard of him either until 2001, when we received a copy of this novel. Originally published in 1967, it was a critical sensation, but somehow the "buzz" on Thomas Savage never reached most of us average slobs, the general reading public. Fortunately, readers and author have another chance to get together, since Little, Brown reissued the novel (long out of print) June 2001. Set in 1920s Montana, *The Power of the Dog* tells the story of two families who come together in a distinctly unharmonious fashion. Its utterly convincing narrative voice offers a chillingly precise look into the demanding lives of its strong, complex characters. As the story progresses, you might find it tough to determine if the main character is a villain or a victim, but he will scare you silly nonetheless.

⁓ Read*Smart*Guide® *available at* www.goodbookslately.com

Sula
Toni Morrison. Penguin USA: 2002 (paperback—reprint). 192 pages.

Many book groups have read *Beloved,* Morrison's haunting novel about one woman's terrible choice to save her children from the horrors of slavery. *Sula* has received less attention, but it shares the strange beauty and fascinating characters that make Morrison's fiction a favorite among book groups—we think this novel makes for the perfect introduction to Morrison; it's short, sweet, accessible, and quirky as all get out. *Sula* is set in the small town of Medallion, Ohio, during the years spanning World War I to the civil rights movement; and it tells the story of Nel and Sula, whose friendship endures the hardships of social change and personal transformation. *Sula* may be a slim little book, but make no mistake—it raises complex questions about race, sex, death, poverty, education, and that knottiest of all dynamics, friendship between women.

⁓ Read*Smart*Guide® *available at* www.goodbookslately.com

CLASSICS REVISITED: CONTEMPORARY AUTHORS REIMAGINE OLD FAVORITES

Whenever you're reading a story that references an older classic, it's always interesting to explore connections and deviations between the two. If you aren't familiar with the earlier narrative, you may want to ask a book group member who is to summarize some key points. Each of the stories below, however, can also stand on their own merit entirely.

Life of Pi
Yann Martel. Harvest Books: 2003 (paperback). 336 pages.

How to describe this meaty and miraculous novel? Well, it's kind of like *The Old Man and the Sea* meets *The Black Stallion*, only quite a bit better than either of those two respectable tomes. A smallish Indian sets sail for Canada with his family, accompanied by the remaining animals of the former family zoo. A mysterious shipwreck leaves Pi the sole survivor but one; he is stranded alone on a rowboat in the middle of the ocean, with only an enormous and very hungry full-grown male Bengal tiger for company. The water around him is churning with sharks. This heart-thumping story is so strong and so good that you can almost hear the water around Martel churning with people vying to acquire the paperback and film rights. You'll race to finish the novel, but you won't forget it in a hurry—unique, awesome, and utterly necessary. Without giving too much away, we'll tell you this is an ingenious and provocative revision of *Robinson Crusoe*. It is the 2002 winner of the prestigious Booker Prize.

☞ **ReadSmartGuide®** *available at* www.goodbookslately.com

"Tell Us About the Bad Ones"

When we visit a book group for the first time, we ask members to tell us about their favorite and least favorite book choices. The atmosphere in the room tends to turn all warm and friendly as book group members attempt to pinpoint the factors that made a loved book so special and significant. But the discussion of books that bombed can be even more revealing and intriguing. Consider having one with your group soon—you may learn something you didn't know about your members' unique criteria for awesome or awful. The following is a list of some of the common obstacles that may hinder seemingly good books from being great book group books. We don't mean to offend anyone who loves any of the examples we've used. These are simply titles readers have mentioned time and time again as occupationally problematic.

The Nice but Nothing to Talk About Book

This is generally an upbeat, life-affirming book, well written and fun to read. The characters are easy to understand; the story doesn't force us to think or question too much. Such books can provide a welcome break for a group that has made a serious run of heavy, dark books and discussions. The typical group, however, needs something more challenging and ambiguous to sustain them. We loved reading *The Nanny Diaries,* but it would be tough to build a worthwhile couple of hours of intense discussion around the fact that some rich people are superficial and oblivious to their children's true needs.

The Social Platform Battle-ax

This book has a distinct agenda, a particular ax to grind. The author's purpose is to teach us something, dammit; he or she wants to challenge our complacent convictions. If the writer can't separate the story from the platform, however, if all the characters "stand" for some social good or evil, it's tough to debate their conflicting personality traits or motivations. Ayn Rand's famed celebration of objectivism, *The Fountainhead*, could be fertile book group ground if you want to learn about, you know, objectivism. But every major character in this book represents a specific worldview—either pure and perfect or disgustingly flawed by Rand's philosophical standards. *The Fountainhead* is a compelling story, but never trust anyone who tells you that "it changed my life."

The Initially Intriguing but Eventually Disappointing Story

Nothing spoils a great book like a rotten ending. What makes an ending bad? Maybe it's predictable, or unrealistic, or doesn't seem to "go" with the rest of the book; it seems artificial or overly sensational. Maybe it's so abrupt and unresolved that it seems as if the author just got sick of writing one day and left his or her desk to go on a cruise. Look at reviews from critics or fellow readers; if more than one has remarked on a dud finish, you may want to steer clear. As one reader queried, for example, "After the wonderful and mysterious buildup of *The Sparrow*, all that amazingly creative and compelling intergalactic communication, the big finale is alien anal rape?"

The Extremely Creative but Not Everyone's Cup of Tea Experiment

Certain experimental works are never going to attract any but the most academic or philosophical of readers—wherever you go for book group recommendations, please ignore the pundit who advises that you read *Tristram Shandy*. Of course, part of the reason most of us are in book groups is to expand our reading experience, so it's good to try something new and unusual every once in a while. It all depends on your group's preferences and personality. Lots of readers love Dave Eggers's *Heartbreaking Work of Staggering Genius,* but others can't get past that strange table of contents or object to the proliferation of the word that rhymes with "duck."

The "Extremely Challenging" Literary Classic

Many book group readers struggle with the nagging feeling that they aren't *really* improving their minds unless they are reading the occasional classic. Recently we've been running into all sorts of groups who've struggled heroically with William Faulkner's *Sound and the Fury.* If you're new to Faulkner, this is not the best introduction—large portions are written from the point of view of a severely retarded boy, so it's not exactly easy going. Instead, pick up the infinitely more accessible *Light in August.* Ask a trusted and well-read friend, teacher, bookseller, or librarian to recommend a favorite "classic" novel or to choose which novel might be the most welcoming introduction to a particular famed author's oeuvre.

The So Universally Loved It Creates a Vacuum Book

Alice Sebold's *Lovely Bones.* Leif Enger's *Peace Like a River.* John Irving's *Prayer for Owen Meany.* Harper Lee's *To Kill a Mockingbird.* Each of these novels has earned a hallowed, well-deserved place in book group history. These are *not* bad book group books; in fact, they can be potentially the greatest of book group books. But unless you arm yourself appropriately, they may disappoint your group in the discussion: "We all loved that book so much it was hard to talk about it." Do your job as a participant, a leader, a researcher, or host. Make sure that your group has access to a stimulating list of discussion questions or points of consideration to turn to once the initial communal bliss has run its course.

Ahab's Wife or, The Star-Gazer
Sena Jeter Naslund. HarperPerennial Library: 2000
(paperback). 688 pages.

Everything you always wanted to know about existentialism but didn't ask for fear that someone might actually tell you. But seriously, folks. The story of *Ahab's Wife* represents a phenomenal step forward for the reworking of the classic novel. In Melville's *Moby-Dick,* we learn that the vengeful Captain Ahab, he of the one leg and the terrible grudge against the white whale that took it, left a young "girl-wife" behind in Nantucket when he went to sea aboard the *Pequod.* In the few spare details Melville offers about Mrs. Ahab, Sena Jeter Naslund apparently found enough inspiration to create a rich, complex, and very surprising character, the ever free-thinking Una Spenser. *Ahab's Wife* remains spiritually and technically true to much of Melville's masterpiece, but for those of you who could never quite make it through *Moby-Dick,* let it be said that this novel is consistently interesting and intriguingly readable. Naslund's novel brings a vital and volatile period of American history to life, but this time it's from a woman's perspective. And because Una is a very special sort of woman, she brushes up against many of the most fascinating people, movements, and events of her time. Pick this one up and dive right in—don't be scared off by the leviathan size, either. There are lots of pictures.

❧ **ReadSmartGuide®** *available at* www.goodbookslately.com

The Hours
Michael Cunningham. Picador USA: 2000 (paperback). 230
pages.

A breathtaking reworking of Virginia Woolf's classic novel *Mrs. Dalloway, The Hours* is the winner of the 1999 Pulitzer Prize. Read the book and follow up with the equally delightful movie.

❧ **ReadSmartGuide®** *available at* www.goodbookslately.com

Summerland
Malcolm Knox. Picador USA: 2002 (paperback). 272 pages.
The new *Great Gatsby,* Australian-style! Can the sufferings of the
rich ever grow dull?

MEMOIR: WRITERS BRAVE THE ROCKY
TERRAIN OF THEIR OWN LIVES

(See chapter 3, page 89, for reading considerations and discussion
questions on memoir.)

Don't Let's Go to the Dogs Tonight
**Alexandra Fuller. Random House: 2003 (paperback). 336
pages.**
The first thing we ought to say about this memoir by Alexandra
Fuller is that it's got to be the most brutally honest reminiscence
of Rhodesia by a white African that has ever come out of that
lovely but unlucky region. The second thing would be that it's unbelievably well written and defiantly readable. Even if we can't
sympathize with Fuller's account of her family's role as unques-
tioning rulers of their own small domain and the native Africans
who populate it, it doesn't matter, because Fuller doesn't ask us
to. This is the story of the childhood of a young woman who isn't
afraid to admit that she was the center of her own universe, that
she was primarily concerned with protecting her own personal
comfort, just as children who are well fed and much loved do
everywhere. Only it just so happens that this particular child's
comforts were inextricably connected with her white family's relative position of power over their black neighbors, a power that
slowly deteriorated as an anticolonial war heated up.

 ReadSmartGuide® *available at* www.goodbookslately.com

Girl, Interrupted
Susanna Kaysen. Vintage Books: 1994 (paperback). 169 pages.

If you saw the movie, you saw a somewhat sensationalized rendering of Kaysen's more sophisticated, more subtle remembrance of the time she spent in McLean Hospital during the late sixties. Kaysen steers clear of the dramatic revelations and tear-jerking images that a record of a teen's descent into alleged insanity might so easily evoke. She doesn't make her stay at a mental institution sound like a day at the zoo, but she doesn't ignore the potential for humor in her unusual history, either. Instead, Kaysen presents us with a meditation on madness that is both realistic and surreal, as the adult author tries to make sense of the thought processes that weakened her adolescent self to the point of frightening mental instability. Challenging her readers to examine the nature of what distinguishes the healthy mind from the unbalanced, she encourages us to consider the flimsy boundaries that divide those who see things differently from those who see things as they are—wait till you read the book to figure out which is which.

🖢 **ReadSmartGuide®** *available at* www.goodbookslately.com

Me Talk Pretty One Day
David Sedaris. Little, Brown and Company: 2001 (paperback). 288 pages.

Has your group gotten bogged down, reading the deepest, darkest, and most emotionally demanding books? Well, it's time to climb out of your funk and have some fun. In this comical feast of essays, Sedaris brings his personal history to life, leaving no psyche unturned in his attempts to make sense of the random and ridiculous events that comprise our allegedly purposeful existence. Sedaris starts off with tales of his North Carolina childhood, during which he wages mostly successful campaigns against such adversaries as his determinedly upbeat speech therapist and his skeptical midget guitar teacher. As a young adult, Sedaris finds work as a perfor-

mance artist, bringing both lack of talent and lust for amphetamines to his career. In later stories, we find Sedaris teaching a writing class using *One Life to Live* as an inspirational model, moving to
France and turning into a scary "man-child" who can speak only in
nouns, and attending a soccer match in which men play against a
team of wily cows. Sedaris is outrageously nonstop fun to read, but
he also manages to make a lot of interesting observations on some
of the most inevitable human needs and desires.

Running with Scissors
**Augusten Burroughs. Picador USA: 2003 (paperback). 320
pages.**

Young Augusten wants to create his very own beauty empire, just
like Vidal Sassoon, but gets stuck with Mom's shrink, Dr. Finch,
and his Masturbatorium instead.

Naked in the Promised Land
**Lillian Faderman. Houghton Mifflin: 2003 (hardcover). 368
pages.**

An aspiring lesbian studies scholar discovers that she can put herself through college as a pinup gal and through grad school wearing pasties.

Cherry
Mary Karr. Penguin USA: 2001 (paperback). 276 pages.

This sequel to Karr's debut memoir (*New York Times* best-seller
The Liar's Club), an account of teenage years in rural Texas, is
Ellen's favorite memoir of all time, thus far.

Double Down: Reflections on Gambling and Loss
**Frederick and Steven Barthelme. Harvest Books: 2001
(paperback). 198 pages.**

Two college-professor brothers give in to the powers of addiction,
big time, in this frenzied tale of academics run amok in the "real
world" of real American casinos.

SHORT STORIES: THE BEST COLLECTIONS FROM WRITERS WHO KEEP IT SHORT AND SWEET

(See "Short Stories" in chapter 3, page 76, for reading considerations and discussion questions.)

Drinking Coffee Elsewhere
Z. Z. Packer. Riverhead: 2003 (hardcover). 238 pages.

"By our second day at Camp Crescendo, the girls in my Brownie troop had decided to kick the asses of each and every girl in Brownie Troop 909." So begins "Brownies," the first story in Z. Z. Packer's much-awaited debut—a collection of smart, edgy, beautifully crafted stories that capture the harrowing personal journeys of her young black characters. Published in the *New Yorker*'s debut fiction issue and in *Best American Short Stories, 2000*, Packer's stories are provocative and one-of-a-kind, recalling the best of Toni Morrison and Alice Walker. Each story is narrated by an outcast character struggling to find his or her place in a hostile world: the result is often furiously funny and always surprising. In the title story, Dina joins other new freshmen at Yale for orientation games; when asked what inanimate object she'd like to be, she chooses a revolver and thus begins her weekly visit to the university psychiatrist. "Every Tongue Shall Confess" features Clareese, the cross-eyed, devout choir director at the Greater Christ Emmanuel Pentecostal Church of the Fire Baptized, who finds love in a most unlikely place. In "The Ant of the Self," teenaged Spurgeon sets off to the Million Man March with his loser con-man father and discovers not his proud black male self but "the ant of the self—that small, blind, crumb-seeking part of ourselves." Packer's narrators are all wonderfully unique, but as the stories accumulate, the thematic core of the collection becomes visible: *Drinking Coffee Elsewhere* is a fierce exposé, a look at what it's like to be young, black, wickedly smart, and lost in America.

Darling?
Heidi Jon Schmidt. Picador USA: 2002 (paperback). 304 pages.

Take a close look at the Rorschach blot on Schmidt's cover. What you see may say something about your perspective on love. Do you see a human heart, a fragile rose petal, a bloody mess? Schmidt's stories themselves are kind of like a Roschach blot: it's hard to decide if they're heartwarming, scathing, funny, or tragic. The collection begins with the tale of complicated love between sisters that reaches a climax over a charbroiled feast of songbirds (yum!) and closes with a story that echoes with the bittersweet laughter of lovers at a funeral party. As one admiring writer points out, Schmidt's stories address "the frustrating, hilarious, embarrassing, transcendental business of living with love." Schmidt's wit is brilliant, her themes provocative, her female characters terribly flawed and wonderfully sympathetic. It's tough to write about love and have anything new to say, but Schmidt does just that.

The Toughest Indian in the World
Sherman Alexie. Grove Press: 2001 (paperback). 250 pages.

Alexie has been selected by the *New Yorker* as one of the best American fiction writers under forty; we think he's one of the best writers around, period. These stories will certainly challenge many people's preconceived notions of the contemporary Native American experience. Alexie's American Indian characters live in the city and the suburbs as well as on the reservation. They are journalists, lawyers, country music lovers, homosexuals, athletes, frequent flyers. Like the rest of us, they have their tragic and noble and savage qualities, but Alexie's brutal honesty and deadpan wit ensure that we see these people as individuals rather than as symbols of a lost cause. Alexie is a fierce writer, never pausing to flinch in the face of injustice, brutality, or ugliness; but he's also very funny, appealing, inspiring, and worth your reading time.

⚶ **ReadSmartGuide®** *available at* www.goodbookslately.com

The Woman Who Gave Birth to Rabbits
Emma Donoghue. Harcourt: 2002 (paperback). 254 pages.

Mary Toft didn't mean to become the woman who gave birth to rabbits. But enterprising friends and family persuade this ordinary eighteenth-century English housewife to share her miraculous offspring with the world, much to her eventual shame. This astoundingly persuasive collection of short stories inspired by strange nuggets of history proves that Irish author Donoghue has a similarly miraculous talent to share with jaded readers everywhere; she could be justly lauded as the Woman Who Gave Birth to Insane Jealousy for all the short-story writers whose jaws dropped slack on their chests as they read this collection. A famous Howgarth engraving of the alleged bunny producer set Donoghue's wildly creative gears in motion to create the title story; and in each of the others she draws upon some other, mostly forgotten historical remnant of Great Britain's meaty past to produce the tale behind a plague ballad, a theological pamphlet, or an articulated skeleton of the world's littlest little person. Put on your boots and get ready to go grave robbing with an enthusiastically curious master of the earthiest in historical fiction.

You Are Not a Stranger Here
Adam Haslett. Bantam: 2003 (paperback). 240 pages.

"The mental health establishment can go screw itself on a barren hilltop in the rain before I touch their snake oil or listen to the visionless chatter of men half my age. I have shot Germans in the fields of Normandy, filed twenty-six patents, married three women, survived them all, and am currently the subject of an investigation by the IRS, which has about as much chance of collecting from me as Shylock did of getting his pound of flesh. Bureaucracies have trouble thinking clearly. I, on the other hand, am perfectly lucid." That's from the first paragraph of the first story of Adam Haslett's mind-blowing new short-story collection. The story is "Notes to My Biographer," and the speaker is a manic-depressive septuagenarian who is determined that no one—especially not the son who still loves him—shall thwart his manifest destiny as one of America's greatest inventive geniuses. From the roller-coaster ride of this first story, Haslett's collection picks up speed and delivers knockout punch after knockout punch, chronicling the bizarre attempts of the desperately alienated and terribly lonely to find some way to connect to their fellow human beings. This is a harsh but absolutely amazing, ultimately touching book, a must read for anyone who wants to meet the future of American letters.

Interpreter of Maladies
Jhumpa Lahiri. Houghton Mifflin: 1999 (paperback). 198 pages.

Deserving winner of the 2000 Pulitzer Prize, featuring a bevy of immigrant characters, mostly from Bangladesh, India, and Pakistan, struggling to make sense of lives that seem strangely out of touch with mainstream society's expectations.

⫸ **Read*Smart*Guide®** *available at* www.goodbookslately.com

Birds of America
Lorrie Moore. Picador USA: 1999 (paperback). 291 pages.

The uniting factor in these twelve stories of every imaginable shape and variety is the presence of a different bird in each—we see these quirky characters first from above, then Moore swoops down, and we suddenly share their point of view.

Book Group Troubleshooting: The Wolf Comes to Town

I f you aren't overly squeamish about lots of violence, gore, and nasty words—so long as they're packaged in an interesting and clever way—then you very likely may have seen Quentin Tarantino's 1997 film *Pulp Fiction*. Actor Harvey Keitel plays a character known as the Wolf in this movie, a man "who takes care of things that people need taken care of." He cleans up troublesome messes, such as the interior of the car that Samuel L. Jackson's and John Travolta's characters manage to splatter with the brains of an accidental gunshot victim. We're guessing your book group hasn't had to confront the problem of scraping brain chunks off your upholstery—if so, please call us from the prison pay phone because we definitely want to interview you for our next book— but on the other hand, it's likely that if you've been together for a while, you have run across a book group mess or two in your time. Fear not, for the Wolf is in town, offering services free of charge, with the help of the many book group members around the country and the world who have faced just that particular problem and have learned, from experience, how to take care of it. Got a book group problem? Our readers have an answer.

FINDING NEW MEMBERS

Q: *For so many years, we had more members than we could comfortably accommodate. Now, all of a sudden, we are down to six people and really need some new blood. How do we find new members?*

Book Group Members Respond

"When someone resigns, we talk about who has asked to join and make a decision among ourselves. Our goal is to have a diverse group with a full range of ages and experiences."
—*Karen, East Quogue, New York*

"Members invite their friends. They aren't 'voted in' or anything. They just come back if they like it."
—*Kimberly, Arlington, Virginia*

"All readers are welcome to our bookstore group, and I post the information and display the book in the bookstore."
—*Ettabelle, Stow, Ohio*

"Each of us is responsible for 'recruiting' by word of mouth."
—*Kate, Fairfax, Virginia*

"We advertise at the library and on the e-mail list that circulates to the private community that I live in."
—*Eileen, Canadian Lakes, Michigan*

"Ask each of your members to bring a potential new member to a meeting—probably one or two at a time. The member can present it as an invitation to join the club for a meeting or an evening, not necessarily for good, until the group has time to decide whether this person is a good mix with the rest of you."
—*Sascha, Casper, Wyoming*

"Our [on-line] book group leader still sends out invites on different Web sites. We welcome anyone who is not looking for a heavy intellectual discussion. We like to have fun during our chat." —Beth, Mount Laurel, New Jersey

MINIMIZING SPORADIC ATTENDANCE

Q: *Why do people join book groups if they don't want to attend? We have had a real problem with this.*

Book Group Members Suggest

"Personally call or e-mail and remind members of the upcoming meeting three or four days beforehand." —Katherine, Dallas, Texas

"No big deal—it's not a job." —Jim, Griffin, Georgia

"Things that help are food and the book selection. If attendance gets slim, maybe the group could decide to suspend meetings for the summer or whatever. I do think there is a critical level of attendance that is necessary for a good discussion."
—Lisa, Hailey, Idaho

"Make it MANDATORY to RSVP. If someone misses consistently, ask them privately if they're still interested in being a member. Sometimes they are looking for a way out and just don't know how to bring it up." —Shelly, Dallas, Texas

"If a member has an apparent problem with this, call her and say, 'We missed you and hope you will be able to make the next meeting.' If you do this each time she misses, and if you make her feel welcome each time she comes, she'll take the hint." —Diane, Elko, Nevada

"Provide better food and wine, and in more generous quantities."
—Nancy, Trenton, New Jersey

"Perhaps this says something about your group as a whole, not just the absentee members? Maybe you need to pay a little more attention to ways to keep a stimulating discussion rolling."

—Gary, San Francisco, California

CHOOSING GREAT
BOOK GROUP BOOKS

Q: *Our book choices are so hit-or-miss. How do you pick a winner each time?*

Book Group Members Speak Up

"You have to expect a few losers. Your winner may be someone else's loser."

—Jennifer, Osage City, Kansas

"I subscribe to several book newsletters and check several book Web sites on the Internet. Also, we all have favorite authors whose books we enjoy reading."

—Anna, Oak Ridge, Tennessee

"We try to have variety in our picks. For example, this year we are reading a classic of our choice and we also read poetry. In the past we have read an autobiography of our own choice. We have also read a children's book. We have each read a book about our ethnic background. In addition we have read Oprah books, best-sellers, and just recommendations of others. It has worked very well."

—Anne, Plover, Wisconsin

"Because our members have lived all over the world, one year we tried to pick a book from each continent." —Kim, Windlesham, Surrey, England

"Look for books that have discussion questions available. I think having a theme for a series of books aids discussion, like Family, History of the Mystery, Steinbeck Centennial, Movies from Books, etc." —Lisa, Hailey, Idaho

"We look for books with controversy . . . stories that invite multiple interpretations, operate on several levels, are open to literary interpretation. Deal with some conflict, moral or broad issue."
—*Dalene, Kansas City, Missouri*

"Find yourself a trusted source: a particular newspaper book critic whose other choices you have liked, a wise friend who is well read and has picked many great books for you over the years, a knowledgeable bookseller who reads as much as any of her most avid customers, or a savvy book group Web site."
—*Margaret, Green Bay, Wisconsin*

"To my mind, the whole beauty of being in a book group is to read books that you would NEVER have chosen for yourself in a million years. And some of those books may not be so great, but still, you learned something from trying a kind of book or an author that you have never tried before."
—*Franklin, Fort Lauderdale, Florida*

"Make use of awards lists, get to know something about the kinds of books that each award tends to represent—your group may enjoy National Book Award short-list winners but not Nobel winners, for example."
—*Anna, Doe Bay, Washington*

"Choose books that no one in the group has read—that's what makes it interesting and fun for everybody."
—*Janice, Great Falls, Montana*

"Make a rule that at least one person in the group has read it and thinks it would be a good fit for the group. If she thinks it's good enough for her to read twice, then that's a pretty good sign!"
—*Veronica, Denver, Colorado*

STREAMLINING THE PROCESS OF CHOOSING BOOKS

Q: *We're a new group, but we've actually had a decent track record, so far, in terms of the books we've picked. Our real problem is the process of actually picking them—we have no established system, it's* *all frantic slapdash at the last minute, and it makes me exhausted just thinking about it.*

Book Group Members Advise

"Let everyone have a voice in choosing the books. Otherwise, you'll miss out on lots of good stuff. Everyone has different tastes and different sources, and you should make use of them."　　　　　　　　　　*—Jennifer, Temple, Texas*

"Once or twice a year, people bring books to recommend. Our rules are that some-one has to have read the book, and it must be available in paperback. This fall, each person recommended a book, and we have our list for the next twelve months."
　　　　　　　　　　　　　　　　　　　　　—Bev, Fort Collins, Colorado

"We've used two methods. Previously we've each submitted several titles, and then we voted, and the books with the most votes were the ones we'd read. Then every-one picked one of the 'winners' and signed up for a month to be the leader. Starting this coming year, we each pick one book, and then the one who chose the book for a specific month will be the leader."　　　　　　　　*—Marsha, Aurora, Colorado*

"Vary it and be flexible. For example, when a book wins a literature prize, be open to discussing it in lieu of something already chosen."
　　　　　　　　　　　　　　　　—Kim, Tewantin, Queensland, Australia

"Sometimes the hostess will announce the choice. Other times the hostess may bring several titles for the group to vote on, and sometimes the hostess will choose an author and we may read any of that author's books."
　　　　　　　　　　　　　　　　　—Julie, Concord, North Carolina

"We do not meet over the summer. Instead, a small book-selection committee will meet and come up with [some choices]. At our first book club meeting, the books are presented, and the entire membership votes on which book they want from each category. From there we make a reading schedule for the rest of the year."
　　　　　　　　　　　　　　　　—Kim, Windlesham, Surrey, England

"We e-mail our choices to our group leader. She puts the choices in a hat, and the one she pulls out is our selection. The person who picked that book is the leader of that discussion."

—Anonymous

"Each time, one member chooses two to four books for the group to vote on. That member may get his/her ideas from reviews, Web sites, previously read and loved books, recommendations from others."

—Ruth, Richmond, Virginia

"Planning a year ahead of time is too long because sometimes a truly tempting book rises to the surface in the middle of the year, you've only just heard about it, and everyone's dying to do it for book group, but you're all "booked up" (ha ha) for the next eight months. We tried a six-month schedule one time, but now we always make sure that we have just the NEXT THREE months' books chosen—adding one book for that third month at each meeting."

—Anonymous

LOCATING BOOK GROUP RESOURCES AND SUPPORT

Q: *We're a fairly new group and need some help with book choices and getting organized. Where do we go for a little outside support?*

Book Group Members Recommend

"First place to go, if you live in a town that is fortunate enough to have a good independent bookstore, would be that very same good independent bookstore. Lots of these stores have devoted special displays or programs just for book groups, and even if not, smaller booksellers are generally on a first-name basis with many of their customers and know which books are working best for whom."

—Jack, Lawrence, Kansas

"Check out the Web site of the publisher of the book you're reading—or the author's Web site, if he or she has one, and most of them do. Lots of these Web sites provide discussion questions or links to other book group resources."

—*Dana, Sacramento, California*

"Don't forget your local library—call ahead and ask to meet with the librarian in charge of the fiction section—or whatever section you're interested in. Let him or her know that you represent a book club and need help finding the best books and resources to research books for book club discussion." —*Angela, Dayton, Ohio*

"All you need is a computer and an Internet hookup. There are so many great new Web sites for reading groups and reading group guides and resources." [Please note: you can find a complete list of these Web sites in appendix 3, "Book Group Resources."] —*Karly, Wichita, Kansas*

"We've been getting almost all our book club recommendations from *Good Books Lately* for over three years now, and we think they're the most consistently great picks to be found!" —*Sally Pollock, Kansas City, Missouri, (Ellen's mother-in-law)*

PREPARING TO LEAD THE DISCUSSION

Q: *I joined a book group recently, and most members have been involved for years. I'm leading my first discussion next month, and I'm a bit nervous. How do you suggest I find information on the book and prepare a really good discussion?*

Book Group Members Suggest

"If I'm presenting, I do quite a bit of research online. If it's appropriate, I bring in a guest speaker. In the case of *Ahab's Wife*, I plan to read *Moby-Dick* because of the references to it." —*Anonymous*

"When it's my turn to lead the discussion, I usually go to the library to do some research on the author and the book. Read through some criticism and biographical info to share. I try to bring some pictures if I can find some."

—*Kathy, Pflugerville, Texas*

"If I'm leading, I'm all over the Web. I look for stuff about the author, the time period, discussion guides, etc. If I'm just attending, I try to read the book as close to the book group date as possible, as I have a brain like a sieve and tend to forget everything."

—*Nancy, Lafayette, Colorado*

"First it helps to read the book! I'm in charge of the questions, so I look up or create discussion questions as well. I put out an E-mail to the group about a week before the meeting to remind everyone. I try to make an invitation that has something to do with the theme of the book."

—*Elaine, Denver, Colorado*

[Our Suggestion—see appendix 3, "Book Group Resources."]

FOCUSING ON THE BOOK WHEN SOCIALIZING TAKES OVER

Q: *How do you get an extra-social book club to settle down and devote some time to serious book discussion?*

Book Group Members Recommend

"No such thing. If the books are interesting, there will be enough serious book talk. We have never had this problem. While we eat dinner, we go around the table and each person says whether she liked the book and why. Once everyone has had her say, we have a general discussion. We socialize before and after." —*Lisa, Denver, Colorado*

"Have a routine and stick to it. We have a potluck dinner for one hour (6–7 p.m.), then begin discussing the book at 7 p.m. whether everyone's finished eating or not."

—*Kay, Blue Springs, Missouri*

"We have a happy balance. Because we did not know each other prior to starting the book group, we find we are not distracted by socializing. We may find that personal experiences, such as having been immigrants to a new country, will be discussed when a similar theme is drawn out in a book. It is very enlightening to hear it from a true perspective." —*Cate, North Parramatta, Australia*

"Try to bring the subject back on track. One time the diversion was flatly refused, so we let the meeting turn into a social gathering. That wasn't preferable, but who wants to be the book club police?" —*Katherine, Dallas, Texas*

"We had a problem with this and sent an E-mail explaining that while we love the social aspect, the real reason for getting together is to discuss the book. We suggested that if someone has not read the book, that they do not socialize during our discussion period." —*Angela, Canton, Georgia*

[For Internet groups:] "We have an easy way of dealing with this. We simply head the subject line OT (off topic) and others can choose to read or not read the message. We as moderators only 'get heavy' if the subject goes on too long or is too political." —*Kim, Windlesham, Surrey, England*

LIGHTENING UP A TOO-SERIOUS
BOOK GROUP

Q: *Believe it or not, our group is too serious—that is, too serious for me! We spend almost all of our two hours talking about the book, and I'd like to find a way to encourage more social time and interaction.*

Book Group Members Respond

"Wow! So there is a parallel but reversed universe that exists invisibly alongside of ours! We can't get anyone in our book group to shut up about their sex lives long enough to settle down to serious book discussion."—*Betsy, Andover, Massachusetts*

"Perhaps you need to choose some different kinds of books when it's your turn—something really funny, or really personal. Take advantage of the 'looser' talk to encourage members to open up a bit about their own lives."

—*Angela, Albuquerque, New Mexico*

"We don't often have this problem! Make sure you have plenty to drink . . ."

—*Jennifer, Temple, Texas*

"Why not establish a social hour before each meeting? That way, any members who are interested in socializing and getting to know one another better can feel free to do so without worrying about wasting discussion time."

—*Paul, St. Louis, Missouri*

"Frankly, I'm glad I'm not close friends with the women in my group. I like them all very much, but it's the fact that we're not friends outside of book group that allows us to be so honest when we're discussing books, especially when sensitive issues are raised. I guess it's sort of the safety of relative anonymity."

—*Charlotte, Bismarck, North Dakota*

"Once a year we read a 'foodie' book and have a potluck where everyone brings a food that has significance for them and gets a chance to say why. On that night, we are mostly socializing, and there's not too much book discussion."

—*Lisa, Hailey, Idaho*

"A small subset of members who knew each other went out to dinner several times with a member who knew very few members. This helped a lot."

—*Bev, Fort Collins, Colorado*

"Use the books to get to know one another. Talk about yourself and your own experience when you're talking about the book. It can be hard to keep a balance between the personal and the literary, but I've found that it's worth it. Our discussions are richer when we include our own life experience."   —*Steve, Little Rock, Arkansas*

"Have a party (Christmas is our time) at least once a year, where you just get together and socialize. We also have had outings to plays and movies based on the
books we are reading."   —*Angela, Canton, Georgia*

GETTING WHAT YOU WANT OUT OF
YOUR BOOK GROUP

Q: *I'm not getting what I expected to get by joining a book group—
feel like my needs and goals aren't being met—what do I do?*

Book Group Members Advise

"Unless your group is a psychic book group, chances are that others don't know
that you're not satisfied. SPEAK UP and let them know that you'd like to see some
changes, or find another group that's more your style."

—*Tasha, Cheyenne, Wyoming*

"If you don't feel like addressing the group at large, take someone you like or would
like to know better into your confidence, ask for his or her help in finding a way to
change the dynamic a bit."   —*Stacy, Park City, Utah*

"[Y]ou need to get the group at large to talk about its goals as a club. Does the
group hope to read a wide variety of different kinds of books from different perspectives or backgrounds? Does the group want to keep up with all the hottest
book group best-sellers? Create a block of time, perhaps every six months or so, in
which your group will have an open but structured discussion about what each of
you would like to see happen in the next six months or so, both in terms of what
you read and how you talk about it."   —*Mary, New York, New York*

"We wrote down the reasons we joined the group and shared them with each other.
Then one member typed these up. Once a year or so, we revisit these goals and
discuss them to make sure we're on track."   —*Kim, Glendale, Colorado*

ADJUSTING YOUR READING TASTES

Q: *I seem to be out of sync when it comes to reading tastes with the rest of my group. They all like books that are very (complex/easy, racy/prude, risky/safe, international/domestic, long/short, etc.) and don't seem to be interested in moving out of that range. Should I be the one to make a change?*

Book Group Members Respond

"If by 'make a change' you mean choose the kind of thing that you would want to read when it's your turn, then absolutely it's time to shake things up. They may not love you for it, but every member deserves to have her day."

—*Shawna, Billings, Montana*

"When you say that they're 'not interested' in moving out of that range, do you mean that you have made a specific request for a slightly different kind of book and they flat out refused to accommodate you? If so, then get out of there and find a new group. If not, then you need to make that specific request."

—*Toby, Aberdeen, South Dakota*

"Are you sure that you're the only member who feels the need for an occasional change? Have you asked around, in a diplomatic and friendly way? Maybe your group would thank you for getting them out of a rut." —*Christina, Albany, New York*

"I can read anything I want at any time, the only exception is the book group book. I have really enjoyed the experience of reading books that are nothing like what I would have usually chosen—one of the main reasons I'm in a book group anyway."

—*Tess, Boulder, Colorado*

DEALING WITH A DIFFICULT OR UNPLEASANT MEMBER

Q: *How do we deal with a member who manages to spoil the dynamic for the rest of us by being overly aggressive and negative?*

Book Group Members Advise

"We did encounter this. Without confronting the person directly, we discussed that some members were feeling that their needs weren't getting met in the group and how could we reorient the discussion. One change was to have a more facilitated discussion since there was a member skilled in this. Another was to chat for the first fifteen minutes, discuss the book, and then end with a social time for whoever wanted to stay for that. In retrospect, a direct confrontation of the offending member by just one person away from the group may have been the better solution."

—*Susan, Denver, Colorado*

"We have only had to 'disinvite' a new person on one occasion—after we had already had a couple of chats with her about the need for mutual respect and the need to tone down her attacks on other people's opinions." —*Shelley, Boulder, Colorado*

"If you're the moderator, then you're also a 'traffic cop' who sometimes must say to the talkative person, 'Hold that thought, Bob. Cheryl has a comment.' Don't let the more zealous talkers drown out the shy folks." —*Kay, Blue Springs, Missouri*

"This can happen, and in our group, the amount of loud, adamant opinion on the part of that member was directly proportionate to the amount of wine served."

—*Anonymous*

"I'm really embarrassed to admit this, but we had a terribly obnoxious member in our book group, and she was so overpowering, we didn't know how to deal with her. So we told her the book group had disbanded, and then we continued to meet without her!" —*Francine, Washington, DC*

"Every group has one—if you can't prevent them from the beginning, you're probably stuck with them."

—*Anonymous*

"Sometimes we go around the room and hear from each person about their opinion of the book when we start our discussion. This helps us to hear from everyone, even the quieter members."

—*Bev, Fort Collins, Colorado*

"Be sure it isn't just you who finds them dominating."

—*Kim, Tewantin, Queensland, Australia*

"There was this one older woman in our book group who drove everyone crazy with her pushiness. Eventually, she could tell she wasn't welcome, so she left the group. We didn't expect what a hole she'd leave behind. The discussions were definitely better when she was there to get us all riled up. So we invited her back, and I'm glad we did (even though she's still overbearing)."

—*Jan, Boise, Idaho*

LEAVING AN UNSATISFACTORY GROUP

Q: *I've tried everything, and my book group still drives me crazy. It's not the kind of group I want, but the problem is that I like the women in the group. I want to leave, but I don't know how to without hurting their feelings.*

Book Group Members Suggest

"Quietly move on . . ."

—*Katherine, Dallas, Texas*

"I was tempted to bail out on my group a few years ago. I'm glad I didn't. Instead of storming out or just disappearing, I told the group that I wasn't happy with the way things were going. We seemed to spend only about ten minutes talking about the book, and many members didn't even bother to read it. Turns out, I wasn't the only one who was disappointed. We reorganized the group, made some rules, and now we're all getting what we'd hoped."

—*Jen, Grand Rapids, Michigan*

"If you're just joining, ask for a past list of books the group has read. Make sure the group's taste is compatible with your taste." —*Anonymous*

"Depends on why you're leaving the group. I don't think you have to make a big deal if it's not what you want, but you might want to let your group know why. I know if one of our members left, I would definitely want to know why. We've been together for over ten years, so that would be a real loss, and it would change the dynamic of the group." —*Jane, Roseville, California*

FINDING A NEW BOOK GROUP IN A NEW PLACE

<u>Q:</u> *I was in a super book group, and then I was forced to move because of my job. I want to find a new book group (for social reasons and because I loved my old group so much), but I don't know where to begin.*

Book Group Members Recommend

"Many Newcomer Clubs have book groups. Check the local bookstores, as they may have reading groups." —*Barbara, Winter Springs, Florida*

"[I]n talking with people at the health club, etc., I've learned of groups, and there is also one in my neighborhood. It seems that most libraries have a book group, so that's a good source." —*Marsha, Denver, Colorado*

"Years ago I had a terrible time finding a new book group when I moved from Washington, DC, to a small town. I joined several before I found one that was what I wanted, so my advice is: be picky and be patient!" —*Linda, Des Moines, Iowa*

"Check local bookstores, small-town newspapers. If all else fails, start your own." —*Angela, Canton, Georgia*

"I know I could have found a bookstore or library group when I moved to San Francisco—it's such a great book town—but I'm glad I didn't. Instead, I started my own book group as a way to meet my neighbors. I passed out invitations, and, to my surprise, more than twenty people showed up for the first meeting. The group has been going for over five years, and we have ten members who come every month. I feel connected to my neighborhood now because of my book group."

—*Harriet, San Francisco, California*

"If I were in a new town and wanted a book club to become a member of, I would go to the public library and see if they had information on existing book clubs. If not, I would probably seek people out at my church who I felt were of like minds and interested in forming a group." —*Betty, Grand Saline, Texas*

"Ask around at your place of employment; look in a local newspaper or your homeowners' association newsletter." —*Marilyn, Englewood, Colorado*

Index of Literary Terms:
Learning the Language

Allegory. An extended metaphor that represents an abstract idea in the form of a concrete image. Most allegories are decisively heavy-handed. You may remember Bunyan's *Pilgrim's Progress,* a tale of the trials of a man named Christian. Christian is the concrete image that represents Mankind, and his struggles allegorize the Progress of Mankind (or at least the Christian sector of Mankind) toward Ultimate Reward or Punishment. It's hard to miss the message. **Fables** and **parables** are types of allegories that emphasize the instructive aspect of the genre.

Alliteration. The repetition of a consonant speech sound, such as "slyly he slipped his side slide into the slalom." Writers, both of fiction and nonfiction, story and poetry, occasionally play with alliteration to produce a particular sound effect. *A little goes a long way, however; just think how annoying it would be if you got too much of that on a single page.*

Allusion. A generally brief reference to something or someone else outside of the current story, a person, place, thing, idea, or event in history or fiction, generally brief. A writer might make an allusion to the Bible, to the plays of Shakespeare, to wars, historic figures, popular cultural trends or sayings, anything else that the author feels may enrich his or her work. Allusions (the name of our company is another example) imply cultural knowledge and experience that is shared by both author and reader, functioning as a kind of shorthand to describe a particular moment or emotion.

Ambiguity. The thing you look for in a good book group book and find in great writing. Ambiguity in a literary work allows for two or more simultaneous interpretations of a word, phrase, action, character, or situation, both or all of which can be supported—this is key—by the actual text and context of the story.

Archetype. A term used to describe certain allegedly universal symbols that evoke deep and sometimes unconscious responses in the reader. The idea is that there are certain characters, images, situations, and themes that symbolically represent certain universal meanings and basic human experiences that we all share, no matter where or when we live. Common literary archetypes include the brave but inexperienced young hero who takes on an important quest—as does Lancelot in the King Arthur stories, as does the adolescent narrator of Leif Enger's *Peace Like a River*—or the lovely, innocent, but inspiringly resourceful young heroine who foils her evil suitors or captors by means of a trick—think of the many clever ingénues in fairy tales, or the trapped but not defeated protagonist of Margaret Atwood's *Handmaid's Tale.*

Assonance. The repetition of identical or similar vowel sounds, slightly harder to pick up on than **alliteration.** Assonance might be something like "oh, no, she goes slowly in the snow." It doesn't have to rhyme, but does have to share those repetitive vowels.

Absurd, Literature of the. This is a term often applied to certain works of drama and fiction that share the sense that the human condition is by its very nature essentially absurd, and can best be expressed in literature by works that are absurd themselves. Samuel Beckett is probably the most famous proponent of this mode, hitting the high mark of Absurdist theater in his 1955 play *Waiting for Godot*.

Atmosphere (also known as Mood). The emotional tone or mood that infuses a section or a whole of a literary work: sarcastic, ominous, reminiscent, frenzied—just to name a few.

Bildungsroman (also known as the Coming-of-Age Novel). The coming-of-age novel is one of the most eternally popular, and with good reason. A bildungsroman (from the German *bildung* "education" + *roman* "novel") deals with the development of a young person, usually from adolescence to maturity. Many of these stories are recognizably autobiographical (think of Charles Dickens's *Great Expectations* or Richard Wright's *Black Boy*).

Biography, Autobiography, and Memoir. Biography is usually the story of a famous or important person's life written by an insider or scholar. Autobiography and memoir are the stories people write about themselves. Memoir is generally concerned with personalities and actions other than those of the writer, whereas autobiography stresses the inner and private life of the subject. For the most part, a memoir is an account of a specific arena or period of person in the writer's life. For a detailed look at memoir, turn to page 83.

Canon. Simply put, the canon is made up of all the books that we study in school, those that teachers, critics, and other experts have decided are important and meaningful to a particular culture or country. But who has the right to decide which works are major and which are not? And what criteria should be used to make these distinctions? As you might guess, the whole idea of the literary canon has come under fierce attack many times in recent years, especially from those who point out that the vast majority of the authors that make up the Western canon (North American and Europe) are dead white men, and that their works fail to reflect the experience of society as a whole. Today, the emphasis is on "opening" the canon to include previously excluded groups. Many book groups feel the need to read both "the classics" (the books we were supposed to read in school) and "for diversity" (books from around the world that represent many previously unfamiliar cultures and viewpoints). In fact, each individual book group is in the process of forming its very own personal canon—the books that its members have designated as major, important, and worthy of their time and consideration.

Character.   For a detailed discussion of the different types of characters you'll find in literature (whether fiction or nonfiction), see chapter 2, page 51.

Comedy.   A comedy is a work of fiction that is intended to amuse, interest, and entertain us. We are pleasantly diverted rather than profoundly concerned by the characters' troubles. Within the general spectrum of comedy, there are some familiar subtypes. We owe the **romantic comedy** to William Shakespeare, who popularized this genre that involves a love affair gone wrong through misunderstanding and mishap, but which will all be sorted out in the end, as even Bridget Jones will discover. The **comedy of manners** also involves a love plot and the interference of such stock characters as the old and grumpy parents, the clever servant, and the wealthy rival, but is generally set in a sophisticated upper-class echelon of society and owes much of its humor to the wit and sparkle of fast-paced dialogue—think Oscar Wildes' *Importance of Being Earnest* or contemporary novelist Diane Johnson's *Le Divorce*. **Satiric comedy** (in which Hunter S. Thompson has reveled for much of his career) pokes fun at political policies, philosophical practices, or culturally deviant stances that interfere with the ordinary happiness and productivity of people in a particular society. The most over-the-top and ludicrous flavor of comedy is often called **farce,** which makes use of highly exaggerated **caricatures** of characters, improbable and fantastic situations, sexual mix-ups, off-color humor, and crazy physical confrontations—it's easier to do on screen than in a book, as the Marx and Farrelly brothers have demonstrated. **Black comedy** is an edgier brand of comedy, comedy with a bite and a sting. Unlike other comic forms, it does sometimes have a more serious purpose or message at its heart and can involve some fairly realistic and disturbing violence and/or evil. American author Sherman Alexie is one of the current literary masters of black comedy, as is promising newcomer memoirist Augusten Burroughs.

Connotation and Denotation.   In literary terms, the **denotation** of a word is its primary literal meaning, such as you might find in a good dictionary. Its **connotation** can be much wider and broader, all the words, ideas, or feelings that this word commonly evokes or implies. So while the dictionary definition of "ghetto" denotes a part of a city in which a minority group of people are forced to live by economic or legal necessity, it may also connote a wide variety of associated images or ideas—such as fear, family, drugs, pride, violence, home— depending on who is doing the connoting. Book group discussion can go a long way on connotation as your members debate the more intricate, implied meanings of a certain quotation or event.

Creative Nonfiction.   This is a somewhat ambiguous term of recent vintage, referring to literary works that are nonfiction in subject but creative in style, given life and form by the author's particular voice and choices in telling the story, the author's imagined construction of scenes or events. For a closer look at creative nonfiction, turn to page 92 in chapter 3.

Critics and Criticism.   Criticism is the catch-all term to describe writing or studies concerned with defining, classifying, analyzing, interpreting, and evaluating artistic works; in this case, works of literature. It's important to remember that critics are not necessary "critical" in the negative or pejorative sense, despite what seems like the inability of so many cultural critics to enjoy some good clean simple fun. There are numerous and overlapping schools of literary criticism—feminist criticism, cultural criticism, historical criticism, postmodern criticism, just to name a few—each distinguished by the critic's approach to evaluating and understanding literature, based on his or her particular idea of what is most important and valuable to examine and consider. As a book group member, you can and should make use of critical reception to any book that your group is reading—gather a few reviews from the Internet or your library, and watch the sparks fly as your friends enjoy that most innocent of pleasures, tearing to pieces the opinion of a person who isn't in the room.

Deus Ex Machina.   A Latin phrase meaning "a god from a machine." Originally used to describe the tendency of certain Greek playwrights (Euripides, in particular) to end their dramas and resolve their plot conflicts by means of a god lowered to the stage by a mechanical apparatus, who would then dole out moral evaluation, judgment, and commands for the future. It's now used to describe any forced or improbable plot device, such as when a building falls down upon the main character, thus ending the story.

Domestic Novel.   A domestic novel does not have to be confined to a domestic setting, i.e., the home, but it does refer to a novel about a family. The primary subject, theme, and concern of a domestic novel is the family dynamic, the relationships, alliances, and battles between certain family members.

Empathy and Sympathy.   While many of us use these two terms interchangeably to express our fellow feeling with a literary character or situation, **empathy** can be described as the "involuntary projection of ourselves into another": we feel what the other feels, we participate in his or her or its physical or emotional reality. **Sympathy** is slightly more detached: we *understand* what someone or something feels instead of *feeling with* that someone or something. You can sympathize with the anxious discomfort of a fictional character or a real person making an awkward public speech; but if you start to become physically uncomfortable, perspire, and blush, then you have moved one step further into empathy.

Epic.   This is an adjective frequently applied to novels or films of great length and general meatiness. It first arrived on the scene in the form of **epic poetry,** a long narrative poem on a weighty subject (such as *Beowulf* or the *Odyssey*), and featuring a heroic figure who holds the fate of a people in his mighty hands. You may remember that the epic is associated with certain traditions, which could be interesting to think about in terms of discussing one of today's "epic" novels. An epic hero is a figure of great national or even international importance; the epic setting is grand in scale; the action generally involves superhuman deeds in battle or dangerous missions daringly accomplished. In the traditional epics a God or gods generally get into the action, aiding or thwarting the hero with supernatural agency. Finally, you can't forget the epic style—grand, formal, ceremonial in tone and pattern.

While most heavy-hitting novels don't make use of all of these epic traditions, some do aspire to the title by telling a story of grand and "epic" proportions, covering a lot of space, focusing on action that may affect a nation or a people, and featuring a protagonist who seeks to kick some serious behind. Thus, *Moby-Dick* and *War and Peace* are frequently and fairly called epics, and so are some of today's novels, such as Isabel Allende's *House of the Spirits* or Russell Banks's *Cloudsplitter*.

Epiphany. A point of realization for a main character, the classic "Aha!" moment. Originally used by Christian thinkers to signify the manifestation of God's presence within the natural world, epiphany has become the standard term for the description of the moment when a character first begins to see something specific in the world around him or her in an entirely new way.

Epigraph. A quotation set at the beginning of a section, chapter, story, or entire literary work to suggest a central theme or question of that piece of writing. Epigraphs are somewhat common, and thus easily overlooked, but it is always a great idea to consider them carefully—sometimes a wonderful starting or concluding point to a discussion of a character, theme, or the book as a whole.

Epistolary Novel. A novel written in the form of a series of letters, such as Alice Walker's *Color Purple* or Mark Dunn's *Ella Minnow Pea*.

Essay. Any short composition in prose that attempts to describe an event, discuss an opinion, or persuade us to accept a thesis or conclusion on any subject. Essays can run the gamut from the very serious to the very funny, such as the travel accounts of Bill Bryson or the tales of personal dysfunction from David Sedaris. If you or your book group needs some extra help considering or discussing essays, please see the specific sections on this activity in chapter 3.

Fable. A short, fictional (nonhistorical) tale that teaches a specific moral; often features animals or inanimate objects as characters. Remember Aesop? We have him to thank for the collection of *Aesop's Fables* that bears his name, but the tales themselves stem from a much older, oral tradition of folklore.

Figurative Language (Simile, Metaphor). Fancy words or imaginative language used to describe something or someone. A **simile** is a comparison between two distinctly different things, which uses the words "like" or "as": "My love's like a red, red rose." A **metaphor** is slightly more subtle—one kind of object or idea is used in place of another to suggest a likeness or analogy between them, without using "like" or "as." So if poet Robert Burns had said, "My love *is* a red, red rose," technically, that would be a metaphor. Writers go to some incredible trouble coming up with unusual and creative ways to compare and express things, so it's always a good idea to keep an eye open for their most distinctive and arresting efforts.

Folktale. A short story of unknown authorship that has been transmitted by word of mouth throughout a group or groups of people. Simple definition notwithstanding, this term has become a veritable grab bag for all kinds of popular stories with some history within the oral tradition. Folktales are pretty much universal, told all over the world, and include myths, fables, fairy tales, and tales of cultural heroes, whether historical or legendary. The more recent urban and suburban legends could also be included in this category, as can off-color jokes and bawdy tales of longstanding and seemingly endless fascination.

Formula Fiction. This is what you read when you just want a good escape. Formula fiction follows a pattern of conventional reader expectations; hence, you know what is going to happen. Formula literature offers happy endings: the girl gets the guy, the detective bags his man, the sheriff saves his town, the explorer defeats the alien intruders—and the reader is pleasantly entertained but not unpleasantly surprised.

Genre. A word that's tossed around all the time in academia, but not so much in the sphere of more practical readers. However, it's a useful one to know. The term refers to a category of literature, a literary form, such as the novel, the short story, the poem, the memoir, just to name a few. We can divide pretty much any genre into further subcategories if we want to, such as the historical, the postmodern, or epistolary novel; and some critics might argue that these smaller categories can constitute a series of distinct genres all their own. This is a matter of personal opinion, since the classification of works of literature by genre has enjoyed a long and hotly debated history, as different critics over the years have employed a variety of different criteria to define and classify texts by genre categories. Your book group may occasionally enjoy a good debate surrounding the concept of the alleged genre that a particular book supposedly belongs to, according to either the author or the critics.

Gothic Novel. "Gothic" originally meant "Germanic," but later came to refer to anything that smacked of a certain dark medievalism. The traditional Gothic novel is set in a gloomy castle, the malodorous dwelling of a suitably beautiful and innocent heroine who is forced to reside in it due to the tragic deaths of her elders and must suffer the dastardly intentions of nasty and nefarious villains (who are, of course, determined to get into her bloomers), and the capricious visits of horrifying ghosts, ghouls, and poltergeists. The term "Gothic" has been extended to describe the type of fiction that may lack the dripping medieval castle setting, but which depends on the development of an ominous sense of gloom and terror; which features melodramatic, unnatural, and violent events; and which is populated by protagonists who are losing the last of their mental marbles. Thus, we can find remnants of the Gothic tradition everywhere from the work of Stephen King to the terrors of the Blair Witch team to the fashion expressions of certain black-clad, sun-phobic, pierced and studded teenagers the world over.

Historical Novel. You sometimes see this title applied to any novel that makes use, in some way, of events, settings, and/or people from the historical past. But a true historical novel not only takes its setting, characters, or events from history but depends on a specific historical moment to shape character and story. In order to determine if a novel is truly historical, or simply a novel set in the historical past, just ask yourself whether you could place the story of the novel in a different period or location and come up with pretty much the same results. Could you, for example, imagine Margaret Mitchell's *Gone with the Wind* without the Civil War, or Tracy Chevalier's *Girl with a Pearl Earring* without Johannes Vermeer or seventeenth-century Delft? Unlikely.

Hyperbole and Understatement. **Hyperbole** is the Greek word for "overshooting," and it's when you exaggerate something in an extravagant manner for either serious or comic effect (both inherent in an athlete's promise to give "200 percent" to the game). Many authors and critics make use of hyperbole to emphasize a point or enhance a mood. The opposite of hyperbole is **understatement,** which is when a speaker deliberately represents something as much less important or immediate than it really is, usually for an ironic effect— Mark Twain's comment that "the reports of my death are greatly exaggerated." **Litotes** is a form of understatement that negates its opposite, such as "he's not the brightest bulb in the pack," to say that someone is stupid, or "this is not my favorite way to spend the evening," when you're waiting to pass your gallstones in the emergency room.

Imagery. An extremely common term and confounding concept when it comes to discussing literature. At one time imagery was generally associated with poetry for the most part, describing the "mental pictures" that were conjured up in the reader's mind by the poem, as well as perhaps the image of the poem that is created by the poem as a whole. But we can talk about imagery in terms of almost any artistic or creative man-made project—story, music, visual arts, theater, film, even advertisements. For in the first and most narrow definition of the word, imagery signifies only descriptions of visual objects and scenes, those mental pictures we create in our heads and associate with the work of art itself. But if we go by a broader definition of the word, imagery can be used to reference any evocative literal descriptions, visual or verbal allusions, the use of simile and metaphor—how the work makes us see; what it makes us feel; how or if it conveys sound, pressure, temperature, solitude, a bitter taste or delicious smell. The most recent definitions of imagery focus on the use of figurative language, the dependence on simile and metaphor to convey a particular theme, motif, central idea. For example, if you were to look for all the examples of creative metaphors for death and transformation in Alice Seabold's *Lovely Bones,* you would be hunting for figurative imagery for quite a long time.

In Media Res.　Borrowed from classical epic poetry, such as Homer's *Iliad,* this phrase describes an introduction to a story that starts "in the middle of things."

Interpretation.　A word on literary interpretation in general, and for your book group in particular: most of the time, there are many ways to interpret particular events, actions, or characters in a good book. This is because a good writer knows how to keep things subtle, ambiguous, and complex, just like, unfortunately, life is often frustratingly opaque, ambiguous, and complex. So, in most cases, there is more than one possible "reading" of a certain literary moment, but, of course, not every reading is valid. What do you do when a fellow member comes out with a completely wacky reading of a particular book or situation? You could try asking, very gently and politely, "Are you saying that Shakespeare had the psychic foresight to predict

World War II? Or are you just commenting on Shakespeare's insight on the horrors of war in general?"

Irony. The enduring truth in both life and literature that things are not always what they seem to be. As a verbal device, irony reveals a reality very different from what we supposed to be true. For a detailed look at the different types of irony (**verbal, situational,** and **dramatic**) please see page 42 of chapter 2.

Literature. A basic but potentially loaded term and concept. While most people agree that literature has something to do with words, writing, and verbal expression, there are many opinions on what exactly that "something" is. Some definitions include anything that is written down on the page (at the doctor's office you can pick up some "literature" on the subject of high blood pressure); some embrace all fictional narratives but exclude nonfiction; others admit all published creative efforts, whether song, play, story, or poem. Many definitions of literature also depend on the criteria of quality—a written work is only considered literature if it is "good," or "true," or "lasting" in some way. Personally, we tend to have a foot in this camp. We believe that the best of literature, whether fiction or nonfiction, is infused with and motivated by the desire to provoke the tough questions rather than the easy answers. Great literature, old or new, encourages a great book group discussion because it encourages a wide variety of possible interpretations.

Magical Realism. This is a literary term that, like postmodernism, has inspired its fair share of heated debate. The term became widely applied to literature in the 1940s, referring to the juxtaposition of the factual and the fantastic, the historical and the mythical, the real and the magical. Although we now typically associate **magical realism** with Latin American fiction, authors like Italo Calvino, John Fowles, Günter Grass, Salman Rushdie, Toni Morrison, and even Annie Proulx have written fiction that shares many of its characteristics.

In its most basic sense, magical realism rejects pure rationalism; it infuses the world of the ordinary with the extraordinary. The insanely lovely Rosa in Isabel Allende's *House of the Spirits* has green hair, which only compounds her mermaidlike appeal. A secretive gentleman goes everywhere accompanied by a cloud of yellow butterflies in Gabriel Garcia Marquez's *One Hundred Years of Solitude*. No one in either story, not even the narrator, attempts to explain these bizarre phenomena—they simply acknowledge that they exist. Several Latin American writers have pointed to the very spiritual but chaotic histories of South American countries as the source for their people's implicit acceptance of supernatural manifestations. As Lois Parkinson Zamora and Wendy B. Faris explain in their introduction to *Magical Realism: Theory, History, Community* (Luke University Press, 1995): "The supernatural is not a simple or obvious matter, but it *is* an ordinary matter, an everyday occurrence—admitted, accepted, and integrated into the rationality and materiality of literary realism."

Malapropism.   When a person is attempting to use words that are a bit beyond his or her level, trying to sound smart but instead coming off as ridiculous. A malapropism is a type of **solecism,** that is, a conspicuous and unintended mistake in the standard use of the language. It is named for the character Mrs. Malaprop in Richard Brinsley Sheridan's comedy *The Rivals* (1775), who attempted to impress others with her prodigious word power, producing such gaffes as "a progeny of learning" and "as headstrong as an allegory on the banks of the Nile."

Melodrama.   Melodrama is a term applied to any story that relies on implausible events and sensational action for its effect. The conflicts arise out of plot rather than any attempt at unique characterization, and usually a virtuous individual must confront and overcome a wicked oppressor.

Memoir (see Biography).

Metaphor (see Figurative Language).

Modern and Postmodern.   Ah, the intellectual wars fought over these two seemingly simple and innocuous terms! Scholars and critics (of all the arts, not just literature) have been struggling to nail down definitive perimeters for the modern and the postmodern for decades, but no one can seem to agree exactly what these guidelines should be. Most experts concur that what we identify as the **modern period** in European and American cultural offerings spans the years between the beginning of World War I and the end of World War II, and is associated with a wide variety of *-isms:* futurism, Dadaism, expressionism, formalism, and surrealism. Reacting against the social and artistic conventions of the Victorian Era, modernist writers such as James Joyce, Virginia Woolf, and T. S. Eliot tried to create an art that would capture the psychological disillusionment and fragmentary experience of the modern world, using stylistic techniques such as stream of consciousness. In general, modernist fiction and poetry are characterized by a sense of alienation, loss, despair, and historical discontinuity.

Under modernism's general sense of pessimism lurks the hope that art itself can somehow repair the rules of a world broken by war. While modernist art seeks to construct elaborate forms that create—at least within themselves—order out of chaos, a new mythology from an abandoned mythology, postmodernist art often denies the very idea of order and the need for transformative myth. What some may identify as the **postmodern period** is less well defined by scholars and theorists (perhaps because we are allegedly still living in it), but, in general, it refers to radically experimental works of art and literature produced after World War II. Postmodern art blurs genre distinctions (architecture that combines Grecian, Gothic, and Colonial features), uses "pop art" and popular culture as subject matter (think Andy Warhol's cans of Campbell's soup), and, often, accepts the idea of a chaotic and fragmented world. Well-known postmodern writers include Don DeLillo, Kathy Acker, John Fowles, Thomas Pynchon, Donald Barthelme, Harold Pinter, Margaret Drabble, John Ashberry, and Jori Graham.

Motif. A **motif** is a conspicuous element—a visual image, a type of incident, a plot device, or a particular kind of character—that reappears frequently in a work or works of literature. Certain kinds of stories depend on shared motifs—the dumpy maiden who turns out to be a beautiful princess is a common motif in fairy tales and the wise mentor who dies tragically is a common motif of many coming-of-age stories. You can also have a motif that appears only in a particular story or book; John Irving loves motifs and returns repeatedly and poignantly to certain objects (a dressmaker's dummy), animals (bears), and ideas (a young man who lusts inappropriately for a near or distant family member) in each of his novels. **Theme** is sometimes used interchangeably with motif, but the terms are more useful if a distinction is made: motif is a reappearing element, while theme is a main idea or central concern of the work.

Myth. In classical Greece, *mythos* referred to any story or plot, whether true or fictional. In our current literary usage, however, a myth is generally thought of as one story in a larger **mythology,** a group of stories that were once believed to explain and define the natural order of things for a certain group of people. Myths could explain why things happen as they do, why people and plants and animals are as they are, or why bad things happen to folks who are minding their own business. If the protagonist of an ancient story is a person rather than a supernatural being, the traditional story is generally called a **legend** rather than a myth. Most of us modern movers and shakers don't have much use for myths or mythology anymore, but writers and poets have persisted in playing around with ancient and classical myths for their plots, episodes, and allusions because myths do carry a certain cultural weight. The modernists, as you may remember, loved messing about with the mythic heroes of yesteryear. James Joyce made use of *Ulysses* to write his own prize-winning work of the same name, and T. S. Eliot dragged up a whole crate of mythic corpses in his modern-epic poem *The Waste Land*.

Narrator (versus Author). The reason you want to be careful about distinguishing the narrator from the author of a particular story is that the two are often quite different. We also want to remember that not all narrators or narratives are necessarily reliable or straightforward. For a complete look at the different kinds of narrators and narrative styles, turn to page 48 in chapter 2.

Naturalism and Realism. Naturalism refers to a literary movement in the late nineteenth and early twentieth century in America, England, and France; and while this movement did create a certain type of "realistic" fiction, the two terms are not synonymous. In **realism,** the characters have some degree of free will; in **naturalism,** characters have little or no control over their situations. In a naturalistic world, things happen *to* people, aided by both the hereditary and environmental sources acting against them. There are three basic assumptions in **naturalist fiction:** everything real exists in nature, human beings are animals driven by fundamental urges (fear, hunger, and sex), and only the fittest (and most ruthless) survive in the competitive jungle of the modern world. The naturalist universe is an amoral one, and naturalist writers usually represent their imagined worlds in a detached, objective manner, avoiding commentary on morality or justice. Well-known American naturalist writers include Theodore Dreiser, Jack London, and Eugene O'Neill. **Realistic fiction** emphasizes authentic characterization and creates what most readers perceive as a plausible world. Characters are situated in a specific time and place, and their motivations are established in order to make their development both believable and moving. The democratic ideals of most realists lead them to value the individual and to concentrate on the surface details, common actions, and minor catastrophes of middle-class society. Realistic novels usually do not share the pervasive pessimism of naturalistic novels, and their tone is often satiric. Realists of repute include Mark Twain, Edith Wharton, George Elliot, Wallace Stegner, T. C. Boyle, Anita Brookner, and William Trevor.

Onomatopoeia. Onomatopoeia refers to the use of a word that resembles the sound that it denotes—rattle, bang, sizzle—but can also consist of more than one word. A particularly clever writer can create a line or even a whole passage in which the sound of the words also convey their meaning.

Parable. A short, realistic, and illustrative story intended to teach a moral or religious lesson. A type of allegory, it differs slightly from a fable in that a true parable is composed or told in response to a specific situation in an allegorical manner, which may explain why Jesus Christ was such a big fan of the form.

Paradox. A **paradox** is something that just doesn't make sense, no way, no how, yet it does all the same. A paradox could be a statement, a concept, a thing, or a person who possesses contradictory or seemingly incompatible elements. An **oxymoron** is a kind of verbal paradox: "jumbo shrimp" or "living death."

Parody. A humorous imitation of another, usually serious work of literature or drama. A parody can take any form because the writer will imitate the tone, language, and structure of the original in order to deflate the subject matter. Parody can be used as a form of literary criticism to expose the faults and flaws of the original work, but it can also be affectionate in its acknowledgment that a particular story or scene has become so well-known and such a part of our society that it is merely a target of fun, not malice.

Pastoral. Think shepherds, sheep, maidens, green fields, and a simpler, sweeter place and time. Original credit for this literary staple goes to a Greek poet by the name of Theocritus, who in the third century BC wrote poems celebrating the life of Sicilian shepherds (*pastor* is Latin for "shepherd.") Centuries of poets and writers latched on to this longing for an idealized lost way of life, including Shakespeare. In most of his comedies the characters retreat into a "green world" of nature and magic, emerging significantly altered in some way—as they do in *A Midsummer Night's Dream.* The term has been expanded to include any work that contrasts the pleasures of a simple life to those burdens associated with hectic modern complications; you could say that both *Bel Canto* and *Corelli's Mandolin* are novels that pulse with a strong pastoral sentiment.

Picaresque. In this type of novel or narrative, a rascally protagonist wreaks a path through a series of episodic events, living by his or her wits, untroubled by lengthy reflection or dramatic reform. Famous picaresque heroes include Cervantes's Don Quixote, Daniel Defoe's Moll Flanders, Mark Twain's Tom Sawyer (but not Huck Finn, who actually learns something in his travels), and Thomas Berger's narrator in *Little Big Man*.

Plot. As we all know, plot refers to the ordering of events in a story, fictional or nonfictional; plot is "what happens." See chapter 2, page 55, for an in-depth discussion of all the intricacies and devices of plot.

Poetic Justice. When a character gets what he or she deserves, especially if it is not the result that he or she was necessarily looking for. Poetic justice involves a situation that is resolved in such a way as to satisfy the aphorism "what goes around comes around."

Point of View. The point of view of a story, of course, is the point of view, the perspective, from which it is told. For a detailed look at all the different possible points of view, and how each shapes a story, see page 48 in chapter 2.

Prose. Prose simply means "not poetry." Prose is the ordinary, straightforward language that most people use when speaking or writing, devoid of intentional rhymes, regular controlled rhythms, or any arrangement by verse or line.

Realism, Realistic Novel (see Naturalism and Realism).

Regionalist Fiction. Also known as **local-color writing,** regionalist fiction captures the habits, speech, culture, history, folklore, and beliefs of a particular geographical area. Even though popular writers such as Mark Twain, Kate Chopin, Sarah Orne Jewett, and Robert Frost are known as regionalists, this kind of "local color" writing has been criticized by some scholars who regard much of it as decorative and sentimental and who argue that it lacks "serious" literary value. Increasingly, regionalist writers such as Kent Haruf, Barry Hannah, and William Gay are defying the old stereotypes by infusing their work with deep moral questions, complex characters, and innovative style.

Satire.   The literary art of making someone or something look ridiculous, to diminish or degrade a subject by encouraging an audience's contempt or scorn. **Satire** usually invites us to laugh, just like comedy, but satire uses this laughter like a weapon against some human frailty. You might not think of Jane Austen's *Sense and Sensibility* and Joseph Heller's *Catch-22* as having much in common; but each novel, in its own way, satirizes dominant popular sentiments of its day. **Lampoon** is a form of satire that generates humor by exaggerating or distorting aspects of physical appearance or character traits, making a **caricature** out of a particular character.

Setting.   The setting of a novel, poem, or dramatic piece is composed of three things: location, location, location. No, just kidding. The setting is composed of location, time, and the unique set of social circumstances in which its action occurs. To learn why setting can be one of the most vital of all elements that shape a story, see page 57 in chapter 2.

Simile (see Figurative Language).

Social Novel.   The social novel usually has an ax to grind with somebody. In this kind of novel, the social, political, and economic conditions of a certain time or era will typically play as large a part as the main characters; in fact, detrimental social conditions will have a dramatic impact on both characters and events. More often than not, the social novel will also offer up some explicit or implicit thesis for social reform. Harriet Beecher Stowe's *Uncle Tom's Cabin* and John Steinbeck's *Grapes of Wrath* are classic examples of this "platform" style of novel. Some relatively recent offerings in this tradition would include T.C. Boyle's *Tortilla Curtain*, in which oblivious white Americans tangle with heroic Mexican immigrants, or Barbara Kingsolver's *Prodigal Summer*, in which environmentally good people battle the environmentally evil.

Stream of Consciousness. As it has been defined since the years following World War I, this term is the name used to describe a narrative mode that attempts to create and capture a character's messy mental journey, the full range and speedy flow of his or her perceptive and reflective process, without any tidying up or organization by the narrator. Faulkner does this to great effect with his idiot narrator Benjy in *The Sound and the Fury*. Virginia Woolf is particularly famous (if not always beloved) for her incredible efforts in this kind of narration; she was one of the early pioneers of this style in her novels *To the Lighthouse* and *Mrs. Dalloway*. Michael Cunningham copied Woolf's fluid style in his novel *The Hours*, a tribute to *Mrs. Dalloway*. Love it or hate it, both authors won a Pulitzer, so somebody in the know approved.

Style and Tone. Style refers to *how* a particular author, speaker, narrator, or character says whatever it is that he or she has to say. The author's **tone,** his or her attitude toward the people, places, and events in a narrative, is revealed by style. If you need to brush up on some of the basic intricacies of style and tone, see chapter 2, page 39.

Surrealism. If you are even remotely familiar with the work of painter Salvador Dali, you are well on your way to understanding the concept and aspects of surrealism in art—be it visual or verbal. The surrealist artists wanted to revolt against all perceived restraints on their creativity, including boring standards like logical reason, traditional morality, and cultural conventions and norms, especially as they applied to artistic expression. Basically, they just wanted to freak out big time. We can still trace the influence of many a literary surrealist in the work of modern writers who have broken with conventional modes of narrative organization to experiment with free association, nonlogical and nonchronological order, dreamlike sequences, and the juxtaposition of bizarre or seemingly unrelated images or events. Writers such as Henry Miller, Thomas Pynchon, Williams S. Burroughs, Dave Eggers, and even Zadie Smith have all, to some degree or another, borrowed from this surrealist tradition to create a unique type of storytelling.

Symbol. In the technical sense, a symbol is any word or thing that signifies something else. Thus, strictly speaking, all words are symbols. When you're talking about books, however, the term *symbol* is used to describe a word or phrase or image that is of greater or wider or deeper significance than just that simple word, phrase, or image. The key thing to remember about symbols is that they often possess *many* possible meanings and nuances, depending on who is doing the looking. Melville would not have written *Moby-Dick* were he not interested in myriad possible symbolic associations with that great white whale. Don't worry if you run across something that might be a symbol but eludes your immediate understanding—keep it in mind or jot it down, and share your question or idea with the rest of the group.

Synecdoche. A relatively unknown but incredibly useful word and concept. Synecdoche refers to "a part that signifies the whole," and is a kind of figurative language that most of us use more frequently than we may observe. When the first mate aboard a ship yells, "All hands on deck!" he is making use of synecdoche, the hand being just part of a person, yet being used to signify the person as a whole. Even if you're not a first mate, you may have counted "heads" for the number of people at a party or a dinner table, or kept "an eye" out for a friend. You can also have some fun with the concept of synecdoche by trying to choose a sentence or a paragraph that you think is at the center of a book as a whole—as you read, look out for that synecdoche line or lines, and think about why they are emblematic or representative of the author's text in its entirety.

Theme. A theme is simply a main idea or central concern of a literary work. A novel, story, or memoir may be home to a wide variety of themes, or it may house one or two major central preoccupations. See chapter 2, page 59, for detailed thematic inspiration.

Transcendentalism. Emerson and Thoreau, we owe it all to you. Transcendentalism is a philosophical and literary movement that took root in Boston and Concord and that was popular and prominent among the egghead circles of New England from the mid-1830s until just before the Civil War. Transcendentalism was not so much a strictly defined philosophy or style of writing as it was an adherence to those aspects of human perception that transcend the physical sensory experience, such as moral truth and a confidence in the validity of knowledge that is grounded in feeling and intuition. Emerson and company were primarily interested in reacting against the social conformity, rampant commercialism, and depressing materialism that they perceived as gradually taking over the American life and spirit. Sound familiar? If the popularity of such books as Alex Garland's *Beach,* Jim Crace's *Quarantine,* and Ron Hansen's *Mariette in Ecstasty* is any indication, we're still pretty fascinated by those who dare to step outside societal norms and forge their own rules for living.

Tragedy. Loosely speaking, this is when bad things happen to good people. The term is used to describe literary and dramatic works (especially the latter) in which the main character, or *protagonist,* will meet with a disastrous end. Aristotle argued that a tragedy is a work that makes use of incidents that arouse sympathy, pity, and fear, and that makes a catharsis possible for the audience; ideally, you leave the theater feeling exhilarated rather than depressed. Aristotle also claimed that the most effective protagonist, or **tragic hero,** will be neither angelically good nor disgustingly bad, but rather a mix of both, so that the audience will be able to identify with his dilemmas and sufferings. This hero may be well-intentioned, but he gets in trouble because of his **tragic flaw,** the personal failing or error in judgment that leads him down the thorny path to disaster. For the Greeks, the flaw of **hubris,** or excessive pride, often led to the hero's mistaken confidence that he can ignore a divine prophecy or flaunt a moral law.

Tragedy has changed some since Aristotle's time. By the sixteenth century, Shakespeare was already wreaking havoc against the classical Greek definitions. The protagonist of *Macbeth,* for instance, is not what you'd call a basically good guy. Rather, he's a greedy social climber who takes advantage of good luck to hatch an evil plan. As you discuss a "tragic" story, you might want to think about whether the protagonist does indeed possess the classic requirements to make him a tragic hero. Do we need our modern heroes of tragedy to personify that mix of good and bad character traits? For today's readers and audience, must the tragedy always be the fault of the man (or woman), or can the protagonist simply lose the battle against outside forces through no fault of his or her own?

Book Group Resources: Finding Help When You Need It

BOOKS

Books on Book Groups

Book Clubs: Women and the Uses of Reading in Everyday Life. Elizabeth Long. Chicago: University of Chicago Press, 2003. Long is a sociology professor at Rice University, and her book examines the socioeconomic forces that have shaped women's book clubs in the United States, with a particular focus on post–Civil War groups.

The Book Group Book: A Thoughtful Guide to Forming and Enjoying a Stimulating Book Discussion Group. Ed. Ellen Slezak. 2nd ed. Chicago: Chicago Review Press, 1997. Slezak's book is less a guide and more a collection of amusing anecdotes about the book group experience. The book's strength is that the author lets individual book group members speak for themselves.

The Complete Idiot's Guide to Starting a Reading Group. Patrick Sauer. Indianapolis: Alpha Books, 2000. Too bad it's out-of-print— this is a fairly comprehensive handbook on how to get a book group going. Like all books in the Idiot's Guide series, the text is rather simple and is accompanied by silly drawings and such.

The Go On Girl! Book Club Guide for Reading Groups. Monique Greenwood, Lynda Johnson, and Tracy Mitchell-Brown. New York: Hyperion, 1999. The Go On Girl! book club is probably the best-known African-American book group in the United States, and this book tells the story of the group's formation and shares some expert tips.

The Mother-Daughter Book Club: How Ten Busy Mothers and Daughters Came Together to Talk, Laugh and Learn Through Their Love of Reading. Shireen Dodson. New York: HarperPerennial, 1997. If you want to start a book group with your nine-to thirteen-year-old daughter, this is the book for you. Although the reading suggestions are dated, the book includes some great advice.

The New York Public Library Guide to Reading Groups. Rollene Saal. New York: Crown, 1995. One of the first books to come out about book groups (it was pre-Oprah!), this book is out-of-print but still worth a look as a beginner's primer.

The Reading Group Book: The Complete Guide to Starting and Sustaining a Reading Group. David Laskin and Holly Hughes. New York: Plume, 1995. Comprehensive (if a bit out-of-date), this handbook balances hands-on advice with thematically organized, annotated lists of recommended titles

The Reading Group Handbook: Everything You Need to Know to Start Your Own Book Club. Rachel W. Jacobsohn. Rev. ed. New York: Hyperion, 1998. With its first edition published in 1994, this is perhaps the best known "how-to" guide on reading groups, and it sets the stage for many of the guides that follow. Jacobsohn facilitates book groups in the Chicago area and heads the Association of Book Group Readers and Leaders.

The Reading Groups Book. Jenny Hartley. Foreword by Margaret Forster. 2002–3 ed. London: Oxford University Press, 2002. If you want to know what's going on with book groups in the UK, this is the book for you. A bit academic, but filled with some amusing and interesting survey results.

Talking About Books: A Step-by-Step Guide for Participating in a Book Discussion Group. Marcia Fineman. Salt Lake City: Talking About Books, 1997. This self-published book does a good job describing some very basic ways to get a discussion started.

Books on Reading

The Book That Changed My Life: Interviews with National Book Award Winners and Finalists. Ed. Diane Osen. Introduction by Neil Baldwin. New York: The Modern Library, 2002. Ever wonder what your favorite authors like to read? This is the book for you— filled with surprising book choices and fascinating discussions of what makes a book "great."

A Feeling for Books: The Book-of-the-Month Club, Literary Taste, and Middle-Class Desire. Janice A. Radway. Chapel Hill: University of North Carolina Press, 1997. Radway is a feminist literary scholar who was among the first to discuss the history of women's reading habits.

A History of Reading. Alberto Manguelo. New York: Viking Press, 1996. If you're interested in the history of reading practices, and you want to go back—way back—check out Manguelo's book.

How to Read a Book: The Classic Guide to Intelligent Reading. Mortimer J. Adler and Charles Van Doren. New York: Touchstone, 1940. This classic of the genre introduces the reader to the fundamentals of reading comprehension—an interesting historical artifact.

How to Read and Why. Harold Bloom. New York: Touchstone, 2001. Called an "aesthetic self-help manual" by *Publishers Weekly*, this handbook from our most celebrated (and often crankiest) literary critic shows his passion for reading.

The Lifetime Reading Plan: The Classic Guide to World Literature. Clifton Fadiman and John S. Major. Rev. ed. New York: Harper-

Perennial, 1997. Originally published over forty years ago, this book is great fun to read if you're interested in the formation of the canon. The books that are included (and omitted) may create some healthy debate about "great books."

Reading the Romance: Women, Patriarchy, and Popular Literature. Janice A. Radway. Chapel Hill: University of North Carolina Press, 1984. Another book by Radway, the current academic expert on the culture of women's reading.

So Many Books So Little Time: A Year of Passionate Reading. Sara Nelson. New York: Penguin Putnam, 2003. Sara Nelson is a self-proclaimed "readaholic" and a veteran book reviewer who makes a New Year's plan: to finish one book a week and record her thoughts as she reads. This clever and unusual memoir is the result of her enviable endeavor.

Women Who Love Books Too Much: Bibliophiles, Bluestockings & Prolific Pens from the Algonquin Hotel to the Ya-Ya Sisterhood. Brenda Knight. Berkeley: Conari Press, 2000. This light-hearted book is filled with unique illustrations and anecdotes about women reading through the ages.

Books on What to Read

Bloomsbury Good Reading Guide. Kenneth McLeish. London: Bloomsbury, 1991. Over three thousand books are cross-indexed in this guidebook, giving the reader a chance to find new authors.

Books of the Century: A Hundred Years of Authors, Ideas, and Literature. Ed. Charles McGrath and the staff of the *New York Times Book Review.* New York: Times Books, 1998. If you think the *New York Times* is a bit stodgy (or if you think its reviewers can write no wrong), this collection of the paper's literary reviews will educate and entertain you.

The Reader's Choice: 200 Book Club Favorites, a Treasury of Top Picks by More Than 70 Reading Groups Nationwide. Victoria Golden McMains. New York: HarperCollins, 2000. A professional book reviewer, McMains writes plot-driven synopses with an occasional nod to style and too-quick glimpses of her personal reading experience. A few questions for discussion are tagged on at the end of each description.

Reading Group Choices: Selections for Lively Book Discussions. Donna Paz. Nashville: Paz & Associates, 2002. This guidebook is published semiannually, which makes it current. Keep in mind, though, publishers pay to be included in its pages.

The Reading List. Contemporary Fiction: A Critical Guide to the Complete Works of 110 Authors. Ed. David Rubel. New York: Owl Books, 1998. A good source of basic information on current literature, this book includes some biographical information, a brief synopsis of each title, and some quick observations from critical experts.

The salon.com Reader's Guide to Contemporary Authors: An Opinionated, Irreverent Look at the Most Fascinating Writers of Our Time. Ed. Laura Miller with Adam Begley. New York: Penguin, 2000. What salon.com does so well: it challenges us to rethink our understanding of highbrow and lowbrow. Filled with original, well-written, and unique observations about literature and its impact on our world.

What to Read: The Essential Guide for Reading Group Members and Other Book Lovers. Mickey Pearlman. Revised and updated. New York: HarperPerennial, 1999. Includes thirty-eight thematically arranged and annotated lists of recommended books—the only weakness is that the lists are dated and don't include new titles.

A Year of Reading: A Month-by-Month Guide to Classics and Crowd-Pleasers for You and Your Book Group. Elisabeth Ellington and Jane Freimiller. Chicago: Sourcebooks, 2002. A great inspiration for book groups who want to plan their reading schedule far in advance—thematic reading suggestions are especially helpful.

BOOK MAGAZINES AND REVIEWS

Black Issues Book Review. The authoritative voice in the world of African-American literature.

Bookmarks Magazine. Over two hundred book reviews a month distilled in every issue.

Bookpage. A monthly book review distributed nationwide by more than two thousand bookstores and libraries.

Books & Culture. A premiere review of Christian fiction and nonfiction.

New York Review of Books. One could argue that it's a bit more literary than *The New York Times Book Review*—tends to review more esoteric books.

New York Times Book Review. The granddaddy of all book reviews—authors' careers are made and crushed in the pages of this review.

Publishers Weekly. The industry's main source of news. Be aware the reviews (unless starred) are usually plot driven and descriptive rather than evaluative.

WEB SITES

Web Sites for Book Groups

Bookbuffet.com

http://www.bookbuffet.com. A membership-driven Web site that provides book news and space for book group members to talk online.

The Book Group List

http://books.rpmdp.com. In the words of Angie, the site's creator, "Simply put, we put together a list of books and a reasonable schedule in which they should be read in."

BookMuse

http://www.bookmuse.com. Subscribers to this site get access to reading guides on various contemporary and classic works of literature.

Good Books Lately

http://goodbookslately.com. Here's what we offer that no one else does: one-on-one support for book group members, over the phone and via E-mail. Our discussion guides—Read*Smart*Guides®— are available for quick and easy download. We're thrilled to introduce exciting interactive resources for book groups as we develop the National Book Group Association of America at our site.

Reading Group Choices

http://www.readinggroupchoices.com. The on-line version of the book—see above.

Reading Woman

http://www.readingwoman.com. A grassroots, homemade site of book group readers devoted to "the power of good literature . . . when we find a great read, we want everyone to know about it."

On-line Book Groups

Book Clique Café

http://www.readinggroupsonline.com. Provides support for active on-line reading groups. Affiliated groups use different combinations of Internet modalities to create book discussions on the Web: chat rooms, message boards, listserv/e-mail discussions, and Web pages.

Bookies, The

http://www.geocities.com/bookiestoo. A well-maintained, open-to-the-public on-line book group with this mission statement: "BookiesToo is a long-standing book discussion group that is friendly and welcoming. We enjoy stimulating book discussion and we love to chat about anything that is book-related! Our discussion schedule includes two books per month. We primarily discuss literary fiction but members may nominate books from any genre for discussion. The group then votes from among all nominated titles to arrive at a schedule."

Rachel's Compendium of Online Book Discussions, et al.
http://www.his.com/~allegria/compend.html. A user-friendly list, compiled by an enthusiastic and personable reader. We'll let Rachel explain in her own words: "Once upon a time . . . I had a book club of my own. It was very cool, a lot of fun, and took an awful lot of time that I ultimately decided that I couldn't afford to spend. But in the course of working on my book club, I became interested in other book clubs on the Internet. So I thought, 'Why not put together a page that lists different book clubs on the Internet?'"

Salon.com Table Talk
http://tabletalk.salon.com. A collection of public discussion forums (you'll need to register at salon.com to become a user) on all kinds of subjects: Books, Health and Science, Mind and Spirit, Mothers Who Think, Social Issues, White House. Pretty much something for everyone, and from what we can tell, the bulletin boards are filled with thoughtful and thought-provoking threads.

Yahoo Clubs
http://dir.groups.yahoo.com/dir/Entertainment___Arts/Humanities/ Books_and_Writing?show_groups=1. Lots of erotica book forums on this list, but don't let that dissuade you! There are over fifteen hundred on-line book clubs listed, so chances are, you'll find one that's right for you.

Book-Related Web Sites

AcqWeb's Directory of Book Reviews on the Web
http://acqweb.library.vanderbilt.edu/acqweb/bookrev.html. If you're looking for a book review online, this is a great place to start.

Atlantic, The
http://www.theatlantic.com/books. The "Books—Critics" section is filled with free, full-text reviews and author interviews on both popular and obscure books. An excellent resource.

BookBrowse.com

http://www.bookbrowse.com/index.cfm. Great place to look for book reviews (if sometimes frustrating because the whole review is often not included). We'll let the folks at this innovative site describe what they do: "BookBrowse carefully selects from the most interesting current books and provides you with multiple reviews and a substantial excerpt of each. So don't judge a book by its cover—read it for yourself at BookBrowse.com."

BookCrossing

http://www.bookcrossing.com. With a slogan like "generosity is addictive," you know this site is up to something good. Here's the idea: "The 3 Rs of BookCrossing: (1) *Read* a good book (you already know how to do that); (2) *Register* it here (along with your journal comments), get a unique BCID (BookCrossing ID number), and label the book; (3) *Release* it for someone else to read (give it to a friend, leave it on a park bench, donate it to charity, 'forget' it in a coffee shop, etc.), and get notified by E-mail each time someone comes here and records journal entries for that book. And if you make <u>Release Notes</u> on the book, others can <u>Go Hunting</u> for it and try to find it!" The software development firm that maintains the site claims that "between three hundred and five hundred new members from around the world join daily," and you can search by country, city, town, and neighborhood. You never know—the book you've been looking for may be waiting for you in your local Laundromat!

BookSpot.com

http://www.bookspot.com. Part of the StartSpot Network, this site gathers all kinds of links to information on books: prizewinners, best-sellers, author Web sites, on-line retailers, etc.

BookTV.org (C-SPAN's "Booknotes")

http://www.booktv.org. The on-line companion to C-SPAN's popular and ubiquitous Book TV.

Bookwire

http://www.bookwire.com. Published by Bowker, this is a strong book industry resource if you're looking for "behind the scenes" information.

Good Book Guide

http://www.thegoodbookguide.com/gbg/default.asp. *The Good Book Guide* magazine complements this independent site and was established more than twenty years ago "to guide readers through the maze of books published each month—and with more than ten thousand new titles issued every month, that mission is even more valid today than in 1977."

MostlyFiction

http://www.mostlyfiction.com. This site includes a newsletter and on-line forum and features reviews written by readers and chapter excerpts from a large number of books.

On-line Booksellers

Alibris

http://www.alibris.com. You don't actually buy books from Alibris, but they'll hook you up: "Alibris connects people who love books, music and movies to thousands of independent sellers around the world. Our proprietary technology and advanced logistics allow us to offer over 30 million used, new and hard-to-find titles to consumers, libraries and other institutions."

Amazon.com

http://www.amazon.com. Pretty soon, you'll be able to buy any-thing—*and we mean anything*—at Amazon.

Barnes & Noble

http://www.bn.com. The on-line presence of the brick-and-mortar chain. Recently added an impressive book group element to the site, including a free weekly "book club pick" E-newsletter.

Book Sense

http://www.booksense.com. "Independent stores for independent minds" is their motto, and the folks at Book Sense strive to keep the old-fashioned art of hand selling alive. When you buy a book through this site, you support your local independent bookstore.

Half.com

http://half.ebay.com/index.jsp. When you need to save some dough, this is the place to go.

Powell's City of Books

http://www.powells.com. Portland's humungous independent bookstore has a great E-bookstore and often features well-conducted interviews with celebrated authors who visit the store.

Used Book Central

http://www.usedbookcentral.com. Great place to buy—and sell— used books online. Especially good for college students looking for discounted textbooks.

Discussion Guides

Barnes & Noble Reader's Companions

From what we can tell, this new series provides plot synopses and thematic descriptions for several contemporary works of fiction (such as *Lovely Bones* and *White Teeth*)—may be more useful for students than book groups. Available at Barnes & Noble stores.

GradeSaver

http://www.classicnote.com. A site that's really designed for college plagiarists—oops, we mean students!—this can be a good source of biographical information on well-known authors. Includes summary and analysis of mostly canonical books. Very similar to *CliffsNotes,* but available online for free.

Reading Group Guides

http://www.readinggroupguides.com. A very handy tool when you're looking for a publisher reading guide. This site gathers guides from major publishers on one site—no more bouncing back and forth between Penguin and HarperCollins or trying to figure out how to navigate enormous sites like Random House.

Read*Smart*Guides®

http://www.goodbookslately.com/recommendedbooks/readsmart guides.shtml. We think Read*Smart*Guides® are the best book group resource out there, but then again we might be a little biased. Check out the end of this book for a list of available discussion guides and visit our Web site for a free sample.

SparkNotes

http://www.sparknotes.com. You have to set up an account and log in each time, but once you do, you have access to free "study guides." Very similar to *CliffsNotes*—the difference being that *SparkNotes* are available for newer, less canonical books (but like *CliffsNotes,* they're designed for students and consist mainly of plot overviews).

Publisher Reading Guides

Anchor Books
http://www.randomhouse.com/anchor

Ballantine Reader's Circle
http://www.randomhouse.com/BB/read

Book Group Corner (bantam, broadway, dell and doubleday)
http://www.randomhouse.com/resources/bookgroup

HarperCollins
http://www.harpercollins.com/hc/readers/index.asp

Houghton Mifflin
http://www.houghtonmifflinbooks.com/readers/_guides

Picador
http://www.picadorusa.com

Random House
http://www.randomhouse.com/randomhouse

SimonSays (Simon & Schuster)
http://www.simonsays.com/Sections/Areas.cfm? AreaID=4

St. Martin's Press
http://www.stmartins.com/smp/rgg.html

Time Warner
http://www.twbookmark.com/books/reading_guides.html

Vintage Reading Group Guides
http://www.randomhouse.com/vintage/read

TELEVISION BOOK CLUBS

"Booknotes" *C-SPAN*
Not really a book club, but perhaps the most reliable source of regularly televised author readings from bookstore readings across the county.

"Exxon Mobil Masterpiece Theatre Book Club," *PBS*
Different organization in different markets, some invite viewers to the station for untelevised book discussion.

"Martha's Favorite Books!" *Martha Stewart Living*
Features one book per week, fiction, nonfiction, and poetry—word is that Martha chooses the books, so expect a high literary tone.

"Read This!" *Good Morning America*
Profiles regional book clubs and has club recommend next book. Chooses word-of-mouth favorites like *The Lovely Bones*.

"Reading with Ripa" Book Club, *LIVE with Regis and Kelly*
Michael Gelman, executive producer of *LIVE with Regis and Kelly*, says, "You won't hear about nonfiction with deep, meaningful messages. Any hint of a life-affirming message will lead to disqualification from book club."

"Today Book Club," *Today Show*
Well-known authors choose their favorite lesser-known writer, providing a wide range of fiction and nonfiction.

NEWSPAPER & MAGAZINE
BOOK CLUBS

Each print-media book club works differently. Many feature regular reviews of books chosen specifically for book groups. Some announce a book ahead of time with questions for discussion—to which readers respond—and then select responses are published the following month. Others have readers gather together for a real face-to-face book group discussion, during which a reporter jots down their comments and excerpts them in a feature article. More and more newspapers and magazines are joining in. We've included a brief list of the best-established book groups, but we encourage you to check the book section of your local paper to see if you, too, can join the fun!

Atlanta Journal-Constitution, AJC Reading Room
Boston Globe, Books & Reading
Essence magazine
San Francisco Chronicle, The Chronicle Book Club
Star Tribune, Talking Volumes
USA Today Book Club
Washington Post

RADIO RESOURCE

***Fresh Air with Terry Gross,* NPR**
http://freshair.npr.org/. The one, the only, Terry Gross. Perhaps the best interviewer out there. You may think it's a bit odd she does her interviews only over the phone, but no one can compare. Her daily program features interviews with novelists, journalists, film-

makers, musicians, and artists, and you can always count on her to ask smart questions of her often inspiring guests.

LITERARY ORGANIZATIONS

Association of Book Group Readers and Leaders (ABGRL)
http://lcweb.loc.gov/loc/cfbook/coborg/abgrl.html. Based in Chicago with over five hundred members, ABGRL is a "cooperative information clearinghouse to provoke, inspire, and reward individual readers and members of book discussion groups."

CAE (Book Groups for Adult Education)
http://www.cae.edu.au/bookgroups/index.php. A huge and impressive site devoted to supporting on-line book groups in Australia.

The Great Books Foundation
http://www.greatbooks.org. The well-known site with information on both junior and adult Great Books, a program "dedicated to helping people learn how to think and share ideas by educating them to become participants in, leaders of, and advocates for shared inquiry."

"One Book" Reading Promotion Projects
http://www.loc.gov/loc.cfbook/one-book.html. The Library of Congress "Center for the Book" sponsors the increasingly popular community-wide reading programs in states and cities across the country.

BUSINESS BOOK GROUPS

Business Literary 2000
http://www.bkpub.com/literacy. A program developed by the Consortium for Business Literacy. Almost two dozen small-business book publishers are involved with the program, and its purpose is to promote literacy in the workplace and to make reading central to corporate America. Study guides are available for popular business books featured in the program.

Available Read*Smart*Guides®

You're just a click away from getting the comprehensive and fun-to-read information you need to enliven and empower your book discussion. Our Read*Smart*Guides® are now available for on-line purchase and instant download at www.goodbookslately.com.

Ahab's Wife or, The Star Gazer by Sena Jeter Naslund
Amy and Isabelle by Elizabeth Strout
Angle of Repose by Wallace Stegner
Atonement by Ian McEwan
Bee Season by Myla Goldberg
Bel Canto by Ann Patchett
Close Range: Wyoming Stories by Annie Proulx
The Curious Incident of the Dog in the Night-Time by Mark Haddon
Disgrace by J. M. Coetzee
Don't Let's Go to the Dogs Tonight by Alexandra Fuller
Everything, Is Illuminated by Jonathan Safran Foer

Girl, Interrupted by Susanna Kaysen
Girl with a Pearl Earring by Tracy Chevalier
The Group by Mary McCarthy
Homestead by Rosina Lippi
The Hours by Michael Cunningham
The House of the Spirits by Isabel Allende
In the Time of the Butterflies by Julia Alvarez
Interpreter of Maladies by Jhumpa Lahiri
The Life of an Ordinary Woman by Anne Ellis
Life of Pi by Yann Martel
Make Believe by Joanna Scott
Mariette in Ecstasy by Ron Hansen
Memoirs of a Geisha by Arthur Golden *(free sample available online)*
Plainsong by Kent Haruf
Plum & Jaggers by Susan Richards Shreve
The Poisonwood Bible by Barbara Kingsolver
The Power of the Dog by Thomas Savage
Quarantine by Jim Crace
Sula by Toni Morrison
The Tortilla Curtain by T. C. Boyle
The Toughest Indian in the World by Sherman Alexie
White Teeth: A Novel by Zadie Smith

This list is current as of Fall 2003. Please check our Web site for more information and an up-to-date list of all our discussion guides.

An Invitation to Our Readers

If you'd like to contribute to future editions of *Good Books Lately: The One-Stop Resource for Book Groups and Other Greedy Readers* or to our monthly e-newsletter *LATELIES* please contact us. We'd love to hear from book group members, book group facilitators, booksellers, librarians, publishers, and authors: call, e-mail, or send juicy book group anecdotes, reading recommendations, helpful literary resources, and smart book group advice to:

GOOD BOOKS LATELY
PO Box 12259
Denver, CO 80212-0259
(303) 744-8000
kira@goodbookslately.com

ELLEN MOORE (at right in the picture) is teaching English and completing her doctorate at the University of Denver, working on a dissertation on the subversive power of book groups in the marketplace. Ellen has worked as a teacher, counselor, and activities director for several different age groups. She enjoys forcing people to get along and have fun—but only if they really want to. Ellen can be reached at **ellen@goodbookslately.com.**

KIRA STEVENS has eight years experience teaching college English and is finishing her doctoral dissertation—on "The Oprah Effect" and the cultural history of book groups—at the University of Denver. Kira worked at Denver's renowned Tattered Cover Book Store for ten years, helping to organize the store's annual book club seminar. Her compulsive love for organization and detail runs rampantly unchecked by modern pharmacoloy, to the delight of all her coworkers. Kira can be reached at **kira@goodbookslately.com.**

Visit both Ellen and Kira on the Web and check out the Good Books Lately Web site, with lots more Read*Smart*Guides®, an expanded Greedy Reader Menu, and much more at www.goodbookslately.com.